GYPSY MOON

Pamela Rose Anders

Real Publishing Company
Dallas, Phoenix

Gypsy Moon

First paperback edition: September 2011

The characters and events portrayed in this book are real. Some of the characters represent composite characters. Some dates have been changed.

Pamela Rose Anders, Author
John Behr, Editor
Steve Hammond, Editor
Cover design by Pamela Rose Anders
Graphics by Pamela Rose Anders
Back cover photo by Erica Montgomery Photography

ISBN-13:
978-0578091402

ISBN-10:
0578091402

Real Publishing Company

For my children, Cheryl, Gregory, and Steven; without whose love, understanding, acceptance, and support, I would never have made it through this journey.

And to all those who, through their own strength and courage, inspired me to finish this book. Without them, Gypsy Moon would have remained unfinished.

If you have a song, sing it.
If you have a story, tell it.
If you have an image, paint it.
If you have a vision, realize it.
If you have a dream, live it.
Don't die with the music still inside of you.

Table of Contents

Chapter One
The Upside-Down Year

October 1961 -

It was morning recess at Eberhart Elementary School. A five-foot tall, wrought iron fence surrounded the schoolyard, with the playgrounds and entrances separated by the fence: One side for the boys, and one for the girls. Between the playgrounds grew a thirty-foot buffer of grass, with a walkway in the center that led to the faculty's entrance.

Screeching, frolicking students filled both playgrounds. On the boys' side of the fence, there was basketball, football, and roughhousing. Conversely, on the girls' side, there was hopscotch, jump rope, and volleyball. On both sides of the wrought iron fence were the social and the antisocial, the popular and the unpopular, the bullies and the victims.

The first of three bells rang, indicating that it was time for the children to gather up their equipment and head back to class. A second bell would sound in five minutes, with the expectation that the students would be at their seats and prepared for class to resume. The third bell was the tardy bell. Any student who was not at his or her seat at the sound of that bell would most assuredly be paying a visit to the principal's office.

As the playgrounds cleared, and boys and girls made their way back toward the entrances, a slight, dark haired boy remained standing at the dividing fence, his deep hazel eyes peering blankly through the vertical bars. The boy was neither liked nor disliked, bully nor victim. He was tough and athletic; a formidable opponent in a fistfight, with lightning fast reflexes and superb hand-eye coordination, yet uninterested in fighting or participating in sports. He was highly intelligent, but an under-achiever; only putting forth a minimum effort. He was friendly, humorous, and kindhearted, yet preferred solitude.

As on most days, he stood alone at the fence, watching the girls play on the other side. Teachers took note of this, observed him, and speculated that he had entered puberty, and perhaps developed an early interest in the opposite sex. However, this was not the case. He could not understand, nor could he explain, what made him feel the way he did. He chose to keep his feelings a dark secret to himself, which if revealed would surely result in ridicule and chastisement.

Fallen leaves skipped about the playgrounds and gathered around his feet. The cool, autumn breeze blew gently across the school grounds. Beyond the iron bars that imprisoned him, the girl's playground was clearing in a sea of pastel colors, converging upon the girls' entrance. He stared blankly for a moment, and as he expected, the ghostly figure appeared from a swirl of leaves beyond the fence. He had seen her many times before, angelic in appearance, with a soft face, warm smile and long flowing hair. She was there, but not actually there.

She smiled, and waved invitingly, long blond hair cascaded across her rosy cheeks in the breeze. As she had done on previous occasions, she raised her arm slightly and motioned for him to come over. However, as had been the case on previous attempts, he was unable to negotiate the strong bars that held him in place. He waved slowly as she smiled one last time, before she dissolved; leaving in her wake the leaves that had danced at her feet just moments before.

"Hey, Mair, who ya wavin' at?"

Philip turned his head without answering. It was Joe Amato, an eighth grader. His younger brother, Frank was in Philip's class. Joe, one of the more popular boys in school, had developed an avid interest in automobile racing. Joe would one day go on to become a renowned, national drag racing champion.

"You're gonna turn into a girl one of these days if you keep staring over there all the time," he laughed, while walking toward the school entrance.

Philip shrugged, "Yeah, sure," while following Joe and the throng of boys into the building.

In the hallway, boys and girls emerged from their respective entrances to make their way up three flights of stairs leading to the second and third floors. The first floor held the kindergarten, first and second grades. It also housed the library, gym, and offices. There was no cafeteria at Eberhart as most students lived close enough to walk home for lunch. Those who packed a lunch ate in the library. The second floor contained the third, fourth and fifth grades, while the third floor held the sixth, seventh and eighth grades. Ms. Stockdale's sixth grade class, situated on the west end of the third floor, had windows overlooking Homan Avenue.

As the mob of students reached the third floor, they dispersed, heading to their classrooms. Philip followed the stream into the sixth grade class, as Ms. Stockdale stood guard at the door.

Geraldine Stockdale was the tallest of the teachers, extremely thin, but large-breasted. She appeared so top-heavy, that Philip wondered how she managed to walk without toppling over. She kept her dark brown hair in a short cut, styled in tight curls. She seldom smiled, giving the impression that she was either a very unhappy person, simply hated her job, or perhaps a combination of the two. There was no joy in Ms. Stockdale's class. She would immediately dispatch any frolicking or joking student to the Principal's office.

As Philip entered the classroom, he noticed a message written in large block letters on the chalkboard, which he read aloud.

WE WILL DISMISS 30 MINUTES EARLY FOR LUNCH TODAY. DON'T FORGET TO WEAR YOUR HALLOWEEN COSTUME TO SCHOOL THIS AFTERNOON.

"Well, what do you know? He can read!" Ms. Stockdale mumbled sarcastically, as he walked past her. She did not like Philip and made no effort to hide the fact. She glared at him as he made his way to his desk in the back row of the classroom.

Ms. Stockdale preferred to separate the genders in her class, girls in front, and boys in back. There were five rows with seven desks in each and his was right in the middle, directly in front of the pencil sharpener, attached to the wall. Above the pencil sharpener was a photo poster of President Kennedy captioned with his famous words, *"Ask not what your country can do for you -ask what you can do for your country."*

To the right of the Kennedy poster was a White Sox pennant from 1959, the year they were defeated in the World Series by the Los Angeles Dodgers.

Philip slid into the seat of his wooden desk and settled in. He glanced to his right and left, noticing that yesterday's homework assignments, graded by Ms. Stockdale during recess, sat on everyone's desk. One assignment consisted of fifty arithmetic problems, which Philip had completed with ease, and a history assignment, which he had also breezed through. The graded assignments were on everyone's desks except for his. Did he forget to turn it in? Quickly checking his notebook, he confirmed that it was not there. He was certain he had turned it in that morning. Why had she not returned it to him? The answer came quickly as his fellow classmates settled into their seats.

"Philip Andrew… Can you come up here please?"

The use of his middle name and the tone in her voice was ominous. He knew he was in trouble, as he made his way to the large wooden desk at the front of the class. The tall curly headed woman, with the large breasts, and the angry look on her face, stood in front of her desk glaring at him.

He noticed his two homework assignments atop it. Each was marked with a large "INCOMPLETE" at the top, in thick black ink.

"Philip did you even read the comments I wrote on your homework assignment yesterday?" she snarled angrily.

Philip nodded slightly, "Yes Ma'am."

She picked up her black marker from the top of her desk and circled the name line with accentuation on the top of each assignment. "I gave you fair warning! This is unacceptable! I will tell you once again, you are to put your name, not your initials, on your work."

She offered the papers to him, which he meekly took. "From now on, if any of your assignments are turned in like this," underlining each of his initials on the paper to emphasize her point, "they will be marked as incomplete. You will put Philip Mair or Philip Andrew Mair, I don't care which, but no initials! Is that clear?"

"Yes Ma'am," he muttered softly.

"Good, now go back to your seat," she said as she shooed him off with a flick of her boney hand.

Philip turned and began the long walk back to his desk expertly avoiding eye contact with the other students, with practiced perfection, who were most assuredly staring at him. Mike O'Brien occupied the desk to his right, Eric Leschi to his left. Both boys were grinning at him as he slid into his seat.

"You sure know how to piss off a teacher, guy!" Eric said in his heavy German accent with a cupped hand over his mouth.

Philip just silently nodded as he slid the incomplete homework assignments into his notebook.

The remainder of the morning consisted of a geography lesson, followed by a quiz. Philip was careful to print his full name on the top of each sheet, but now with an emphasis on the first letter of each name, which he enlarged and bolded,

"Hopefully this will make her happy," he thought to himself, as he filled in his answers.

It took him under 20 minutes to complete the quiz, at which time he laid down his pencil and sat erect in his seat. Several minutes later, Ms. Stockdale glanced at her watch, and stood up to instruct the class to pass forward their answer sheets. After collecting all the sheets, she gathered them up, placing them on her desk. After a quick glance at the wall clock behind her, she rested on the edge of her desk, her long thin legs stretched out before her.

"Okay now, let's quietly put on our coats and get ready for the lunch bell."

As if in unison, thirty-four students were on their feet, heading to the large coat closet that took up nearly the entire wall next to the door. With the rustling of vinyl, leather, cloth and the sound of zippers zipping, the lunch bell rang, as the mass exit began. The hallways and stairways instantly filled with bodies. The sounds of hundreds of hungry, excited kids of all ages eager to get home, to gobble down a quick lunch, so they could put on their Halloween costumes, filled the air. Philip made his way down the three flights of stairs, following the throng of students out into the cool October air.

Candy walked along the sidewalk in front of the school with two of her friends, as Philip fell into step several feet behind her. She glanced quickly over her shoulder, rolling her eyes at the sight of her pesky little brother behind her. Candy was one year and twenty-two days older than Philip, and like most siblings, they fought constantly. Although cut from the same cloth, they were worlds apart in persona. She was the honor student; he was the troublemaker. She was popular; he chose to be a loner.

They turned right at Homan Avenue walking the half block to Sixty-Fifth Street where the "Patrol Boys" controlled the flow of kids across the busy avenue. They were eighth graders that wore white baldrics signifying their position of authority to stop automobile traffic, allowing the kids to cross safely. It was an honor to be a Patrol Boy, and most of the younger boys dreamt, of one day wearing the baldric, but not Philip.

On the southeast corner of this intersection stood the Yellow Store, a school supply and candy retailer, so nicknamed because of its yellow brick exterior. A grumpy Polish woman, named Gertie, who had little patience for her young clientele, ran the Yellow Store.

"Hurry up", she would harshly admonish a youngster methodically selecting twenty-five cents worth of penny candy from the vast selection beneath the glass.

This day however, she closed the Yellow Store, as she did every Halloween. Gertie cringed at the thought of actually giving away candy to the trick-or-treaters. She simply closed the store, rather than give anything to those freeloading little grubbers.

Philip did not like crowds, so he found a spot away from the other students on the wall of yellow bricks. He leaned there casually, while awaiting the bulk of the crowd to cross the street. Candy and her friends, now several hundred feet ahead of him, walking briskly home, so they could eat, and put on their costumes.

The wind, blowing from the west, had swept the fallen leaves from the street, pushing them against the wall of the Yellow Store, creating a large pile of dead leaves around Philip's feet. He kicked away the leaves from the area directly below the window of the store, exposing the concrete at the base of the yellow bricks. During the summer, a car had lost control and crashed into the Yellow Store, creating a hole in the brick building, and damage to the concrete footing. Philip happened by soon after the repair crew had departed, and had been unable to resist. Using a fallen twig from a nearby tree, he had etched his initials for all eternity into the still wet cement.

Now, swinging his foot back and forth like an eraser, he cleared the spot so he could once again look at his artwork from three months earlier. There it was, as clear as the day he wrote it.

He had etched his initials twice along with the year, with the second set inverted, as if it was a mirror image of the first. 1961, when inverted was still 1961, an anomaly that he found fascinating. It was his upside down year.

The walk home from school was one block north and three blocks west, a total of a half mile. There were twenty-nine trees, two mailboxes, three stop signs, and seven streetlights along the way. Philip had verified these facts, on his way to and from school, time and time again. As he walked down Sixty-Fourth Place towards the brick, bungalow-style house in which he lived, he noticed the grey 1957 Studebaker parked in front. It was Eddie's car, which meant that Mom was home with her current boyfriend.

Eddie Chepchore, or "Chops," as his friends in the neighborhood bars knew him, grew up in the neighborhood, had attended Eberhart Elementary, and had gone to nearby Lindblom High for two years before dropping out. His father had been a Chicago cop until he died suddenly of a stroke in 1959, leaving his Studebaker to Eddie, and the rest of his estate to Eddie's mother.

Eddie never cared much for work, preferring instead to spend his days and nights in "O'Brien's on 63rd Street," one of many neighborhood taverns within walking distance of Philip's house. Although he was well into his thirties, he still lived with his mother, who continued to give him a weekly allowance.

Philip walked through the front door into the parlor past Candy's room. Even with her door closed, he could hear her rustling inside, as she put on her Halloween costume. Mom was in the kitchen. Eddie was in the hallway bathroom as Philip attempted to slip by unnoticed into his room.

Eddie emerged from the bathroom just as Philip passed the door.

"Hey sport! What's up?" Eddie said, as he punched Philip in the shoulder, knocking him into the wall.

"Not much, Eddie," Philip rubbed his shoulder, as he continued walking toward the kitchen in the hopes of escaping Eddie and finding some food.

"Your mom has a surprise for you sport. Go ask her!"

Philip hoped her surprise would be that she was dumping Eddie. Then he wouldn't have to hear himself being called "sport" anymore.

"Hi, Mom." She was sitting at the kitchen table in her waitress uniform, adjusting her wig in a mirror. Today she had chosen a long brunette style from her vast collection. There was a highball in front of her. A Pall Mall lay burning in the ashtray.

Jackie Mair was an attractive woman in her mid-thirties, who had been married and divorced twice. Her first husband was the father of her two children. Harold Smith was a trumpet player and waiter from Tennessee, who had vanished when Candy and Philip were infants. She later married a grumpy movie theater manager named John Mair, who had gone through the motions of changing the kid's surnames from Smith to Mair. That marriage had dissolved last year, and she was now in the process of changing the names back to Smith.

"Guess what?" She did not give him a chance to guess before

continuing, "Eddie's friend with the boat is going to take you and Eddie to Lake Wabesa fishing this weekend. His uncle has a cabin out there." She looked across the room at Eddie, who was attempting to open a bottle of beer with a pair of pliers.

Philip stood motionless, as his mother took a long drag on her cigarette.

"It will be just you three guys, a nice guy weekend. Won't that be fun?" The words erupted from her mouth in a cloud of exhaled smoke. Philip ducked.

Eddie, as had most of Mom's previous boyfriends, had made it his mission in life to be a substitute father to Philip, and hoped to provide all the activities that boys are supposed to enjoy. A month earlier, they had gone to a nut farm in Algonquin to hunt squirrels. Philip had spent an entire day carrying a shotgun around, gazing into the trees in search of rodents with long fluffy tails, presumably to shoot dead. The day had ended with Eddie having shot one squirrel, and Philip never having even fired the gun. That night, the two of them sat by the fire, as Eddie gutted the rodent to cook it on the fire. The two of them shared the equivalent of one chicken wing for dinner, followed by Eddie teaching Philip how to roll a cigarette.

"I'm gonna make a man outta you!" Eddie had proclaimed proudly, while swigging a bottle of whiskey.

The only part of this man training that Philip enjoyed was learning how to drive. At first, it was on Sundays in closed shopping centers. Eddie would let him drive the Studebaker around in circles in the empty lot. Soon, Philip drove around the block, then through the neighborhood. Before long, he had become a twelve year old chauffeur, shuttling the drunken Eddie from bar to bar on Saturday afternoons.

Philip's thoughts drifted back to a morning last winter when he was awakened by a loud knock on his bedroom door. Eddie walked in and opened the blinds.

"We're gonna have some fun today," he grinned

Philip looked outside into the bright sunlight, rubbing his eyes in an attempt to focus. There was a sheet of ice outside; trees and shrubs glistened. There had been an overnight ice storm.

"C'mon, get dressed. Let's go for a drive."

The Studebaker slid from side to side, as Eddie drove to an empty parking lot on Cicero Avenue. Once in the lot, Eddie floored the accelerator and began spinning in circles. Philip held on for dear life as Eddie turned the wheel first to the left, then to the right, and back again. The world seemed to be spinning out of control as the car spun madly, narrowly missing light poles. As Philip gripped his seat and clenched his teeth, Eddie laughed, yelling "whoooooooo whoooooooo."

"Now, it's your turn, Sport." The car had come to a stop. Philip released his death grip on the seat.

Eddie opened the driver's side door to hop out, walked around to the passenger side, to open the door.

"Go on, slide over, it's your turn to drive."

Philip slid over to the driver's seat. He craned his neck, as he peered through the windshield at the icy parking lot. A knot had developed in his stomach, and his hands were clammy, as he gripped the steering wheel.

Eddie settled into the passenger seat. He reached behind to retrieve a brown paper bag from the backseat. He extracted a bottle of Seagram's, removed the cap, and took a long swig. Philip felt ill, as the smell of whiskey permeated through the car.

"Okay let's go." Eddie took another swig.

With his foot on the brake, Philip put the car in drive, while gingerly releasing the pressure on the brake pedal. The wheels began to spin slowly, eventually catching hold, causing the car to lurch forward at idle speed. He gently applied pressure on the accelerator pedal, and the car began to move forward gracefully and smoothly. Philip kept both hands locked on the steering wheel as he guided the Studebaker forward in a straight line across the lot. His right foot now hovered over the brake pedal.

"C'mon Sport. You drive like an old woman."

Before Philip knew what happened, Eddie had reached the accelerator pedal with his left foot, pressing it to the floor. Suddenly, the car began to fishtail as it spun on the ice. Philip, paralyzed with fear, gripped the wheel ever harder, trying to keep control of the car as a chortling Eddie took another swig of whiskey.

"Let's do some donuts now." Eddie reached over to the driver's side to grab the steering wheel, twisting it from side to side, making the car slide sideways, first one way, then the other. Eddie turned the wheel to the left suddenly, and the car just barely missed a light pole. Philip thought he was going to die any moment. Eddie laughed. Finally, he took his foot off the gas pedal and sat back. Philip gently stepped on the brake and stopped the car. His entire body was trembling.

They spent the next two hours driving in circles on the icy parking lot. Philip drove, Eddie drank whiskey. Soon, Philip had mastered the ice, power sliding gracefully around the parking lot, resulting in a nod of approval from his drunken instructor.

As Philip drove home from the lot, on now salted streets, Eddie took the last swig from the bottle, tossing it into the backseat. "You drive like a champ, Sport. You'll be the king of the road someday."

Philip had other plans for his future, but before he could respond, Eddie let out a snore from the passenger seat. He parked the car in front of Eddie's house and walked the two blocks back home.

Now, nearly a year later, Philip pondered a guy weekend in the middle of a big lake, on a boat, fishing with Eddie and his friend. He had three days to come up with an excuse. Perhaps stomach cramps would work.

"How late you working tonight, mom?" A change of subject was in order.

"I don't know, probably late though. I may go out with Eddie afterward, so don't expect me home until morning."

Eddie winked at Philip, smiling wickedly.

Philip found a saucepan on the stove with warm tomato

soup in it. Candy had already taken her share, so he poured the remainder into a bowl. He grabbed a spoon from the drawer to sit next to his mom. He studied her face as he ate the soup. She had soft skin, high cheekbones, and beautiful eyes.

"And please have this place cleaned up when I get home! It looks like a pig sty."

Philip nodded as he looked around the kitchen at the overflowing ashtrays and beer bottles scattered over the counter tops.

"I put your costume on your bed. It's the skeleton that you wore last year. Hopefully this year it won't be so big on you." Jackie said as she peered into a small mirror while applying her eye makeup. Philip watched intently.

Candy emerged from her room in a Snow White costume.

"You two want a ride back to school? I'm getting ready to take your mom to work." Eddie finished a beer, and placed the bottle on the counter top directly above the trash basket, while belching loudly.

"Sure!" Candy was rinsing her soup bowl at the sink.

Philip stared at his bedroom door, in deep thought.

"I still need to put on my costume. I'll just walk back." he replied.

Philip gave his mom a hug and a kiss on the cheek and headed toward his room. Eddie stepped in front of him to offer his hand for a handshake. Philip sighed and stuck out his hand.

"See you this weekend sport." Eddie grinned as he pumped Philip's hand, gripping it tightly. Philip thought a bone would break. He considered the possibility of having a sore hand this weekend.

Philip stood by the window, watching the Studebaker pull away before heading to his room. He picked up the skeleton costume from his bed to hold it up in front of the full-length mirror on his wall. His mom was right; it would probably fit better this year than it did last year. He glanced at the clock on his dresser. School resumed in thirty minutes; he had better get his costume on.

Fourth grade teacher, Rosemary Malpe, was in the teachers' lounge cranking the handle of the mimeograph machine, making purple copies of a social studies quiz, when Ms. Stockdale burst in. As she entered, the second bell sounded in the hallway. Mary Roberts, the gym teacher, was sipping coffee with Principal Helen Smith. They both set down their cups, and gazed at the breathless teacher standing before them.

"Helen, you have got to come to my room. Now! You have got to see this!" exclaimed Ms. Stockdale while trying to catch her breath, after having trotted down three flights of stairs.

"What is it, Geraldine?" Ms. Smith liked to get right to the bottom line and had little patience for guessing games.

It was too late. Ms. Stockdale opened the door and was already heading back into the hallway.

"Just come to my class now please." she said, as she disappeared into the hallway.

Ms. Smith sprang to her feet, catching the door just before it completely closed, reopened it, and followed Ms. Stockdale into the hall. Ms. Malpe and Ms. Roberts followed closely behind. They all now wondered what in the world could be going on in the sixth grade class. The sound of three pairs of high heels clacking up the stairs, accentuated by the squeaking of Ms. Robert's gym shoes, echoed through the halls of Eberhart Elementary school, as Geraldine Stockdale led the charge to her classroom.

The athletic Mary Roberts followed closely behind, trailed by Rosemary Malpe, and the elderly Helen Smith, with her thin white hair streaming behind her head like fantails. As the four of them reached the third floor, the sounds of their flight caught the attention of seventh grade teacher Margaret Garvey, who popped her head out of her classroom door. Margaret, attaching herself to the gaggle of teachers now swarming down the hall toward Ms. Stockdale's classroom, asked plaintively, "What's going on?"

"I don't know." Ms. Malpe and Ms. Roberts replied in unison.

The sixth grade class was abuzz with giggles and conversation, which came to an abrupt halt when Ms. Stockdale opened the door to enter her classroom. With something akin to a well-practiced field drill, Ms. Roberts, Ms. Malpe and Ms. Garvey flanked her. The four teachers stood side by side and stared in astonishment at the sight before them.

"Oh my!"

"Good Lord!"

"Unbelievable!"

The line of teachers parted, opening a rift, as a breathless Ms. Smith entered the room to gaze toward the rear of the classroom. She then looked quickly at Ms. Stockdale, then back to the source of the turmoil.

There, in the last row, directly in front of the pencil sharpener, beneath the John F. Kennedy poster, seated between Flash Gordon and Frankenstein, was a girl. She wore a blonde wig, red lipstick, black dress, stockings, black pumps, and clip on earrings.

An obviously shaken Ms. Smith made her way fastidiously to the back of the classroom, while attempting to adjust her glasses to give her eyes a better fix on the strange looking woman.

Frankenstein chuckled while muttering something in German as Ms. Smith stood directly in front of this usurper.

The Principal of Eberhart Elementary School pointed a crooked finger at the girl, who bore a striking resemblance to Jackie Mair.

"Just who…" she stuttered for a moment,

" Just who are you supposed to be?"

Sitting erectly, the girl looked up with dainty poise at the four teachers standing at the front of the class, then directly at the Principal. With her red lips pursed in an ear-to-ear grin, she proclaimed proudly for all the world to hear.

"My name is Pam."

Chapter Two
Coming Around Again

May 2007 -

Pennsylvania is one of my favorite states in which to drive. It is a beautiful part of the country with well-maintained roads, decent speed limits, and a minimal number of weigh stations. In short, it is a truck driver's dream. The beauty of the rolling hills and valleys has never been more awe-inspiring than when there is a fresh blanket of snow on the ground as there was this day.

The sun was making its first appearance of the day, as I sat gazing through the restaurant window at the fresh snow that had fallen during the night. The scenery outside the window reminded me of a holiday greeting card, replete with tree limbs glistening with frosty icicles, and a pristine "White Christmas" panorama.

There were no sounds of sleigh bells, however. Instead, there were sounds of diesel engines rumbling in counterpoint to each other in a throaty chorus, warming up for another day of hauling freight across country. Glancing toward the right of the window, I watched as big trucks lined up at the fuel pumps, their drivers readying themselves for the long day ahead.

The reflection staring back at me in the glass suddenly caught my eye as I gazed back in wonderment.

Is that really me?

The face before me in the window was not the face that I had lived with most of my life. This was a different face. This face had evolved slowly and deliberately over the past three years. Through the religious use of hormones, multiple surgeries, and over a hundred hours of electrolysis, this face was the product of diligence and persistence. The woman gazing back at me in the window had soft skin with flowing blond hair.

Yes, I assured myself, the woman in the reflection was really me!

The sight of another reflection silently emerging in the glass above my own interrupted my reverie. I turned my head and was startled to see a waitress standing at my table. One hand held a glass coffeepot, the other a menu. She smiled warmly as she laid the menu on the table and spoke.

"Good morning ma'am. Would you like some coffee?"

I quickly flipped over the upside down coffee cup on the saucer, and nodded enthusiastically. She skillfully filled my cup without spilling a drop, despite the fact that I was already moving the cup to my face as she poured. I took several gulps before placing the empty cup back on the saucer. She deftly refilled my cup with a practiced hand that comes only with many nights of refueling the caffeine needs of hundreds of truck drivers.

"Thank you, dear." I smiled while sipping the coffee. I set the cup down. She topped it off once more. I was already growing fond of this waitress.

"I'll be back in a few minutes to take your order and to refill your coffee hon."

I looked at her name tag and responded with a wry smile, "Thank you Jacqui, you can just leave the coffeepot."

Jacqui laughed.

I didn't.

I sipped my coffee as I once again gazed through the window. The sun was now in full bloom as the truck stop slowly came alive with activity. Trucks coming and going refueled their tanks to head back onto Interstate 80. The restaurant was nearly full. The travel center was now busy with idling motorists and truck drivers waiting for showers.

Sitting down for breakfast in a truck stop restaurant had become a rare treat for me. My normal routine was to start out earlier than most, leaving between two or three am while eating on the run. That way I could get six or seven-hundred miles behind me before three or four in the afternoon, to be early enough to find a parking spot at the next truck stop. I was usually pretty lucky. By 5:00 pm, most truck stops already filled up making it much more difficult to find a spot.

I had left Allentown at 4:00 am, and made it as far as Mifflinville, on Interstate 80, when my number sixteen tire blew out. I barely heard a burp in my cab, but to anyone who may have had the misfortune of riding along beside me, it would have seemed like the equivalent of a nuclear bomb going off. To my good fortune, the Bloomsburg Travel Centers of America (TA) was only about ten miles ahead on exit 232, which I easily made on my remaining seventeen wheels. The repair shop informed me it would be at least two hours before they could get me back on the road.

Jacqui returned with coffeepot in hand, as I emptied my cup. She did not miss a beat, refilling it the second I set it down, asking, "Are you ready to order?"

I had not even looked at the menu, but I knew what I wanted, "Eggs up easy, crisp bacon, hash browns, and sourdough toast."

"You got it, hon." Before I could respond, Jacqui had spun around to fill the cup of a male driver sitting in the booth across from me. She disappeared, only to reappear merely seconds later, as she swiftly took his order while on her way to the kitchen.

I decided to head over to the travel center to kill some time while waiting for my breakfast to arrive. As I slid out of my booth and straightened my clothing, the man in the adjacent booth surveyed me from head to toe. His teeth were on the table next to his coffee cup and he nodded his approval with a toothless grin.

I feigned a smile as I walked toward the travel center near the restaurant entrance.

Nearby was a small alcove containing an arcade. Truck drivers, and the occasional road weary motorist, could stop there to relieve, or add to their road stress. Several men were busy shooting electronic geese, driving race cars, or destroying planets. A chorus of beeps, boops, sirens, blasts, explosions, and crashes tumbled aloud from the arcade, accompanied by moans and screams of profanity as the ducks flew away unharmed, race cars crashed, and alien planets fought back.

Beyond the arcade was the travel center, where drivers waited in line to complete fuel transactions, purchase showers, cash checks, and stock up on energy drinks, chips, and other unhealthy snacks. Every truck stop in the country has a travel center, which is akin to a convenience store geared toward truckers. Here, one can find anything from mud flaps to Oreos. Many of them, appointed with fast food outlets such as Wendy's, McDonalds, and Subway, even sell beer and wine.

It was the day before Mother's Day, and I discovered a stand-up cardboard display of Mother's Day cards at the front of the travel center. I browsed through the cards for a moment, then turned my attention to a bin filled with refrigerator magnets and other novelty items that might possibly pass as Mother's Day gifts. I found a rack displaying plaques with various clever sayings on them, such as Mother of the Year and World's Greatest Mom. I settled on a miniature car license plate emblazoned with the simple word: MOM.

My breakfast was on the table when I returned with my MOM license plate. In the brief time I had been gone, the man across from me had somehow managed to devour his breakfast, and now sipped his coffee, as he worked on his logbook. He looked up at me and nodded as I slid back into my seat.

Jacqui appeared from nowhere with a new pot of coffee to freshen my cup.

"Does everything look okay?" asked the waitress. Business in the restaurant had slowed down, so Jacqui had a little more time to socialize with the remaining customers.

I nodded approvingly,

"My mother's name was Jackie," I commented as I buttered my toast. "Actually Jacqueline, but she was known as Jackie."

"My full name is Jacqueline too," she replied, "but everyone just calls me Jackie. I spell it J-A-C-Q-U-I though."

I resisted the temptation to point out that I had already figured that out, by reading her name tag, but instead nodded politely, lifting my cup for another sip of coffee, "My name is Pam."

"Nice to meet you Pam." Jacqui replied, as she surreptitiously laid my check on the table, then scurried away to tend to a frantically waving customer.

It did not take long for me to eat my breakfast. I glanced at the time on my cell phone, as I chewed on my last piece of bacon, pushing the empty plate to the other side of the table. It was now 6:20 am. I had no idea how long I would be here before the shop replaced the tire on my trailer.

My load was due in Chicago tomorrow morning. I had originally hoped to make it to Gary, Indiana by the end of today where I could shut down at the TA there. Gary is six hundred fifteen miles from Bloomsburg. Now I would probably have to shut down in Angola, Indiana instead, allowing me to continue to Chicago early in the morning.

"Where you heading, pretty lady?" The sound of my two favorite words interrupted my thoughts.

I glanced across the aisle at the man in the adjacent booth. Thankfully, his teeth were back in his mouth.

"Chicago." I smiled at him.

He was grossly overweight and horribly out of shape, as many truck drivers are. A driver sitting behind the wheel of a truck eleven hours a day, with little to no exercise, while living on a diet of mainly junk food, tends to take its toll on their body. I shuddered at the notion of doing this for the rest of my life.

"Chicago? Good grief, girl! What did you do to piss off your dispatcher?" he chortled.

It's no secret that most truck drivers dislike having to deliver to Chicago.

"Actually, I requested this run to Chicago. I have some unfinished business there and I wanted to get there one last time before I finish driving." I hoped he would leave it that.

"Finish driving? Nobody finishes driving until they die. Once you get into this rat race, you can never get out," he laughed.

"Well, I am finished," I responded curtly. "I've been driving over the road for nearly three years and I've had enough! After this run to Chicago I have one more load to Los Angeles and I'm done for good."

"Young lady, what are you going to do when you quit driving? Make babies?"

I smiled. He was doing a good job of using the magic words, albeit unwittingly.

"I'm going back to college to get my legal degree. I'm going to be a paralegal."

"What the hell is a pair a legal? Two lawyers?" He laughed so hard the table shook from his fat belly, as a small-scale earthquake in progress.

The sound of the PA system paging me saved me. I laid a ten on top of my check and quickly slid out of the booth to work my way to the repair shop.

"My name is Hoppy" he said and extended his right hand from where he sat in the booth.

"I'm Pam." I placed my hand into his and clasped it gently.

"Drive safe young lady. I hear there's a spring snow storm heading that way." I could sense his sincerity and was genuinely grateful for his concern for my safety.

"Thank you, I will. And you do the same." I smiled warmly as I walked away. He was a nice old man.

He flicked his hand at me,

"After thirty years of this, I don't even think about it anymore. All I do is crawl behind the wheel and aim." He laughed heartily as

I departed. Jacqui waved at me from across the room at the waitress station and I waved back.

The shop stood apart from the travel center and restaurant, so I had to go outside and walk across the fuel lanes to get to it. It was now 6:45 am and the sun was just beginning to warm things up. A brisk wind made the light powdering of snow from during the night swirl around my feet in tiny dervishes. I spotted my truck, BJ, in the parking lot as I entered the shop.

"You're all set driver." The shop attendant handed me the invoice to sign. People routinely refer to truck drivers as driver. I would have preferred that he called me ma'am.

I signed the invoice, sliding it across the counter to him.

"So, why did you name your truck BJ? We've all been trying to figure that one out." He smiled at me, hoping for the answer so he could share it with his shop mates.

I had forgotten that I referred to her as BJ when I had brought her in a few hours before. Apparently, the potential lewdness of this nickname intrigued the boys in the shop.

"It has to do with her number. It's a little complicated, but if you think about it, it's fairly simple."

He gazed at the invoice and studied the truck number for what seemed like an eternity.

"Three-seven-three-eight? How do you get BJ out of the number 3738?"

I smiled warmly, "Like I said... it's fairly simple. Give it some thought and you'll figure it out."

I headed out the door and across the parking lot to my truck.

BJ is a cherry red, 2006 International. Painted on each door is my name, Pam Anders. Below my name are the words, Queen of the Road along with the number 3738.

BJ started up with a familiar roar. I flipped the windshield wipers on long enough to clear the light dusting of snow from the windshield, as I cranked up the heater. I hopped out of the truck to make my pre-trip inspection, noting that the number sixteen did indeed have a brand new tire. I climbed back into the cab and turned on the satellite radio. Carly Simon was singing the song that had become my mantra, Coming Around Again,

"That's me," I said to myself, "I'm coming around again."

I changed the status on my log. I was ready to roll.

I pulled out of the TA lot and back onto Interstate 80 heading west toward Chicago. I merged onto the freeway, cautiously watching the road ahead, shifting gears until I had reached thirteenth gear. I glanced briefly at the MOM license plate, which I had placed on the enormous dashboard of the truck.

I would travel 242 miles before crossing the Ohio state line into Youngstown where I would pick up the Ohio Turnpike, to cross into Indiana, where I would shut down for the night in Angola. From there, it would be a three-hour drive from Angola to Chicago tomorrow morning. With an early start, and no more blown tires, I would easily make my early Sunday morning delivery.

I had eight hours of driving ahead of me before reaching Angola, plenty of time for deep thought. Hoppy had made a good point. Perhaps all we do is sit behind the wheel and aim the truck. The truck seemed to drive on its own now, allowing my mind to drift, reflecting on the events of the past three years. Time raced by in a colorful blur. I could barely remember events leading to being behind the wheel of a big truck. Wasn't I once someone else? Who was I? Why am I here?

Staring ahead at the fading crescent moon, I thought back to my chance encounter with the mysterious Sorcha, pondering the fortuitous words of wisdom that she had so soberly bestowed upon me. She had been right. I needed to tend to some loose ends. I needed to touch my past. My life, now disjointed, had no apparent connection between past, present and future. There were still things that I needed to tie together. I needed to make amends. Somehow, I had to stitch my wounded life back together, and the only way I could think of to do it was to make this last, very important trip back to Chicago.

I glanced into my side mirror and saw that a Greyhound bus was about to pass me on the left. I turned on my wipers to clear away the spray from the slowly passing bus, as I exchanged waves with the driver. I watched as the bus gradually passed, observing each one of the frost covered windows slide by. Faces peered out of the windows through small circles, cleared of frost by warm hands.

My memory stirred, as windows and faces passed by one by one, until the rear of the bus completely cleared the front of my truck. The right signal on the bus began to blink, and I flashed my lights, a signal for the bus driver to enter my lane safely.

I watched the wet snow spray from the rear wheels as the Greyhound bus slowly disappeared into the distance. My mind drifted backward to a time that had been, yet had never existed. A time and place long ago, and yet not so long ago. I recalled a person who I once was, yet had never really been.

As the bus transformed into a small dot on the horizon, my thoughts shifted to that moment in time at which my journey had begun...

Chapter Three
Transition

January 2005 -

The Greyhound bus barreled southbound on Interstate 15, as it crossed the state line from Nevada into California. After a thirty minute break in Barstow, there would be a brief stop in Victorville to pick up and drop off passengers, continuing on to San Bernardino, where it would arrive at 8:10 pm. Every seat was occupied, mainly with grim faced passengers returning from weekend jaunts to Las Vegas; their hopes dashed, as they contemplated how they would pay their rent.

I awoke from a brief nap and wiped the condensation from my window. The sun was setting behind the mountains, casting an orange glow on the side of the southbound bus, which added an eerie illumination to the passengers' faces.

It had been a long and tedious bus ride. It began yesterday at 5:20 pm when I boarded the first bus in Colorado Springs, after dinner at Golden Corral with Laura and the boys, before she dropped me off at the bus station. The ride from Colorado Springs to Denver took seventy-five minutes.

There was a two-hour wait at the Denver station for the

next bus. Stops in Idaho Springs, Frisco, Vail, Glenwood Springs, Grand Junction, Green River, Richfield, and St. George followed before changing buses in Las Vegas. The wait between buses at the Las Vegas station was four hours long, which I spent sitting on my luggage at the departure gate. We departed Las Vegas at 3:30 pm and were due to arrive in San Bernardino in four hours. After nearly two days of sitting upright on a bus, I desperately needed a shower and a bed.

An assortment of conversations reverberated throughout the bus. Several seats behind me a group of men had struck up a conversation, as they debated which jail served the best food. The sounds of a crying baby came from the rear of the bus. A couple, seated directly behind the driver argued about finances. Teenagers played with Game Boys, while a toddler ran up and down the aisle as his parents snoozed. Such is the flotsam and jetsam of humanity found on a Greyhound bus.

The woman in the aisle seat to my left snored peacefully. I leaned back and closed my eyes, hoping to sleep for the final hours of this unbearable journey. Sleep had been elusive up until now, and apparently would continue to evade me as my mind drifted rapidly between the conscious and subconscious. Thoughts of what once had been, what might have been, and what may be yet to come, raced through my mind. Ten months of hormone therapy had slowly altered my physical appearance, as well as my emotional state. I was at a point where I appeared neither male nor female, yet legally I still presented as male.

My name is Philip Anders, although my birth certificate says Philip Andrew Smith. Mom had remarried when I was six, and changed my sister and my surnames to Mair. After that marriage ended, she changed our names back to Smith. In 1976, I legally changed my name to Philip Anders, which was a variation of my middle name. Soon, I would be experiencing the most dramatic name change of them all.

I had just begun to doze off when I felt my cell phone vibrating in my pocket. A glance at the caller ID told me it was the home phone. I had called earlier and left a message for them to call me.

"Hi" I tried to sound cheerful.

"Hey are you in California yet?" It was my youngest son, Steven.

"I just crossed the California state line. I've got another four hours to go." I glanced out the window in time to see a sign stating that it was sixty-four miles to Barstow.

"I miss you already."

"I miss you too, Steven. More than you will ever know." I did not know what else to say.

"I'll call you tomorrow morning. It will be too late to call you when I get to San Bernardino. Can I talk to Greg?"

"Sure… I love you."

"I love you too." I could hear the phone clunk onto the kitchen counter. Steven yelled for Greg to come to the phone.

"Hello?"

"Hi Greg, how's it going?"

"I'm okay. What are you doing?"

"I'm still on the bus. I should be there in about four hours. What are you up to?"

"I'm playing against Steven on PlayStation."

"Well, I won't keep you. I just wanted to say hi to you guys and let you know that I love you, and miss you."

"I love you too."

"Say hi to mom for me, okay?" I was certain she was close by, preferring not to participate in the phone call.

"I will."

"Goodnight. Love ya."

"Love ya."

I pressed the end button and placed the phone back into the pocket of my jacket.

"Kids?"

The woman seated in the aisle seat to my left had awakened from her slumber, and apparently had tuned in on my conversation.

"Yeah." I replied unenthusiastically.

I turned away from her and peered through the window at the darkness outside, starring at nothing. I did not feel like engaging in a conversation with a stranger, but she persisted.

"How old are they?"

"I have two boys, thirteen and twelve, and a daughter thirty-four." I had diverted my attention from the darkness and turned to face her. She appeared to be slightly older than me, with warm, twinkling eyes and a pleasant smile. Her gaudy attire and jewelry led me to believe she was returning from a visit to the slot machines in Vegas.

"Wow, the boys are a year apart, huh?"

"Actually, they are sixteen months apart. Gregory will be thirteen in April." I did my best to smile sincerely, but failed miserably.

The inquisition continued.

"Where do they live?" She had accurately assumed my separation from them.

"The boys are in Colorado Springs. My daughter lives in Daytona with her two sons."

"How about you, where do you live?" Betsy asked.

I was afraid she was going to ask this question. I turned toward the window again, staring blankly as I tried to conjure up an appropriate response. Her reflection in the darkened glass of the window held an expression of patience, as she awaited my reply.

"At this point, I am really not sure. It looks like I may be living on the road for a while." I spoke to her reflection in the window, but then turned to face her again. She looked at me curiously, waiting for me to elaborate.

"I'm going to learn how to drive a truck. I am going to be an over the road truck driver, and probably just live in the truck."

I had not spoken to anyone since my bus trip had begun, and it was surprisingly refreshing to find myself carrying on a conversation with someone. I was pleased when she pressed on.

"That sounds exciting." She extended her right hand,

"By the way, my name is Betsy. I'm a retired schoolteacher

and live in LA. I have a son, a daughter, and four grandchildren. My son and his two kids live in San Diego, and my daughter and her two kids live in Portland." She had just given me her entire story in one breath.

I reached across my lap with my right arm and shook hands with her.

"I'm Philip." The utterance of that name made me cringe. I was eager to move forward with my transition and shed that male name.

"It's nice to meet you. What did you do before you decided to become a truck driver?"

I pondered for a moment before answering her. In reality, I never made a conscious decision to become a truck driver. My publishing business had disintegrated, and my wife wanted me out of her life, and out of the house. I was facing unemployment, poverty, and homelessness. Driving a truck seemed to be my only salvation. At least it would be a good steady income, along with a place to sleep, albeit in a sardine can on wheels.

"I spent the past 22 years in the magazine publishing business." I had a feeling this was going to open a floodgate of questions, and Betsy did not disappoint me.

"Wow! That sounds interesting. What kind of magazines?"

"I worked on magazines in the computer industry for a number of years, some travel magazines, a few trade publications. I eventually became the publisher of my own business magazine."

"Why did you get out of it?" I knew that one was coming.

I answered with a half-truth, "I owned my own publishing company in Colorado Springs, where I published a monthly business magazine that failed. After that, I just gave up and decided it was time to get out of the business."

She nodded as she absorbed my abridged account of the situation, unaware that I had only told her part of the story. The reality is, I had confided in one of my trusted colleagues and told him I was planning a transition to become a female. After promising to keep it confidential, he apparently blabbed around town about it.

As news spread that the male publisher of Front Range Business was about to become female, advertisers dropped out, and many of the freelance writers expressed their disinterest in submitting any future articles. It did not take long after that for the magazine to go into a death spiral.

The driver's voice crackled over the PA, announcing that we would be pulling into the Barstow truck stop in just a few minutes, where there would be a twenty-minute break. Betsy stood, and reached into the overhead for her belongings.

I gathered my leather satchel from under the seat in front of me. The entire bus erupted into activity, as forty-nine passengers suddenly came to life, eager to get off the bus long enough to stretch their legs, visit the restroom, and grab a quick snack. The bus swayed gently from side to side as we exited the freeway onto Lenwood Road and into the TA truck stop.

Sitting upright in the cramped seat of a Greyhound bus, for hours at a time, over a period of two days, makes one appreciate fresh air and the ability to stretch their legs. These occasional stops along the way were a blessing, and I took advantage of every twenty-minute respite from the confines of the bus made available to me.

I headed to the restrooms, more specifically to the men's room, for my much-needed potty break. There was a line to get into the women's room, and for the moment, I was happy to be able to go to the men's room where there was no line. Betsy was in line, and we exchanged smiles as I entered the men's room. Inside, I headed to a stall and locked the door. I had long ago given up on standing at a urinal, instead choosing to sit on the toilet in the confines of a private stall. After exiting the stall, I washed up as best I could, before heading out in search of food.

I headed over to the Subway counter where four staff members and a manager were efficiently serving a line of people. Fast food employees in truck stops train to be ready in a moment's notice, in case a bus arrives. I ordered a six-inch cold cut combo with provolone cheese, which the staff graciously wasted no time in making. Soon I was on my way back to the bus.

As I boarded the bus, Betsy was already in her seat munching on a large bag of potato chips, and she stood so that I could slide into my window seat more easily. I began eating my sandwich as the bus began to pull out of the truck stop and back onto the Interstate. I did not realize how hungry I really was; as I managed to devour the sandwich by the time the bus had merged back onto the freeway.

From Barstow, it would be another two hours until we arrived at the station in San Bernardino. From there, I would have to catch a cab to the La Quinta Hotel on Hospitality Lane, where the Human Resources Department had made a room reservation for me. Tomorrow morning I would start my truck driver training. I should have been nervous, but at this point, all I could think of was a hot shower and a bed.

"So, do you already have a job as a truck driver, or do you have to look for one after you complete your training?" Betsy was eager to get the dialog going again.

"Actually, I already have a job with a company and they are going to train me at their own training facility. There is a shortage of truck drivers right now, so the big trucking companies are putting a lot of effort into recruiting and training new drivers."

I rolled my Subway wrapper into a tiny ball and slid it into a trash bag, as I continued.

"After reading an article in the newspaper about the nationwide shortage of truck drivers, I began to investigate companies online. Just about every trucking company that I found had a huge recruiting page, with an online application. I filled out an application with Schneider National Trucking, and within a few minutes of submitting it, my phone rang. It was the recruiting department, just about begging me to join their company as a driver. They ran a quick background check on me, sent me for a physical, and within a few days, they had made a reservation at the hotel, and purchased a bus ticket for me. So here I am." I laughed.

"So they are based in San Bernardino?" Her interest was sincere.

"Their headquarters is in Green Bay, Wisconsin, but they have terminals and training centers all around the country. I am a Colorado resident, so that makes me part of the Western Region. They're sending me to their facility in Fontana, where I will be in training for the next two weeks."

The remainder of the bus ride went swiftly. Betsy and I chatted about everything from cooking to raising kids. She was a delightful woman, and as it turned out, a great travel companion. I was now glad that she had struck up a conversation with me.

The bus pulled into the San Bernardino station at 8:30 pm, twenty minutes late, due to the heavy Sunday evening traffic caused by hundreds of cars returning from Las Vegas. Betsy would be continuing on to downtown Los Angeles, so we said our goodbyes, as I grabbed my carry-on items and exited the bus. It seemed like an eternity waiting alongside the bus for the driver to extract my luggage, which I eagerly grabbed, and walked over to the line of waiting taxicabs.

The cab ride from the San Bernardino Greyhound station to the La Quinta Hotel seemed to take forever, despite the fact that it was only five miles away. After what seemed like several hours, the cab finally pulled into the circular drive of the hotel. I paid the driver and dragged my luggage into the lobby. Thankfully, check in went smoothly.

The front desk clerk ran my credit card, handed me a key and an envelope, left for me by Schneider, and within a few minutes I was in my room.

Two beds, a large dresser, a small refrigerator, and a television filled the room. The beds were the most beautiful sight I had seen in days. I selected the one farthest from the door, and after dropping my suitcase and leather satchel onto the floor, pulled the covers back. I stripped out of my clothing, and took a much-needed shower.

After showering, I brushed my teeth while opening the

envelope from Schneider. Inside was a stack of forms to which was attached a letter welcoming me to Schneider National. The letter included instructions to be in the lobby at 6:00 am for continental breakfast, and to be ready for the company van at 7:00.

After rinsing my mouth and tidying up the bathroom, I gratefully slid under the bedcovers. Having traveled 1,110 miles, on three different buses, over a period of 30 hours, this was as close to heaven as I could imagine. I rested, with my head sunk into the oversized pillows, staring at the ceiling, and pondered the coming events of tomorrow morning. This would begin my new career as an over the road truck driver. Within minutes, I descended into a very deep slumber.

Chapter Four
Fontana

I arose from my slumber and ambled slowly and gracefully toward the bathroom. As I approached the shower, I slipped out of my nightgown, allowing it to float softly to the floor. Stepping naked into the stall, I discovered that the shower was already running, and hot water was spraying out of the nozzle. I used the large sponge on the shelf, gently scrubbing my curvaceous body, as I let the hot water pulsate against my ample breasts. The sound of the water spraying from the nozzle seemed to become louder and louder, as I ran the sponge between my legs and gently caressed my vagina…

I thought I was still dreaming as I opened my eyes to the sound of the running shower. Lifting my head from the pillow, I glanced toward the source of the sound, noting the closed bathroom door. From beneath it, a horizontal shaft of light spilled into the dark hotel room.

From beyond the door came the sounds of spraying water and the clatter of activity. Quickly glancing around the room, I spotted the shape of a suitcase on the dresser that did not belong to me. The adjacent bed now lay disheveled, an indication that it had been slept in.

I was not alone.

The sound of the shower slowed, accompanied by the squeaking of knobs, and the clunk of loose pipes in the walls as the water stopped. After a few minutes of unseen commotion, a burst of light nearly blinded me as the door opened. My eyes slowly adjusted, as the silhouette of a tall, slender man exiting the bathroom began to materialize. He appeared to be in his mid to late twenties, clad only in a towel, and running a brush through his wet hair.

"Hey, sorry to wake you, but I guess it's time to get up anyway."

I looked at the clock next to the bed and realized that I had forgotten to set the alarm. It was 5:05 am.

"I got in around 10:30 last night, but you were sleeping like a rock," he laughed. "I think I could have shot off fireworks in here without disturbing you!"

I waited until he had turned his back to me, then hopped out of bed and swiftly slid into a pair of jeans and a polo shirt.

"My name is Steve, by the way," he smiled as he walked over to my side of the room with his right hand extended. His left hand held an electric razor.

I shook his hand and replied, "My name is Philip. Nice to meet you, Steve. Um… I didn't realize I was going to have a roommate…"

Steve walked back to the other side of the room as he started shaving. He began to speak above the buzz of his electric razor, "It figures that they would double us up, since they're paying for us to stay here for two weeks of training. I guess they need to cut their costs as much as possible."

I nodded affirmatively while opening a packet of coffee and pouring water into the miniature coffee maker that the hotel provided. "Steve, I'll have us some coffee here in a minute."

He turned off the shaver, laying it on the nightstand next to his bed,

"Oh that's okay. I don't touch the stuff."

"Good. More for me!" I laughed while heading into the bathroom with my travel kit in hand, closing the door behind me. I reached into my kit and extracted three prescription bottles, taking one pill from each, and popping them into my mouth. I rinsed them down with water from the tap.

After washing my face and brushing my teeth, I gazed at the face before me in the mirror. Ugly stubble had appeared during the night, which I quickly dispatched with a disposable razor, leaving my face as smooth as newborn baby's skin.

Twenty sessions of electrolysis during the past several months hardly made a dent. I still found it necessary to shave frequently. I hated the sight of whiskers on my face and looked forward to the day that they would be gone for good.

I emerged from the bathroom, tossing my travel kit into my suitcase. I poured myself a cup of coffee, while Steve sat on the edge of his bed flipping through channels on the TV with the remote control.

"So, where're you from Steve?" I took a sip from the Styrofoam cup, and set the cup down to slip into a pair of loafers.

"Fallon, Nevada. You ever heard of it?" He had mercifully turned off the TV, putting an end to the blare. I thanked him silently.

"No, I'm afraid not."

"I'm not surprised. It's a small town, about an hour east of Sparks. You know where Sparks is, right?" He looked at me curiously.

"Oh, yeah, sure, I've been to Sparks many times, Reno too. There are some decent casinos there." I took another sip of coffee, "Do you get over to the casinos very often?"

"No, I don't gamble."

"Okay, you don't drink coffee, and you don't gamble. Next you are going to tell me you don't drink alcohol?" I kidded.

"As a matter of fact, no, I don't do that either." He smiled.

"So what are you? Like… a Mormon?" I said laughingly.

"Yes, I am!" He laughed.

I smiled, "Well Steve, I'm a recovering Catholic and I'll be happy to take care of your share of coffee, gambling and booze. You and I are going to get along just fine."

We both laughed as we walked out the door, heading down to the lobby for our free continental breakfast.

The lobby was filled with people and abuzz with activity as Steve and I made our entrance. There was an alcove to the right of the lobby, containing a buffet table surrounded by several tables and chairs. Every chair was occupied, leaving many of the people to stand while eating.

As we navigated our way through the crowd to the buffet table, I commented to Steve over the din. "I think we need to get down here earlier tomorrow."

"You got that right!" Steve laughed.

"I had no idea there were going to be this many people here!" I said, while surveying the crowd.

Steve handed me a paper plate from the stack, which I accepted gratefully.

"I didn't either, but I guess I'm not surprised. From what I've heard, they have many empty trucks with no drivers, and need to train as many people as they can." He filled a plastic cup with orange juice from the dispenser, before grabbing a banana from the fruit bowl and a muffin from the breadbasket. He plopped both of them onto his plate.

"Yeah, I've pretty much heard the same thing, which is where I got the idea to become an Over-The-Road Truck Driver." I placed a bagel and cream cheese, a banana, an apple and a blueberry muffin on my paper plate. I followed Steve over to the lobby; where we managed to find a bench to sit on to eat our breakfast.

I scanned the room as I peeled my banana, noticing about thirty people of all shapes and sizes. There were a few females, but mostly men. Their ages appeared to range from extremely young to mature. The crowd was relatively silent, with the only noticeable exception being a small group standing nearby, discussing the homework assignmen which they had worked on over the weekend.

"I'm guessing that you guys started last week, since you seem to already have homework assignments?" I said to the group, without addressing anyone in particular.

"Yeah, this is the beginning of our second week. We got a ton of homework piled on us Friday, and it is all due today! You will be getting the same thing. You'll see!" replied a youngish looking male member of the group, as he turned his attention to Steve and me. The remainder of the group prattled on unfazed.

"Your group is pretty small compared to ours." Steve said while glancing around the room. He was chewing on a muffin as he spoke, spraying crumbs from his mouth.

"Our class was as big as yours, maybe bigger," the young man replied. He then made a sweeping motion across the room as if taking a count. "By the fourth day, half the people either quit or were sent home. Now there are only eleven of us left. By the middle of this week, we will probably lose a few more. Who knows, maybe they'll send me packing." He laughed nervously.

"Is the training that tough?" I asked. I took a bite of my bagel, looked at Steve, and back to the upperclassman.

"Driving a big rig is not for everyone. Some people just don't have the knack for it. This company expects nothing but the best. There is no way they are going to give a giant truck to someone, trusting them with customers' freight, if they can't hack it through training. They'll make that entirely clear to you guys right from the start, before you even start the rest of your training."

"I can't wait," said Steve sarcastically while rising from the bench. He took my now empty paper plate from me, added it to his, tossing them both into a nearby trash receptacle.

All conversation ceased as three large white passenger vans pulled into the circular drive outside the hotel entrance. A driver emerged from each van, noisily sliding open the large door on the side of each van, before entering the lobby through the automatic doors. They were dressed alike, in uniforms consisting of blue jeans and a tan shirt. The shirts sported embroidered patches, indicating that they were Schneider trainers. Two of them were male, one female.

One of the males announced, "Schneider school… everybody on board!"

The second week students, apparently accustomed to this routine, boarded the lead van. Steve and I made our way over to climb into the second van.

The female trainer was our van driver. She turned out to be a cheerful, humorous woman, which managed to sooth the nerves of the dozen or so anxious passengers seated behind her.

"Ladies and gentleman, welcome aboard the San Bernardino to Fontana luxury tour. My name is Amy and I will be your tour guide," she shouted while pulling out of the driveway and onto Hospitality Lane.

"The tour will last approximately twenty-five minutes and we will be traveling about thirteen miles. Please fasten your safety belts as we enter Interstate 10, where we will be hurtling along at the amazing speed of five miles per hour in rush hour traffic. If we happen to pass any movie stars' homes, I will most certainly let you know. I will slow down so that you can take pictures."

The entire van burst into laughter as we rode up the Interstate ramp to merge into the flow of bumper-to-bumper morning traffic.

The city of San Bernardino is the county seat of San Bernardino County, and is the eighteenth largest city in California. San Bernardino County is geographically the largest county in the country; larger in area than the combined states of Rhode Island, Delaware, New Jersey, and Connecticut.

Our journey from the La Quinta Hotel to the Schneider training center in Fontana would take us through the cities of Colton, Rialto, and Bloomington. The city of Fontana is nestled within easy access to Interstate 10, Interstate 15, and State Highway

210, which is why it has become the regional hub of the trucking industry.

I gazed silently through the side windows of the van at the slowly passing scenery along the Interstate. It resembled every other city in the United States, peppered with familiar chain restaurants and big box department stores. Traffic zipped in and out of lanes in front of and behind us, each car operated by a driver intent on reaching their own destination faster than the other vehicles on the road.

I turned my attention to the other silent occupants of our van, each seemingly deep in thought as they contemplated what lay ahead during the next two weeks. Steve and I were in the last row of the van. I sat by the window, Steve was in the middle. To Steve's left was the only female on this van. I had spotted her at the hotel as she sat quietly at one of the tables in the alcove.

She appeared quite young, probably no more than twenty-two, with a pretty face and smooth skin. She wore wire-rimmed glasses, with her hair pulled back into a tight bun. She looked more like a librarian than a truck driver, which led me to suspect she would most likely be one of the casualties of the first week of attrition.

Steve struck up a friendly conversation with the 'librarian'. I turned and resumed my reverie of gazing out the window.

"So are you ready for this?" I could hear Steve ask quietly.

"Geez, are you kidding?" she laughed." I have no friggin' idea what I've even gotten myself into!"

Steve joined her laughter, "Yeah, I don't suppose any of us really knows what's in store for us, but we'll find out soon enough I guess."

After a brief silence, Steve continued. "My name is Steve, this is my roommate Philip."

I turned back from the window to smile at the bookish girl.

"My name is Nicole, nice to meet both of you," she smiled.

My curiosity got the better of me.

"Nicole, if you don't mind my saying, you don't strike me as a truck driving kind of woman. What made you decide to be an over the road driver?"

She frowned at me. Steve turned his head, studied me briefly, and turned back to Nicole.

"I dropped out of college, and was having a hard time finding a decent job. My mom is a chippie so she talked me into becoming one too, but I failed the physical so they dropped me from the program. So, I decided to try the next best thing, driving a truck."

Steve and I responded in unison, "Chippie?"

"The California Highway Patrol. CHP. You know… CHIPS!" Nicole looked at Steve and me incredulously as if we had just asked the most ridiculous question in the world.

"Ah, okay. I didn't know they were called chippies." I responded.

Steve added, "Yeah, I thought they were just called bears."

"Yeah, that too. Mom says they get called all kinds of names." Nicole laughed.

The van began its exit from the freeway, turned right onto Cherry Lane, and left onto Valley. As we approached the entrance to the Schneider operating center, all eyes inside the van focused on the large white building trimmed with orange. The building loomed before us, amid a veritable ocean of huge orange trucks. It was a sight to behold. I shuddered with anticipation. The large security gate opened up remotely, allowing our caravan to pull in.

The vans stopped just short of the building, and the drivers ushered us out of the vans into what appeared at first glance, to be a large cafeteria.

To the right, were rows of long tables surrounded by stackable chairs. At the far end of the room was a food service station with trays, paper plates, plastic utensils, napkins, and cups. A large urn of coffee rested on the stainless steel counter. Behind that, a busy kitchen staff efficiently served breakfast to a long line of hungry truck drivers.

To the left of the entrance was a counter, were several staff members attending to the needs of the drivers standing before them at the counter. In the center of one long wall, two television sets were mounted above an array of vending machines. One TV set showed The Weather Channel, the other CNN. Men and women sparsely occupied the tables, some staring at the televisions, some involved in muted conversations, while others simply quietly ate their breakfast. In a corner at the rear of the room was a table occupied by a group of trainers, all wearing the khaki colored shirts.

Straight ahead, directly across from the entrance, a large doorway led into what appeared to be a theater. Inside, I could barely see the last row of chairs, and could hear the sounds of the movie playing.

Amy and the other van drivers instructed us to take a seat and wait to be called into our classroom, as they joined the other trainers in the corner. Steve and I sat at one of the tables. Nicole joined us, along with a young man who introduced himself as Tim, and a girl who Nicole introduced as her roommate, Corrina.

Tim was an extremely obese young man in his early twenties; with several piercings in his ears, lower lip, and tongue. Corrina, a plain looking, unsmiling woman, appeared to be in her mid-forties.

After a few minutes of waiting, a man appeared at the front of the room. He instructed the second week students to go to classroom two, and for first week students to follow him to classroom one. We all rose and followed him into the room. Inside, long tables sat in rows, with three chairs positioned behind each one. In front of each seat, lay training manuals.

I took a seat between Steve and Nicole at one of the tables. After everyone took a seat, the man who had ushered us into the classroom, stood before us to introduce himself. He was an ordinary looking man, who appeared to be in his mid-fifties, sporting a full head of neatly groomed, brilliant silver hair with a matching silver mustache.

"Good morning! Welcome to the Schneider Training Academy, my name is John," he began. "I will be your classroom instructor."

He smiled warmly, carefully making eye contact with each individual in his classroom, as he continued,

"The first thing I want you to do is write your names in your training books. Then, pass your completed paperwork up to me."

Steve handed his paperwork to me; I added mine and handed them to Nicole, who passed the stack to the table in front of us. I wrote my first initial and last name on the front of my training book, resisting the urge to write my new name.

John continued addressing the class as he collected the small stacks of paperwork from the front table. "We're going to spend the first part of our morning together going through some basic orientation, and history of Schneider National Trucking. We will preview what to expect throughout training and what the job of an over the road truck driver entails. This is going to be a very tough and intense two weeks of training, and frankly, half of you will not make it to the second week. Two-thirds of you will never spend a day driving a truck. I am not trying to scare you, I'm just telling you like it is."

I glanced around the room at the other students, noting that every one of us seemed to be doing the same thing, trying to guess who would not be here this time next week.

Tim sat in the back row munching on a donut from the hotel. From the corner of my eye, I observed Nicole, sitting demurely to my left. I turned to my right and exchanged smiles with Steve.

John continued. "Since our beginning in 1935, Schneider National Trucking has grown to become the largest truckload carrier in all of North America. Our fleet currently runs over five million miles per day."

He paused for a moment to let this sink in.

"We need good, dependable drivers to help us with our continued success. By the time this two week training course is over, we will know who among you fits the bill."

We spent the first part of the morning going over basic

trucking terminology, procedures, Department of Transportation (DOT) rules and regulations, and hours of service logging. At one point, a woman entered the room, introducing herself as Diane, the Physical Therapist. Diane spent the next fifteen minutes teaching us exercises that we could do on the truck to help stay fit, and prevent driver fatigue.

After a twenty-minute break, we re-convened. A man joined us now, introducing himself as Gregg Sallavolltia, the head of team operations at the Fontana Operating Center. John left the training room, leaving Gregg now in charge. It did not take me long to conclude that Gregg was clearly on a recruiting mission.

"I am here to talk to you about team driving" he began. "Team truck driving is not the best choice for everyone, but it is a good choice for many people. There are pros and cons to team driving. I am going to talk to you about all of them."

Gregg was a tall, dark eyed, olive-skinned man, with a head full of beautiful wavy brown hair. He had a firm, yet soothing voice, and a commanding presence. Strangely, I found him quite attractive, and even caught myself imagining him as my boyfriend. I was mesmerized, not so much by his presentation, but by the man himself. So distracted to the point that I barely heard a word he said.

"Teams are an important part of our business, so we need to pair people up as much as we can. As a team driver, you will get more miles and earn more money. Teams get the newest and fastest trucks. You will be home more often, if you are a team driver. Plus… as a team driver you will always have someone to talk to, as opposed to solo drivers that spend most of their time in solitude."

Nicole raised her hand. Gregg pointed to her, "Question?"

Nicole was obviously interested in team driving.

"How much driving each day by each team member?"

Gregg smiled as he responded, "From an economic and customer service standpoint, we like to keep our team trucks rolling twenty-two hours a day. That translates to eleven hours per shift for each driver and eleven hours in the bunk. The two hours per day that the truck is not moving is typically spent showering, picking up supplies, eating and such."

Nicole nodded her head enthusiastically while taking notes. Her hand shot back up into the air before Gregg could continue.

"Is it hard to sleep in a moving truck while the other person is driving?"

Gregg chuckled, "I'm not going to try to BS you. It takes some getting used to. You have to learn to deal with road noises, bumps, and the jolts of a truck stopping and starting. Many drivers try team driving for a while and end up going back to solo driving, because they are not getting enough sleep. Like I said, it's not for everyone."

Gregg looked around the room. "Okay, if there are no more questions, I am going to pass around this signup sheet. If you are interested in learning more about team driving, please put your name on the sheet. I will arrange a one on one meeting with you." Greg handed the sheet to one of the students in the first row of tables as he headed to the door. "Good luck with your training and I will be seeing you around the OC."

Regardless of the benefits of team driving, I had already made up my mind that I would be a solo driver. I was going to be going through a great deal of change during my transition, and I would need my privacy.

I looked at Nicole and asked, "So, you're interested in team driving?"

"Yeah, I'm totally interested. I think it would be a blast driving across the country with another chick. Just like Thelma and Louise," she laughed.

"Uh, Nicole… Thelma and Louise drove off a cliff," I chuckled.

Nicole rolled her eyes, "Yeah, um okay, whatever…. except for that part."

"What if they give you a guy partner Nicole?" Steve chimed in.

"A guy partner would be okay, just as long as he understands that we're just trucking partners and that's it!"

A student at the table in front of us handed the signup sheet to Steve, who handed it to me without looking at it. I passed it on to Nicole, who already had a pen in her hand. She eagerly added her name below the names already entered, and passed the paper to the next table.

John returned to the classroom and we resumed training. We spent the next hour learning about the ten-speed transmission in the Freightliner trucks we would drive, and the techniques required for smooth shifting.

Even though I had driven a five-speed automobile for most of my driving life, I found the shift pattern, and double clutching required for the ten-speed to be a bit challenging. Nothing that I cannot master, I told myself.

At noon, we broke for an hour lunch and we all headed off to the driver's lounge. The food in the lounge is not free, but the company paid for our lunch each day during our training. I ordered a cheeseburger and fries, and then joined a group of students at one of the long dining tables.

I found the food in the driver's lounge to be quite acceptable as I munched on my meal. I shared turns participating in the table conversation between bites.

My fellow students seemed to have come from all walks of life, each with a different reason for becoming a truck driver. Few of them had ever aspired to drive a truck over the road, but rather had fallen into it themselves in ways similar to my own.

One older man had been forced into retirement by a company that had gone bankrupt, leaving him with no pension and no savings. One woman, who had been divorced after twenty years of marriage, just wanted to get away.

There were several young, under-educated people, such as Tim, tired of working for minimum wage in low paying, dead-end jobs. Steve had felt trapped in his family's hardware store business for most of his working life, and this was his way of escaping. Nicole was a secretive young girl caught in the throes of trying to discover her path. We all had our stories, but none I heard that day were anywhere nearly as unique as my own.

The remainder of Monday's training consisted of the mechanical aspects of the truck, a checklist of things to look for in a pre-trip inspection, maintaining our logs, and a brief discussion on trip planning.

At the end of the day, we each received a commercial motor carrier's atlas along with homework on trip planning and logging.

By 5:30, we were back at the hotel, where many of us had gathered in the lobby to decide where to go for dinner. The front desk clerk recommended an inexpensive All-You-Can-Eat Chinese buffet a block down Hospitality Lane, so the small group that I was a part of walked down to the buffet. Now that our first day of truck driving school was behind us, we had a lot to talk about during dinner.

After returning to our hotel room, Steve and I worked on our homework assignments together. Steve was having a hard time grasping the Hours of Service Rules, so I did my best to tutor him.

Truck driving is one of the few professions in which the government tells you when to stop working and when to sleep. The Department of Transportation has very strict rules, known as the Hours of Service.

Simply put, a truck driver cannot drive a total of more than eleven hours, after coming on duty, followed by a required break of ten consecutive hours. In addition to this rule, drivers are required to stop driving after fourteen hours from initially coming on duty, even if it was for the most mundane task. As if that is not complicated enough, we are also limited to a maximum of seventy hours on duty over a period of eight consecutive days.

A driver must log as *Off Duty, Sleeper Berth, Driving,* or *On Duty Not Driving.* Each day, drivers record all of this data in the driver log, with each change of status notated on a graph. At the end of a busy workday, the graph often resembles something akin to an EKG.

Tuesday morning began very much the same as the previous day. After a brief re-cap of the previous day's lessons, we moved along to a discussion on air brakes, more on trip planning, map reading, defensive driving, and more about the paperwork the job required.

Next up was our introduction to the Qualcomm. The Qualcomm is a device which somewhat resembles a laptop computer, and is the truck's communications center. Not only is it a GPS tracking device, which keeps the company informed of the truck's location, travel speed, braking efficiency, and fuel consumption, but also works as a two-way text messaging system, linking the driver to the dispatcher. Its main function is to send load assignments to the truck, and for the driver to inform the dispatcher when a load is completed and ready for another. The Qualcomm also has the ability to give the driver concise directions to a shipper's or consignee's location.

One drawback of the Qualcomm, as far as the driver is concerned, is the fact that it records when the truck is moving or if it stops. Many drivers dislike the Qualcomm particularly for this reason, as it can disprove any falsified logbook entries.

After lunch, John ushered in the trainers, and lined them up side by side at the front of the room, introducing each one to the class.

"This is Amy, Rich, Greg, Barry, Brandon, Mary, Pat, and Gennipher. They will be working with each of you, and training you on the actual driving of the truck. Each of them has been assigned two of you to train and will be taking you out on the road."

John proceeded to read off student names along with each trainer assigned to them. Nicole and I were assigned to Gennipher. Steve and another man got Barry. John then sent us all to the driver's lounge to acquaint ourselves with our trainers.

Gennipher, Nicole, and I each purchased a beverage, and sat

down together at one of the tables in the driver's lounge. Our trainer was an attractive woman with spiky auburn hair who appeared to be in her mid to late thirties. My first impression of her was that she would be easy to get along with and would probably be enjoyable to work with. Her friendly smile and easy going disposition put me at ease and made me immediately feel comfortable, and I looked forward to working with her as my trainer.

Gennipher began the dialog, "Okay, let's start out with you guys each telling me a little bit about yourselves, and I'll tell you all about me."

Nicole gave me a quick glance, before she jumped in.

"Well, let's see… Okay, my name is Nicole Riggs. I am 24 years old. I love music, partying and dancing. I was born in Los Angeles, but my mom and I moved to Norco right after my dad died. I went to college to get a degree in criminology, but dropped out during my second year and joined the Navy."

She had not mentioned any of this in her story during our ride in the van. I looked at her with raised eyebrows, eager to hear the rest.

"So you spent time in the Navy?" Gennipher asked.

"Well no, 'cause at the last minute they decided they didn't want me."

"Why?" The trainer asked, before the words could get out of my own mouth.

Nicole glanced over to the other end of the table where Pat was busy telling her personal story to her two new trainees, before leaning in closer to us.

"I don't want this to be a big deal around the OC, but I am telling you guys, because it will probably come up in conversation eventually anyway." She said in a low voice.

I waited patiently for her to continue.

"I'm a lesbian," she went on, "I made the mistake of being honest and told the naval recruiter. He wrote it down in my file. Someone, somewhere up the line, decided that lesbians do not make good sailors, so someone sent me a 'thanks, but no thanks' letter in the mail."

"That really sucks." It was all I could think of to say.

"Well Nicole, if you're worried about what people around here will think of you… don't give it a second thought. There are lots of gays and lesbians in this business. I've heard that there is even a transgendered driver in the Detroit OC"

I instantly perked up. "Really…?"

Gennipher glanced at me "Yup." She then turned back to Nicole. "Okay, so after the Navy rejected you, you decided to become a truck driver?"

Nicole sighed, "Actually no… after that I tried to become a chippie, but failed the physical so I got bounced out of that too."

I was pleased that I didn't have to ask what a chippie is.

Our trainer empathized. "Well, I've heard horror stories about that physical; climbing up ropes, scaling walls, and shit. I wouldn't feel too bad about it if I were you. Anyway, welcome to Schneider," She smiled warmly, "I'm sure you will make a great truck driver!"

"Thank you!" Nicole beamed confidently. She exuded the bravado of a high-school tomboy, yet her eyes belied her confidence; revealing an underlying fear of failure hidden somewhere deep inside.

I suddenly felt a strong sense of compassion for this poor kid. She was a wannabe sailor and enforcer of the law, who liked girls, and looked more like a church-lady than a truck driver. I sincerely hoped that this time she would finally find success.

Gennipher took a sip of her soft drink, turned to me and said,

"Okay, Philip, what about you?"

I took a long pull of my water before screwing the cap back onto the bottle. The two women studied me, patiently awaiting my story.

"Um, well… my name is Philip Anders. I am twice divorced with three children; a daughter, Cheryl and two sons, Greg and Steven."

"Can we call you Phil?" Gennipher inquired while taking

notes.

"Yeah, that would be okay." I shrugged. Neither of them had any way of knowing what name I really wanted to be called.

I continued, "I have been in the magazine publishing business for the past twenty-two years, and I burned out. The reason I chose to become a truck driver, was the freedom it has to offer, minus the pressures I endured throughout my publishing career."

As had been the case with Betsy on the Greyhound bus, I withheld the fuller, more accurate account of why I was here.

"What are your interests?" Gennipher pressed.

"I like music, mainly classic rock. I enjoy golf, gambling, cooking, and skiing." I had the distinct feeling that I would not be doing much of any of those for the next couple of years.

"What kind of gambling?" She continued to press.

"Casino gambling," I said. "I love blackjack and poker." I smiled.

"Welcome to Schneider!" our trainer responded cheerfully, with sincerity and warmth. "Now, I guess it's my turn."

"My name is Gennipher Alman. Just so you know, my name is spelled G-e-n-n-i-p-h-e-r, but if you accidently spell it the other way, I won't kill you, at least not until the second time." She smiled a warm and friendly smile.

Nicole and I both laughed as we wrote her name down in our training books.

She continued, "Before truck driving, I spent time as a professional dancer, the lead singer in a rock band, and as a drag racer." Gennipher paused for a moment while looking at Nicole and me.

"What kind of dancing?" I asked.

"I did tap dancing, jazz, and contemporary. Mostly the dinner theater circuit stuff."

"That's a pretty interesting array of jobs" Nicole responded.

"Yeah, well I also wanted to be in law enforcement, Nicole. I actually took some college courses in Criminal Psychology too."

Nicole nodded silently.

"Anyway, I'm married with animals. I love my animals more than I love my husband. As a matter of fact, I love animals more than I like most people."

"Do you mind if I ask? What's the story behind the unique spelling of your name?" I asked, as my journalistic quest for answers roused from hibernation.

"I don't mind at all. I changed it in high school. Quick! Off the top of your head, how many Jennifers do you think there are in the world?"

"Fifty-billion, maybe?" Nicole took a wild guess.

"Yup. I resisted the social construct of being a girlie-girl. Instead, I raced cars, loved motorcycles and trucks, and couldn't care less about cooking, home economics class, or having kids. I was odd and different, so therefore I chose an odd and different spelling of my name."

My initial impression of Gennipher had been accurate. She was a very cool person, someone with whom I could easily be friends. I wondered how she would react when she became aware of my plans for transition. I felt confident that she would accept it well.

The trainer looked at her watch." Well kids, it's about time for us to get started. Are you ready to learn how to drive a big truck?"

"Totally!" Nicole replied enthusiastically.

"Yeah, I'm ready" I said.

Nicole and I followed her through the door, out into the fresh January air and into the sea of orange trucks.

We arrived at Gennipher's training truck, inside a large fenced off area in the rear of the yard, where several trucks drove around through mazes of cones. Some were busy backing into coned off parking spaces. Trainers in their familiar khaki shirts stood nearby their trucks while coaching their students.

"This is the training area." Gennipher explained. "We'll be doing a lot of our training right here."

After she unlocked the driver door, she showed us how to open the enormous hood of the truck,. There is a latch on each side, just above the front wheel well which, when disengaged allows the hood to be lifted up, and away from the cab of the truck. Beneath the hood was the largest engine I had ever seen.

She went through the entire pre-trip inspection checklist with us, pointing out every pertinent detail under the hood, while explaining each component's function. She taught us what to look for and how to test for potential failure, not just under the hood, but all around the truck. We checked hoses, cables, clamps, couplings, brakes, lights, tires, and steering.

"You are going to need to memorize this entire pre-trip inspection in order to graduate and get your Commercial Driver's License," Gennipher said soberly. "From now on, your pre-trip inspection will become more routine for you than brushing your teeth every day. The difference between a flawless inspection and a lazy one could end with you and or others maimed for life, or dead. You WILL NOT operate a truck without a pre-trip inspection!" She emphasized the words to make her point.

It was now each of our turn to go over our pre-trip inspections with Gennipher paying careful attention, and prompting us when necessary. After she was satisfied with our individual inspections, she showed us how to climb up safely into the cab without falling backwards. I felt as if I was climbing a ladder as I pulled myself into the tractor.

The inside of the cab seemed enormous. I never had a clue how spacious these trucks actually were inside! Beyond the huge cab was a double bunk, a small desk, closet, and a couple of cabinets. It was very much like a miniature RV. This pleased me immensely, since this would essentially be my home for the next few years.

"Okay! Are you guys ready to roll?" Gennipher asked. We both nodded emphatically. The trainer took the driver's seat, Nicole hopped into the back, and I took the passenger seat. I would later learn to know this as the jump seat.

Gennipher started the truck with a powerful roar, and a fierce rumbling, which nearly made me quiver with excitement knowing that soon I would be in control of all of this immense power. After going through a few checks inside the cab, she instructed us to buckle up. She released the air brakes with a loud hiss, and put the tractor in gear, to pull slowly out of the training area and into the main yard. In a few minutes, she had maneuvered the huge truck to the gate.

A female voice crackled over the speaker, "Driver number?"

Gennipher responded with her driver number and the gate slowly clambered open.

"Once you graduate, you will be given a driver number," she explained. After pulling out onto Almond Avenue, she turned right onto Valley and continued, "Once you have your own truck, you will always be asked for your driver number by the fuel desk before you leave. Same thing when you come back."

Nicole had repositioned herself and was now sitting cross-legged on the floor between us so she could hear our conversation above the roar of the engine.

Gennipher drove the truck a few miles to a deserted industrial area where she stopped the truck and pulled the knob to set the air brake.

"Who wants to go first?" she asked.

I was anxious to get started. "I will," I said.

She unbuckled her seat belt and stood up. I unbuckled my belt, sidled over behind the wheel to the driver's seat, nearly shaking with excitement. The inside of the truck was high enough not only for us to stand, but also for me to stretch my arms over my head. She buckled herself into the jump seat. After buckling my seatbelt, I looked over to her for further instructions. She circled her index finger in the air, giving me the signal to go.

After putting the truck in gear and releasing the air brake, I slowly let out the clutch. and graudally applied pressure to the accelerator pedal. As the truck growled into action, I nearly quivered with excitement. I was actually in control of this huge machine.

Within a few minutes, I had shifted gears and was making turns. The shifting was a bit rough at first, but in short order, I had mastered the transmission and clutch, and was shifting smoothly. Gennipher nodded approvingly as she made notes on her clipboard.

Nicole and I spent the next two hours taking turns driving around in circles, up and down streets. Our trainer knew all the areas that were safe for us to practice, and guided us to them. Our techniques were clumsy at first, as we became accustomed to the ten-speed, but with her patient instruction, encouragement, and reassurances, we quickly improved.

On Wednesday, we spent half a day in the classroom, before heading to the yard to couple the rig to a trailer. We practiced driving around pulling a trailer, learning tight turns with a fifty-three foot trailer attached to the tractor. These maneuvers took some doing, not to mention scary, but within a few hours, Nicole and I had both become quite proficient at it.

By Friday, we had become adept at coupling and uncoupling. We now pulled trailers up and down the major streets, and even on the freeways. While Nicole and I took turns driving, Gennipher sat in the jump seat commenting on our performance and taking notes. By the end of the day I felt like I was ready to go on the road, but I still had much to learn and I knew it.

Steve had been struggling with the homework assignments, and relied on me to tutor him each night in our hotel room. On Thursday night, he had confessed to me that his trainer, Barry, had expressed his frustration in his inability to learn how to shift smoothly, lack of understanding of the logging procedures, and his failure to couple properly. Therefore, I was not entirely surprised, when I arrived in the hotel room Friday evening to discover that he had taken his belongings and departed. John's words from our first day, echoed ghostlike in my mind.

"Quite frankly… half of you won't make it to the second week."

My first week of truck driver training was at an end, and I was happy to say that I was quite pleased with my progress. It had been much easier than I had originally anticipated. My initial fears now supplanted by a feeling of bravado. In another week, I would be a professional truck driver.

Nicole had gone to Long Beach to spend the weekend with her girlfriend. With Steve now gone, I had the hotel room for the weekend to myself. I had homework to complete, phone calls to make, and thinking to do. I looked forward to my alone time, and I intended to avoid everyone else as much as possible right up until Monday morning.

Chapter Five
Skid Pad

I came down for breakfast on Monday to find Nicole sitting with Tim and Mark at one of the round tables in the alcove of the hotel lobby. Apparently, they had arrived only moments before me, as their plates of food were barely touched. Tim's plate was piled high with pastries and muffins, as he was busy stuffing a chocolate donut into his mouth. He was wearing an orange, green, and brown tie-dyed T-shirt, which made his enormous body look like a planet. I exchanged greetings with the threesome, as I dropped my leather satchel on the one remaining empty chair and headed over to the buffet.

"Tim and Mark are going to be a team." Nicole informed me, as I set my coffee cup and plate on the table, and sat down. "Only Corrina and that old guy Charlie signed up for team driving. Corrina quit, and Charlie says he doesn't want to pair up with a girl, so I am kind of screwed for a partner." She pouted.

Mark replied, "I'm sure they'll find someone for you to team with, Nicole. We have a week of training left, so I wouldn't stress about it right now."

Mark Blanchard was a 30-year-old carpenter, unable to find work in Mississippi. He moved his family to Hesperia to live with his in-laws until he was able to get back on his feet financially. He hated his in-laws, and hated California even more.

I took a sip of my coffee and turned to Nicole, "When did Corrina quit? She was on the van back to the hotel on Friday and she seemed to be doing fine."

"She was gone when I got back to my hotel room this morning. She left me a note saying she decided truck driving was not for her."

"That leaves us both without a roommate. Steve got the boot on Friday." I replied.

"They're dropping like flies," Tim mumbled through a mouthful of pastry.

I surveyed the hotel lobby while peeling a boiled egg. There were twenty or so new faces, and only half of our original class.

"Well, you can't say John didn't warn us. Apparently truck driving isn't a good fit for everyone, but you never know until you try."

Nicole shifted the conversation back to her dilemma, placing her hand gently on my forearm.

"Philip, have you thought at all about team driving? I think you and I would make good driving partners."

"Perhaps we would, Nicole. We get along just fine in Gennipher's truck during training, but that doesn't mean we would get along living 24 hours a day in a rolling sardine can. Besides, I really need to be a solo driver."

Nicole sighed. "Well, I sure wish you would change your mind."

We spent the first part of the morning classroom session reviewing the homework assignments given to us on Friday, along with further discussion on trip planning and map reading. After our morning break, we spent the remainder of the morning on the various aspects of safe driving. At noon, we broke for lunch, to be followed by an afternoon of driving under the instruction of our trainers. I headed to the drivers lounge with Nicole following closely behind me.

"Can I talk to you privately?" Nicole asked while we ordered our lunch.

"Sure. Is something wrong?" I asked. I sensed a tone of urgency in her voice.

"Let's go sit outside and eat, okay?" Before I could respond, Nicole headed toward the exit with her tray in hand. I followed her through the door and joined her at one of the patio tables. It was a sunny January day, with the temperature in the low seventies.

I took a bite of my tuna salad, "What's up?"

"Is it because I'm a lesbian?" She asked pointedly while popping a french fry into her mouth.

"Is *what* because you are a lesbian?" I knew what she was referring to, but feigned ignorance.

"Is this the reason that you don't want to team with me? Does it have anything to do with the fact that I am a lesbian? I just want to be sure. Go ahead and tell me if it is."

I put the fork down on my plate and took a drink from my water bottle, then leaned toward her.

"Nicole, look into my eyes. Look at my pierced ears. Look at my hair. Look at my long fingernails. Do you honestly think that I am the type of person who would make a decision like this, based upon your sexual orientation? Besides, you don't see me asking anyone else to team with me, do you?"

"Well, you never know. After what happened to me when I tried to join the Navy, I'm kind of leery." She took a bite of her hamburger.

"So, are you gay?" she asked while chewing.

"No Nicole, I am not gay." I was unsure how to answer that question.

"I don't understand. Why are you so against team driving?" She took a sip of her soft drink, before taking another bite of her hamburger, while waiting for a response.

"Nicole, there are some things about me that you don't know, and perhaps will never understand. I really don't care to discuss it right now, but you will find out eventually. Meanwhile, I need to keep my distance from people and just be alone."

Nicole glared at me suspiciously "Are you like, a wanted criminal? Are you some kind of fugitive?"

I smiled, "No dear, I am not a fugitive."

"I know!" She giggled." You're in the witness protection program."

"No" I laughed.

"You're a Russian spy."

"Nope" I said, laughing harder.

"Are you a Martian?" Now we were both laughing hysterically.

"No!" I was almost unable to speak through my laughter.

"A dog disguised as a human?"

"Woof…." I sputtered.

"You're from the future." She poked me in the arm playfully.

"No, no, no."

"You're getting a sex change."

This stopped my laughter. I gazed at her pensively before softly replying.

"Yes."

It took her a several seconds to absorb this revelation before she responded.

"Holy shit! Are you serious? Yer gonna get a sex change operation? Yer gonna change into a girl?"

"Well, it's not quite that simple…. but yes."

"Dude, this is awesome. I have never met anyone having a sex change. When are you doing it?"

"It's not really a matter of when, Nicole. It is more a matter of how. It is a long process and it involves many different stages. I have been on hormones for several months now. The change is gradual over a long period. Eventually I will get my surgery, but that will not happen for at least a year. There will also be laser and electrolysis treatments to get rid of my facial hair. All of that could take years. Plus, I will need some facial reconstruction surgery. It's all very expensive and it's going to take me a while to save the money."

"That is so friggin' cool!" she exclaimed, After pausing for few seconds she leaned forward and whispered "Does Schneider know?"

"No. I did not want that to be a factor in whether or not they hired me. I will just have to see how they react when I come out as a female."

Nicole nodded soberly, "Yeah, I can relate to that."

"Nicole, you are the only person who knows. I hope I can count on you to keep this to yourself. Everyone will know eventually, but for now, I want to keep it a secret. Please?"

Nicole made the motion of locking her lips, tossing away the imaginary key. "Mums the word, dude."

After lunch, we resumed our training in the yard. Gennipher was holding her clipboard and taking notes as Nicole finished backing under an empty trailer. She ensured that the kingpin properly engaged with the fifth wheel, and hooked up the hoses and electrical cable.

"Well kids, you survived the first week. Now you're in the home stretch."

"I'm amazed at how fast this training is going. I can't believe we graduate in four more days!" I said while assisting Nicole with the pre-trip inspection.

"Well, don't get too cocky," Gennipher retorted. "We still have a lot of training today and tomorrow. We are going to spend a lot of time working on maneuvers here in the yard. Thursday we go to the skid pad, then Friday to test out."

After Nicole and I had completed the pre-trip, we all climbed into the truck. I sat on the edge of the sleeper berth, Gennipher sat in the jump seat.

"Today's a good day for a drive on the Interstate. Nicole, takes us to Tom's Farms, Phil can drive back."

Tom's Farms is a tourist destination located near Corona, 25 miles southwest of the Fontana operating center. It is an easy drive on Interstate 15, and offers acres of truck parking, which makes it a perfect location for the trainers to take their students.

Gennipher guided Nicole off the Interstate at the Temescal Canyon Road exit, where she skillfully maneuvered the truck into the parking lot. As we pulled in, several other big orange trucks, along with their students and trainers, also arrived.

Nicole finished parking the truck and set the brakes. Gennipher climbed down and joined her fellow trainers in their cadre, while Nicole and I wandered off to explore the many shops and other attractions. Several of our classmates soon joined us, including Tim, who had already discovered the hamburger stand and was busy devouring a bacon cheeseburger. I purchased a bag of jelly beans from a quaint little candy store, and joined the group of students on a cluster of benches in a garden area.

"I'm really worried about the skid pad," said Charlie, as he peeled the wrapper off a Snickers bar. "I've lived in southern California all my life, and have never driven on snow or ice."

Charlie was a 62-year-old former encyclopedia salesperson. Since the advent of internet search engines, and the subsequent demise of most printed references, he now had nothing to sell. Faced with the impossibility of finding a new career so late in his life, and having squandered 40 years of commissions on gambling and booze, he found his only hope for a new career lay in truck driving.

"Don't feel bad, Charlie. I haven't either," Nicole responded.

Tim chimed in, "I haven't either, but I think I can handle it."

Biting on a piece of peanut brittle, Mark added, "I drove through a snowstorm once while on vacation, but that's about it." Other students joined in.

"I never have."

"Neither have I."

"Philip, you live in Colorado. I bet you have had to drive in ice and snow a lot, huh?" Nicole asked.

"Well not only that, I grew up in Chicago and was taught how to drive on ice and snow at an early age." I laughed at the memory of Eddie. "One of my mom's boyfriends used to come over whenever there was a sheet of ice or snow on the ground. He'd take me to a deserted parking lot where he would show me how to handle it."

I looked over at Charlie, as he was taking the last bite of his Snickers bar.

"Charlie, don't be too worried about it. Just do what the instructors have told us to do. Take your foot off the gas, push in the clutch, and steer into the skid. Most importantly, do not panic. Do not freeze up at the wheel. You have to stay in control."

Charlie tossed his candy bar wrapper in the trashcan. "Yeah, well I guess we'll find out on Thursday won't we."

On Thursday, shortly after lunch, a van appeared near the entrance to the drivers lounge to take us to the San Bernardino County Sheriff's Department skid pad. Rich, one of the trainers, introduced to our class on the second day of training, was driving. Next to him, seated in the passenger seat, was Pat, another person I met that day. The trip to the San Bernardino Sheriff's Department training facility was a thirty-minute drive.

The San Bernardino County Sheriff's Department is one of the few law enforcement agencies in the country to have implemented a state-of-the-art driver training facility for its officers. A three-story building overlooks a parking lot, packed with dozens of shiny new cars and trucks sporting light bars and radar units.

The training area includes a test-driving track, and a specially designed skid pad, made slick using a thin layer of oil and water. In order to offset the half million-dollar investment that the county poured into this facility, the sheriff's office leases it out. Other law enforcement agencies and companies such as Schneider, who are willing to spend the money, use the center to mold their personnel into superior drivers.

We gathered in a waiting area inside the building, which was appointed with vending machines, pay telephones, and an array of tables and chairs. Rich was in the parking lot, readying the two testing trucks.

Pat addressed the students, "As many of you know, driving a car on a slick, icy road can be a terrifying experience. Driving an eighteen wheel tractor and trailer on that same road can turn into a disaster if the driver cannot respond to a potential jackknife situation."

Nicole and I glanced at each other. Her expression exposed a touch of anxiety. I smiled reassuringly at her. Many of the students simply stared blankly at Pat, their faces ashen with fear.

Pat continued, "Each of you will have two turns driving around on the skid pad, once with a trailer, and once without.

Rich and I will be in the truck with you. We have a set of controls that suddenly make the truck go into a skid. It will then be up to you to maintain control of the rig. You all were taught this in class, now it's time to put it into practice."

Pat paused for a few moments and surveyed the eight blank faces in the room.

"Okay, which brave soul wants to go first?" she laughed.

Nicole was game, and raised her hand tentatively. "I will."

"Damn. You go girl!" I uttered as I grinned proudly at Nicole. The girl, who I had once predicted not to make past the first week, now remained the only female student in the class, and the most stalwart of us all.

Pat led Nicole through a doorway that led down the stairs and onto the skid pad. The remaining members of the class gathered en masse at the window to observe Nicole as she mastered the skid pad; first in the bobtail, and then in the tractor-trailer.

For safety purposes, a flatbed trailer was used, strategically rigged to prevent it from completely jackknifing. I beamed with pride while watching Nicole drive around the track with the trailer zigzagging behind her, while skillfully maintaining control. Whoever ended up teaming with Nicole would have a good driving partner.

A grinning Nicole, her face flushed with excitement, burst back into the room with Pat following closely behind her.

"Fuck! That was a blast!"

She turned to Pat, "Can I do it again?"

Pat laughed, "Sorry, only one ride to a customer. Who's next?"

I wanted to get it over with, so I volunteered.

"I'll go."

As I followed Pat to the door, I locked eyes with Nicole, who was still beaming with pride.

We treaded down the stairs, onto the training area. I climbed up into the driver's seat of the bobtail. Rich was sitting on the sleeper berth holding a control box in his hand, connected to the truck through a thick cable. Pat climbed up and sat in the jump seat.

Rich explained the process. "What I want you to do is drive around the track at maximum speed. The engine has a governor on it, so you cannot go faster than 35 MPH. When you least expect it, I am going use this control box to make the truck go into a fishtail. Your job is to maintain control. Got it?"

"Yes" I replied. My hands gripped the steering wheel.

"Okay, let's go," Pat said.

As I turned the ignition key, the engine responded with a roar. I released the brakes and shifted the bobtail into gear. I gingerly drove onto the slick surface of the skid pad and proceeded to maneuver the truck around the perimeter. From my peripheral vision, I could see Pat writing notes onto her clipboard. A quick glance over my right shoulder revealed Rich holding the control box with an evil grin on his face. I was tense with anticipation of what was to come.

"Come on, floor it!" Rich laughed. Echoes of Eddie's voice reverberated in my head.

"C'mon Sport. You're driving like an old woman."

I pushed the accelerator to the floor, and the speedometer reached the maximum speed of 35 MPH.

"Make a hard right turn." Pat yelled from the jump seat.

I turned the wheel to the right, and the truck responded. Suddenly, I felt the wheels lock up, as the rear tandems of the tractor began to slide to the left, and we began to fishtail. I released the accelerator and pushed in the clutch pedal. I steered to the left, and then gently back to the right, bringing the truck back into a straight line. Pat and Rich were both laughing hysterically.

"You're doing fine, let's do it a couple more times before we switch to the tractor trailer." Pat smiled at me from the jump seat.

We did a few more skid maneuvers with the bobtail, before switching to the flatbed trailer. Preventing the tractor-trailer from jackknifing is a bit more of a challenge than simply maintaining control of the bobtail. However, my instincts worked for me, and I managed to handle skillfully each situation Pat and Rich presented to me.

My years of experience driving on slippery surfaces, plus my early training, came in handy as I managed to maintain control, and even power slide around the last curve.

"Wow, you've done this before haven't you?" Rich said from behind me.

I turned my head toward the sleeper berth. "Someone taught me to drive on ice when I was 12 years old. I have been doing it pretty much all my life," I answered, while silently thanking Eddie.

"You're going to be king of the road someday"

"Okay were done," Pat said, "take us back to the parking spot so we can get the next victim." She was grinning mischievously.

I parked the truck, set the brake, killed the engine, and climbed down from the cab.

"You guys really enjoy this don't you?" I asked while walking back to the building.

Rich held the door as Pat and I entered the building. "We take our jobs very seriously. The safety of our drivers is our number one concern. But yes, we really do enjoy this part of our jobs." Pat smiled as we climbed the stairs back into the waiting area.

Nicole was waiting for me in the anteroom with the palm of her right hand in the air, which I slapped enthusiastically with my own right hand. We were both grinning proudly, relieved that this part of our training was finally behind us, rather than looming ahead.

A line of eager students had now formed at the door; somewhat relaxed knowing Nicole and I had managed to navigate through the skid pad without crashing. We watched through the glass, as one by one, the remainder of our classmates conquered the challenge of the skid pad. Our van ride back to the OC was jubilant.

On Friday, a better part of the morning vanished as John administered the written examination. The exam covered every aspect of our classroom training during the past two weeks; including logging, hours of service rules, map reading, trip planning, communications, safety, hazardous materials, and scaling.

I breezed through the exam, turning in my answer sheet to John first. I left the training room, exiting into the driver's lounge. Before long, my classmates joined me one by one.

"How did everybody do?" Tim asked no one in particular.

"I did okay, I'm sure. How about you?" I replied.

"I think I passed" Tim responded.

"Me too" said Nicole.

John came into the drivers lounge to call us back to the classroom. We spent the remainder of the morning going over the questions and answers on the exam. Everyone passed.

Now, it was time for the road test…

Gennipher was unable to administer the road test due to having to give remedial instruction to an employee that received a complaint from a motorist. Barry, having lost both Steve and his other student to attrition, was available to test us one at a time. I went first.

Barry and I walked out of the building and across the lot to his truck. Barry carried a clipboard, while I carried my logbook, flashlight, and gloves. I was a bit nervous, knowing my performance during the next hour likely determined whether or not I graduated from driving school.

Barry broke the silence, "Gennipher speaks highly of you. She says you are a pretty good driver."

"Well, that's reassuring. I am a bit unsure of myself. To be perfectly honest, I'm a nervous wreck."

Barry quipped in true deadpan, "Please don't use the word wreck when we are going on a road test. It makes me nervous."

I laughed, "Okay, sorry."

I hadn't had much contact with Barry during my training ,but from what I had gathered, he appeared to be a pleasant and easygoing man. He bore a striking resemblance to Luke Skywalker from Star Wars, which tempted me to shout, "May the Force Be With You" during my pre-trip inspection. However, prudence won me over, and I decided to reserve my humorous comments for a more appropriate time.

The test, consisting of my knowledge of the pre-trip inspection, coupling and uncoupling, driving on surface streets, making turns, handling intersections, railroad crossings, merging on and off the freeway, and safely changing lanes.

Barry sat quietly in the jump seat and wrote notes on his clipboard, speaking only when giving me a command to turn or change lanes. I was extremely cautious about doing everything by the book. The exam ended with our return to the OC to back the trailer into a tight space, and uncouple.

Barry was stone-faced, as we walked back toward the drivers lounge. The suspense was killing me.

"Well? Did I pass?" I asked.

"You really want to know?" Barry looked at me solemnly.

"Yes," I gulped.

Barry smiled drolly, waiting a few beats, before finally

responding, "You passed," he said.

"May the force be with you!" I blurted.

Barry laughed, "Oh I guess that's another one of those Luke Skywalker jokes."

"I guess you get that a lot, huh."

Nicole was half sitting on the edge of a table looking at me quizzically, as Barry and I entered the drivers lounge. I smiled and gave her the thumbs up signal, as I headed over to get myself a bottle of water. Barry talked with her for a minute, before heading back to the training center to drop off my test results.

"In another hour, it will be finished, Nicole. I have seen you drive and I am sure you will do fine. Barry is very thorough, but also very fair."

"Have you noticed that he looks like Luke Skywalker?" Nicole asked.

"You know? It never occurred to me" I lied with an inward glee.

At 4:00 that afternoon, I sat in the classrom with seven of my classmates with which I had completed driver training. Out of the twenty plus that started with me two weeks ago; eight of us had survived.

"I am pleased to welcome you all as Schneider's newest drivers. Congratulations!" John said proudly. "Your test results will be sent to the California DMV so that you can get your commercial driver's licenses, with the exception of Philip as he lives in Colorado."

John looked at me. "Philip, you are heading to Colorado in the morning to take your CDL test. We've arranged a round trip ticket on Greyhound."

I groaned at the thought of another long bus ride, yet was excited at the thought of seeing my sons, Greg and Steven.

"I will now introduce you to your Service Team Leaders," John said as he dialed an extension on the wall phone.

"We're ready," he said into the phone, before departing the room.

A moment later, a woman entered.

"Hello and congratulations to all of you. I am Sandra Guan, the Service Team Leader for the team trucks. Call us STL's for short. We are basically, the equivalent of a dispatcher. Your STL is the person you will communicate with on a daily basis, and who will send you your load assignments. Those of you who are team drivers, will work with me. The solo drivers will work with Paul Cerny. Paul was going to join us, but he got tied up with a last minute crisis that he needed to take care of."

Sandra was a striking woman in her mid-thirties, with medium length dark brown hair, and creamy smooth skin. Her eyes twinkled warmly as she spoke. She possessed a smile that assured you could trust her. I almost wished I were a team driver.

"I will be having individual meetings with each of the teams on Monday to go over our goals and strategies. Paul will be doing the same thing with the solo drivers."

Sandra smiled at Nicole, "I'm guessing you are Nicole since you are the only female in the room. I understand that you want to be a team driver, but do not have a partner. You indicated on your questionnaire that you would like to team with Philip. Is he here?"

I raised my hand slightly while glaring at Nicole.

"Sorry" Nicole whispered.

Sandra smiled at me warmly, "Are you at all interested in team driving Philip? I can pair you up with Nicole."

"No, I really would prefer to drive solo." I replied.

"Okay, no problem. Team driving is not for everyone. Nicole, don't worry, we have a pool of drivers who need partners. We'll match you up with someone."

Sandra scanned the room and made direct eye contact with everyone. Before exiting, she paused and added, "Please, be safe out there."

On the van ride back to the hotel, Nicole and I made plans to go out to celebrate our graduation from driving school. Her car was at the hotel, and she offered to drive me to one of her favorite nightspots, The Menagerie, in nearby Riverside. We agreed to meet in the hotel lobby at 7:00 pm.

I took a shower and shaved my face as closely as I could. As I looked in the mirror at the male face staring back at me, I truly longed to go out as a female, but I had such a long way to go. Despite my long hair, long nails, and soft skin, I would have to remain in my male presentation for now. I dressed in jeans, a long sleeve shirt, and a pair of slip-on loafers.

When Nicole walked into the hotel lobby, I barely recognized her. Her hair was no longer in the tight bun from two weeks ago, but instead flowed down to her shoulders. In place of her wire rimmed glasses, she now wore contacts. She wore tight jeans and a low cut blouse, which revealed previously hidden cleavage. Nicole stood before me, a stunning beauty.

We drank and danced at The Menagerie until it closed. It felt good to be out having fun after the past two weeks of pressure. In just a few hours, I would be sleeping on a Greyhound bus heading back to Colorado Springs, to get my CDL, and to spend some time with my boys.

Chaper Six
Solo Driver

I arrived in Colorado Springs on Sunday evening, after another joyous Greyhound bus trip. On Monday morning, I took my commercial driving test, and by that afternoon, I had obtained my CDL. I did my best to look feminine in my photo, but to no avail. My driver's license picture looked very much like a man trying to look like a woman.

"In due time" I assured myself.

I spent Monday evening with my two sons, Greg and Steven. I took them to the theater to see the movie, Shrek 2 and out for pizza. It felt great to be spending time with them again.

The night allowed us to catch up after my long absence during training. Unsure how long it would be until I saw them again, I tried making the best of this precious time together. We spent time catching up on everything from school to our pug, Einstein. I changed the subject to a discussion of the lessons in the animated comedy we had just left that evening.

"So, what did you guys think of the movie?" I asked as we feasted on pizza.

"It was okay. I liked the first one better though," replied Greg.

"Not me, I liked this one better," Steven retorted.

"What did you think of the part where Fiona's father revealed that he was really a frog that turned into a human, and Fiona told him that she loved him for who he is inside, and not for his appearance?"

"It was pretty cool I guess" Steven said while finishing the last piece of pizza.

"It was okay, why?" Greg asked.

I was setting the stage for a future conversation.

"Well I think there was a message there that we should all pay attention to. I think love for another person should be based on the person's inside, not on his or her outward appearance. Fiona's love for her father was unconditional, and she did not care if he turned out to be a frog. My love for you guys is also unconditional, and I will always love you, no matter what. I hope that you guys would still love me the same, if I turned out to be a frog, or a bird, or whatever….."

"Of course we would Dad!" Greg exclaimed.

"Are you planning on turning into a frog?" Steven asked while sipping on his soda.

"Maybe… Or maybe something else." I pressed, "Would you still love me if I did?"

"Of course we would," both boys chimed.

Eventually, I would need to tell the boys about my transition. I knew that it would not be an easy thing for them to digest. It was my hope, by planting seeds such as the message found in Shrek, the task would be easier for them to handle.

After we finished our pizza, we headed back to the house to get ready for bed. After tucking the boys in, I headed for the guest room where I would be spending the night. Laura and I had not slept together in over a year. There was nothing outwardly unusual about me sleeping in a separate bed. She had made it clear to me that she did not want me in the house, but sympathetic to my financial situation. She also took solace in the knowledge that I would be gone by early morning to catch the Greyhound back to

San Bernardino.

I entered the driver's lounge at the Fontana operating center on Wednesday afternoon, and spotted Nicole sitting at one of the tables next to a man whom I had not seen before. We exchanged waves as I headed over to grab a bottle of water. Gennipher stood nearby, chatting with other trainers. We also exchanged waves.

As I arrived at the table, Nicole made the introductions, "Philip, this is my new driving partner, Terry. Terry, this is Philip."

"Nice to meet you Terry," I said, setting down my bottle of water to extend my right hand.

Terry made a fist and pounded the edge of my hand, "Yo brother, wassup?"

Terry wore a black T-shirt with the sleeves cut off, the front decorated with the illustrious caption, "Eat Shit and Die." He was wore a New York Yankees baseball cap, with the bill turned sideways.

"Terry just came to work for Schneider. He's been driving for over ten years!" Nicole bubbled, "I'm going to have an experienced driver as a partner!"

I took a sip of my water as I looked at Terry, trying my best to smile, "Welcome to Schneider."

"May I join you guys?" asked Gennipher as she walked to our table.

"Of course, you are always welcome at our table," I smiled, while patting the chair next to me.

Nicole continued with the introductions, "Gennipher this is Terry, he is going to be my driving partner. Terry, this is Gennipher. She was my trainer."

Terry chuckled, "You're a trainer, huh? This is the first trucking company I ever worked for where they have female trainers. I'll probably have to retrain Nicole."

I nearly choked on my water.

Nicole looked at Terry with her mouth agape.

Gennipher glared at Terry, "Excuse me?"

"Hey no offense lady, I'm just saying. Men are much better drivers than women are, it's a fact. Nicole should be grateful to have found a partner that can save her when she gets her ass in trouble out there."

I had never seen Gennipher so angry. She stood up and pointed a finger at Terry,

"Truck rodeo, dude. Anytime you want to strut your stuff; Truck rodeo." She walked away without saying another word. Nicole followed her.

"She sure is a touchy broad, isn't she?" Terry laughed.

I changed the subject, "So, who did you drive for before you came to Schneider, Terry?"

"Well actually, I've driven for five different companies. It's hard to find the right company, ya know. The last place I worked for was okay for a while, but then they hired this little faggot guy as safety manager. He was on my case all the time about my logbooks, so I quit. No offense if you're queer. Are you?"

I ignored the question as I took a swig from my water bottle.

"Nicole is a pretty good driver. I trained with her, so I can tell you first hand."

"Yeah, well you're just a rookie yourself, so what the hell do you know?" he snorted, "Anyway, I need to get out of here and go take care of some business before I hit the road. Nice meeting you." He held out his fist.

I pounded his fist, but felt out of place without a sideways baseball cap on.

"Nice meeting you too," I lied.

Nicole and Gennipher were chatting together at a table near the food station. I joined them.

"That guy is such an asshole. I have never been this furious!" Gennipher fumed.

I nodded in agreement, as I looked at Nicole.

"Nicole, are you sure you want to go out on the road with this guy? He seems a bit creepy to me."

"Give the guy a chance; I think he'll make a good partner. Plus, I need someone with experience" Nicole replied defensively.

Gennipher and I exchanged ominous looks before Gennipher changed the subject,

"Philip, you need to go back to the office and let your STL make a copy of your CDL, so he can get you assigned to a truck."

"Yes, I'm on my way to do that right now. As soon as I get my truck, I'm going to move my stuff in and go to sleep. I've been stuck on a Greyhound bus for the past thirty hours," I said as I stood and headed back to the offices.

Paul, my STL placed a copy of my CDL in my file, and told me to go to the fuel desk to get the keys to my truck. Sly was working behind the fuel desk, and congratulated me on graduating while he made a key for me.

Sly was one of the favorite fuel desk attendants at the OC, and it was not difficult to understand why. He was extremely helpful and friendly to all the students and drivers, while sporting a perpetual ear-to-ear smile. He obviously truly loved his job and enjoyed working with people.

Afer Sly had given me my assigned truck number and key, I set out toward the sea of orange to locate my truck. Miraculously, it did not take me long to find it. I climbed aboard.

I started the engine and performed an inspection for problems. Everything was operational. I began moving my personal items into the various cubbyholes and cabinets, excited knowing this would be my living environment for the next few years. I felt like I was moving into a new house.

A brand new mattress and set of sheets reposed in the sleeper berth. I removed them from the plastic packaging to make my bed. After surveying my new home, I closed the window's privacy curtains, changed into pajamas, and slid into bed for my first of many nights sleeping in the truck.

At 6:00 the next morning, I was jolted awake by the chirp

of my Qualcomm. I jumped out of my berth and peered through groggy eyes at the display. A feeling approaching euphoria roused me from my slumber as I read the message assigning my first load.

I headed into the driver's lounge for a quick shower. After showering, I went back to my truck to drop off my shower bag and take my hormones. As I walked back into the drivers lounge for breakfast, I noticed Nicole already seated at one of the tables, sipping coffee. We exchanged waves as I walked to the food station to grab a tray from the stack. I filled my Styrofoam cup full of coffee, ordered pancakes and sausage, and in less than a minute, had paid, and was on my way to join Nicole at her table.

"Do you guys have a load yet?" I asked, while placing my tray on the table, and sliding into the seat.

"No. Terry said he had some personal shit to take care of at home. He told Sandra not to send us out until tomorrow." I could hear the anger in her voice. She was eager to get on the road.

I removed my plate and slid the empty tray to the end of the table,

"I hope whatever he had to do was important enough to keep you sitting here losing money." I took a bite of my pancakes.

She nodded solemnly while sipping her coffee,

"Do you have a load?" She took another sip, setting the cup down on the table.

"Yeah, I just got it on the Qualcomm this morning. I'm heading up to Stockton." I munched on sausage, washing it down with coffee.

"Lucky you" she said sarcastically.

I was not sure if her sarcasm was because I had a load when she did not, or if it was because, I was heading to the crime capital of California.

"Are you guys packed up and ready to roll when you get a load?" I asked, as I tossed my empty plate onto the tray.

"My stuff has been on the truck for three days. Terry put a bunch of stuff up in his berth yesterday before he left. Some weird stuff too."

I looked at her inquisitively, "Weird stuff?" I raised my eyebrows and looked closely at her.

"Yeah, like a set of dumbbells. He told me he likes to stay in shape, so he takes his dumbbells on the road with him."

"Dumbbells? That's going to weigh down the truck!"

"Yeah, for sure." She paused for a moment, deep in thought.

"Something else?" I could tell there was.

"Yeah, he has this cigar box thingy. You know those wooden boxes that cigars come in, with the little latch on the front?"

I nodded.

She went on, "I asked him what was in it, just out of curiosity you know, and he snapped at me to mind my business. He says it's his personal things."

I replied, "It's probably just what he says, his personal things. Could be pictures of his kids, letters, whatever. I wouldn't be overly concerned about it." Even as I spoke, I felt an odd sense of apprehension that I hoped she did not notice.

I looked up at the clock on the wall.

"Well, it is 8:30. I guess I'd better get going. Give me a call to let me know when you get a load." I grabbed my tray and stood up.

"Sure will. Have fun out there." She waved to me as I carried my tray to the trashcan and dropped it off.

My first run was a preloaded trailer of Puffs Tissue from Proctor & Gamble. I would pick up the load at our Fontana yard to drive to a grocery warehouse in Stockton for a live unload.

After driving around the yard for several minutes, I spotted the trailer number assigned to me and skillfully backed under it. Weeks of training, of hooking and unhooking many trailers, made this a breeze. I checked out the fifth wheel to ensure that I safely hooked it to the trailer. I connected the red and green air hoses, the electrical cable from my tractor to the trailer, and cranked the handle on the trailer to lift the landing gear off the ground. I performed a thorough pre-trip inspection before hitting the road.

I began my log for the day. It was January 27, 2005. 9:00 am.

I changed my status to '*driving*', released the air brakes, put the truck in gear, and slowly pulled the trailer out of the slot. I experienced a rush of anxiety as I did this by myself for the first time. I pulled the trailer through the yard and turned toward the gated exit onto Almond Avenue.

"Driver number?" I recognized Sly's voice on the speaker.

"52736" I responded proudly.

"You look happy." Sly's voice was cheerful as always, as he watched my smiling face on his monitor,

"Be careful out there driver."

"I will. Thank you Sly!" I beamed. It felt good hearing someone call me a *driver*, for the first time after two weeks of intensive training.

The gate rose, allowing me to pull through. I turned left onto Almond, a right on Valley, to Interstate 10 West, which took me to Interstate 5 North toward Stockton. I drove, constantly consulting my array of mirrors, checking windows, while cautiously observing cars alongside and around me.

I wondered what the drivers around me would think if they only knew that a rookie, on his first run, was driving the big truck next to them. I laughed. It felt good to be on the road, on my own without a trainer to coach me.

My destination in Stockton was 380 miles from Fontana. My load was due for delivery at 9:00 am the following day and I had plenty of time.

Schneider has a terminal in French Camp, south of Stockton, where I planned to spend the night. French Camp has no cafeteria, as does our OC in Fontana, so I would need to stop at a truck stop along the way for fuel and food. I now drove a 70-foot tractor-trailer, so pulling into a fast food joint somewhere along the highway was out of the question. My new career now forced me to live on whatever fare each truck stop offered.

At exit 407, off Interstate 5, in Santa Nella, is a Pilot Truck

Stop. According to the truck stop guide, this Pilot features a Taco Bell and a Wendy's. After six hours on the road, I needed to stretch my legs and grab a bite to eat before driving the remaining thirty-eight miles to French Camp.

I pulled into one of the fuel lanes, killed the engine, climbed down from the cab, and swiped my Pilot Rewards Card and my Comate credit card at the pump. I put 50 gallons of fuel into the tank, just enough to give me the reward of a free shower the next morning.

Gennipher taught Nicole and me that the trick to financial survival on the road is to get as many freebies as possible. Truck stop chains give free showers with each 50-gallon purchase as one of those perks. Without the shower credits, I would be paying between $8 and $12 for a shower each day. It does not sound like a lot, but that quickly adds up to a great deal of money.

After completing my transaction, I backed into a parking spot, killed the engine, set the brake, and changed the status in my log. I climbed down from the cab to stretch before walking into the truck stop. After a quick visit to the restroom, I stepped up to the Wendy's counter.

As I stood in line waiting to order, I checked the time. It was nearly 3:30 pm. Why bother going almost a full forty miles on to French Camp, when I was already here at the Pilot? I could spend the night here, better refreshed to drive the remaining sixty-seven miles to Stockton in the morning.

"Can I take your order Sir?" The girl behind the counter smiled wearily, no doubt tired of serving truck drivers all day. I groaned inwardly. She could never have any idea how tired I had become of hearing people call me sir.

"No thanks. I just changed my mind." I had suddenly developed an alternate plan for tonight's dinner.

Earlier, while pulling into the truck stop, I had noticed a quaint building with a Windmill attached to it. The building houses a restaurant named Andersen's, with signs boasting *The World's Best Pea Soup.* I preferred a nice big bowl of soup to a

Wendy's hamburger. Since I would be here for the night, I might as well treat myself. I walked over to Anderson's, happy with my decision.

I ordered a bowl of The World's Best Pea Soup. When the waitress delivered it, I found myself seated before an enormous steaming bowl of thick and delicious smelling soup, accompanied by a basket of onion rolls and a plate of ham, bacon bits, cheese, and scallions. The price was $7.50. With tax and tip, it would come to just about ten dollars.

As I ate, I scratched some calculations onto a paper napkin. Today, I had logged 315 miles, at $.26 per mile, earning a gross of $81.90. I had driven a total of six hours earning $13.65 per hour.

At this rate, if I drove the maximum 11 hours per day allowed, I would gross $150.00 per day. Twenty-five days per month would give me an annual gross income of $45,000.00, on paper anyway. If I kept myself on a tight budget, I should be able to have enough money saved to start my surgeries in about six months. Only time would tell if this projection would come to fruition.

I finished my huge bowl of pea soup, laid a $10 bill on the table, and walked back to my truck feeling satiated. Not only by the soup, but also by the knowledge I would soon be making enough money to pay my bills, support my two boys, and finance my transition. I would discover very soon that it worked out better in theory than it did in reality.

I brushed my teeth in the truck, using one of my many bottles of water to rinse, and slipped into my sleeper berth. I set the alarm for 5:00 am, closed my eyes, and reflected on my prospects for the future.

The pleasant California evening helped me fall into a deep slumber, with a peaceful smile on my face. It was the end of my first day as a professional truck driver, and the future looked promising.

It seemed as though I had just fallen asleep when my cell phone rang. It was Nicole.

"Hey Dude, whatcha doing?"

I looked at my alarm clock. It was 4:47 am.

"I was sleeping," I snarled. "Are you guys on the road yet?"

"No, I am still at the OC, Terry hasn't come back yet!" She was agitated, "Dude, you are not going to believe this!"

"What?" I could not wait to hear what was so important that she needed to call me at 5:00 am.

"Okay. You remember me telling you about that cigar box thingy that Terry put up in his berth with his personal stuff?"

I nodded silently, as if she could see me.

She continued on, as if she had,

"Well, I woke up really early today and decided to organize the truck. I was rearranging things. I accidentally knocked the box on the floor and it popped open. You are not going to believe what was in it!"

"What?" I yawned, desperately in need of a cup of coffee.

"Baggies full of pills. Little baggies filled with tiny white crystals. Drugs dude!"

I was fully awake now. I swung my legs onto the floor and sat up straight,

"Are you sure they're recreational drugs and not just his prescriptions?" I knew it was a silly question, but I had to ask.

"Dude, prescription drugs are not in baggies! They are in little plastic bottles with the person's name on them! These are drugs!" She sounded indignant so I did not press any further.

"So, what are you going to do? You don't want to go out on the road with a truck full of illegal drugs do you? You certainly don't want to depend on a driver who is on drugs." I already knew the answer.

"I'm going to wait until Gennipher gets here so I can talk to her. She'll tell me what to do."

"Yeah I agree. That's the best thing to do right now. In the meantime, you should probably stay away from the truck. Just hang out in the driver's lounge." I refrained from saying I told you so.

"Thank you for not saying, 'I told you so'" she said

gratefully.

I smiled.

She continued, "Is there any way I can talk you into teaming with me?"

This was something I had halfway been expecting her to ask me again, just not so early in the morning. I did the next best thing. I changed the subject.

"Listen Nicole, I need to go grab a cup of coffee and take a shower. I still have an hour's drive ahead of me. I need to get this load to Stockton by nine."

My alarm went off as I spoke. I quickly hit the snooze button,

"Please call me after you talk to Gennipher and tell me what she says. We'll talk about it later."

"Okay will do." She hung up before I could say goodbye.

I carried my huge shower bag back across the parking lot and into the building. The bag contained shampoo, conditioner, body wash, a disposable razor, toothbrush and toothpaste, my blow dryer and a clean change of clothes.

First, I stopped at the coffee bar to fill up a large Styrofoam cup with coffee. I put a lid on it, headed over to the cashier's counter, where I plopped my bag onto the floor.

The attendant smiled cheerfully, "Good morning! Just coffee, sir?"

"Can I have a shower also?" I slid my Pilot card and two $1.00 bills toward the cashier. She rang up my coffee, gave me my change, while swiping my card to deduct the free shower credit that I had earned the previous night.

"Here you go. Enjoy your shower." She handed me a key with a large square plastic fob attached with "#5" written on it in black marker. I thanked her, grabbed my coffee and shower bag, as I headed toward the showers at the rear of the travel center. Shower #5 was just down the hallway, and off to my left. I inserted the key and opened the door to enter.

The typical truck stop shower is equipped with a sink, counter top, toilet, and a walk in shower stall, some with a glass enclosure. Cleaning crews clean and sanitize the room between each use, which is part of the reason a shower costs so much. Towels and washcloths are provided, but are usually flat, rough, and about as absorbent as stainless steel.

After placing my shampoo, conditioner, body wash, and disposable razor on the ledge, I stepped into the shower stall with my steaming cup of coffee in hand. I took a sip and set the cup on the ledge with the other items. I let the hot water spray on my body and began the process of shaving, cleansing my body, and washing my hair. My mind began to churn.

I chose to be a solo driver because I needed my solitude. I was finding that the actual prospect of having a companion becoming more and more inviting. Would Nicole and I be able to get along as driving partners? Would she be able to cope with the challenges that were sure to arise, as I transitioned into a female?

Both drivers benefit equally financially, mentally and physically as a team. The money is better for team drivers, plus you get to enjoy the company of another living person. The benefits potentially far outweigh any possible drawbacks. After all, my goal was to make as much money as possible to pay for my transition.

On the other hand, I would have to cede my privacy and much coveted solitude for the opportunity to make more money faster. It would also force Nicole to endure the backlash of whatever hell awaited me, as I began to present as a female. Despite the apparent benefits of team driving, I still leaned towards remaining a solo driver.

I emerged from the shower and toweled myself dry. My hair was still medium length, so it took no time at all to blow dry. After brushing my teeth, I put on clean clothes, packed my gear, grabbed my coffee and out I went. The obligatory big clock in the truck stop said it was 7:15 am.

Northbound traffic on Interstate 5 remained light, until I reached the outskirts of Stockton, and hit rush hour traffic. The population of Stockton is approximately 290,000, making it the thirteenth largest city in California. It is nestled between Modesto and Sacramento, which leads to a great deal of commuter traffic on Interstate 5 and State Highway 99. Fortunately, I had departed Santa Nella at 7:30, so there would be no problem arriving at my destination by 9:00.

I pulled into the grocery distribution center at 8:50, checking in at the receiving office. I handed my bill of lading to an unsmiling receiving clerk. "Door 38," he mumbled, as he tossed the paperwork onto a pile.

This was a live unload, which meant I would be here for as long as it took the dockworkers to unload my trailer. It could be several hours. The fourteeen-hour clock is still ticking, but I was not earning any money since they only pay us while the truck rolls. Most truck drivers prefer "drop and hook" where you pull into a yard, drop the trailer, hookup to a different trailer, and leave. You do not have to waste time waiting to be loaded or unloaded.

I opened my trailer doors, backed skillfully to door 38, and eased gracefully between two trucks. After feeling the soft thud of the rubber dock bumpers, I pulled the knobs for the air breaks, killed the engine, and changed my log to *On Duty Not Driving.* I was ever grateful for the many hours that Gennipher had spent drilling backing skills into my head. This is one of the most critical proficiencies of a driver. I now needed to wait for them to unload my trailer, so I could get my next load assignment, and be on my way.

I grabbed my cell phone and climbed into the sleeper berth as I dialed up Nicole.

"Hey, what's up?" She said, as if she did not know why I called.

"Have you talked to Gennipher?"

"Yeah, I told her the whole story. She walked out there with one of the security guys and me. I showed them the stuff. The security dude says he thinks the tiny pellets are crystal meth, but he's not sure what the pills are. They gathered it all up and brought it into the office. They're waiting for him to show up so they can call him into the office. Gennipher says they will give him a pee test as a formality, and fire him. They made me take a pee test too."

"You don't need to worry about that do you?" Even though she has always maintained she was drug free, I had to ask.

"Nah, no worries. I just have to find a new driving partner now. Any suggestions?" I could practically hear her winking on the other end of the conversation.

"I'm sure if you ask around the OC, you'll find someone" I deflected.

There was a long pause, Nicole sighed, "So still not interested, huh?"

Now it was my turn to sigh,

"Nicole, do you have any idea what it would be like having a partner like me? Have you thought about the repercussions? Have you thought about how people may react when I start presenting as a female? Have you taken any of this into consideration?" I was trying hard to convince her to look elsewhere for a partner.

"Dude, I'm a lesbian. Do you think I have never had to deal with shit from people? Do you think I can't handle the shit they throw at you?" I had to say, she was determined.

"Besides, who's going to make sure your makeup is put on right? Who is going to help you shop for clothes? Who's going to make sure you don't dress like a dork?" Now she was laughing.

I laughed with her "Okay Nicole. Let's talk to Sandra and see what she thinks ... hold on." A loud bang shook my driver side door.

I hopped out of the sleeper berth to peer out the window.

A large, muscular man stood next to my truck. I opened the window.

"Yes?" I asked curiously.

"Hey! Wassup man?" He smiled and continued before I could respond,

"You've been here for almost half an hour and haven't paid for your lumper yet. You need to get that taken care of, so you can get unloaded and get out of here!” He pointed to my trailer, ”They’re gonna want this hole for other trucks.”

“I need a lumper? Geez, hold on, okay?”

I grabbed the phone from the bed,

”Nicole, I need to go and talk to this guy. You go talk to Sandra and give me a call later.” I pressed the end button, tossed the phone back on the bed to address the man at my window.

“I didn’t realize I needed a lumper. I was wondering why they hadn’t started unloading my trailer yet,” I said while climbing down from the cab of the truck, ”Sorry, nobody told me.”

He looked at me curiously, “How long have you been driving?”

“Counting today?” I laughed.

Yeah sure, counting today” He smiled.

“Two days” I confessed meekly.

“Oh great, another baby truck driver from the womb of Mama Schneider,” he laughed heartily,

”Okay, lemme explain how this works. You are gonna discover that on most grocery deliveries, it is the driver’s responsibility to unload the trailer. Some places let you do the unloading, but that’s not really a good idea.”

He thrust out his right hand. “By the way, my name is Arturo and I run the lumper crew here.”

I shook his hand, “I’m Philip.”

“Nice to meet you Philip.” He continued with his tutelage, ”They told you about lumpers in your training, didn’t they?”

“Yeah, a little bit” I nodded.

“Okay well it’s gonna cost $200 to unload your truck. Schneider will pay for it and recoup the cost from the shipper. Did they give you some blank Comchecks?”

“Yes, I have quite a few of them.”

“Good, go ahead and get an authorization for $200 from your dispatcher. You can find me wandering around the dock when you’re ready. We’ll get you unloaded before you know it.”

Comchecks are blank checks that have no value until the

company issues an authorization number. The recipient must call in to register the check to receive a code to write on the check. Only then, can they cash or deposit the check into a bank. Comchecks are a convenient way for trucking companies to handle transactions with drivers such as paying for lumpers.

I was able to get the authorization number sent to my Qualcomm. Within an hour, I was unloaded. I sent an "empty" message, and waited for my next load assignment to appear. I did not have to wait long.

From the grocery distribution center, I headed to the Toys R Us Distribution Center on the south side of Stockton, to pick up a load of toys destined for Seattle, Washington, eight hundred miles up the coast.

Two days later, after delivering that load, I picked up a load from Kimberly Clark in Everett, to head back south to the OC in Fontana, twelve hundred and ten miles away. I would be there in three days.

Forty-five minutes after departing Everett, my cell phone rang and I answered without looking at the caller ID. It was Nicole.

"Hey dude, where you at?"

"I just left Everett, Washington with a load of toilet paper. I'm heading back to Fontana."

"Yeah, I know. Sandra says you will be back here on Monday?"

"That sounds about right…" I felt a conspiracy afoot, "What's going on with Sandra?" I asked suspiciously.

"She's gonna call you today. She'll tell you all about it."

My phone's call waiting beeped and I quickly looked at the screen. The caller ID said it was coming from the Fontana OC.

"Speak of the Devil; I'll bet this is her calling me now. I'll talk to you later." I hung up with Nicole and switched to the other line.

"Hello?"

"Hi Philip, this is Sandra Guan at the OC, can you talk?"

"Yeah, sure" I did not mention that I was driving through

heavy traffic in Seattle.

"How do you feel about teaming with Nicole? I think you two would make a great team."

"I think it could work. Nicole and I have discussed it some."

"Good, that's why we got you a load back to Fontana. We want to talk to you. Nicole really wants to team with you." She hesitated for a moment and continued, "There is one slight hitch though…"

"Um, hitch…?" I was intrigued.

"We require that team drivers live in the same area. Nicole lives here in Norco, and you live in Colorado, so that wouldn't work." There were several seconds of silence on the line as I digested this new turn of events.

"Would you be willing to move to California?"

"I'm guessing Nicole doesn't want to move to Colorado?"

"It's best if you're here in California since you'll be dispatched out of Fontana. Give it some thought. We can discuss it when you get here Monday. Drive safe and I'll see you then." She hung up.

On Monday, my first week as a professional truck driver will conclude with my arrival back at the Fontana OC with my 30,000 lbs. of toilet tissue. I will have driven twenty five hundred miles along the west coast of the country, crossing three state lines.

I stared through the windshield of my big orange truck as I made my way south on Interstate 5 through Washington, Oregon and back to my home base in Fontana, California. I had a lot to think about over the next twelve hundred miles.

Chapter Seven
Nicole

I pulled the truck into the Fontana yard on Sunday afternoon after an uneventful trip from Everett. Aside from some treacherous ice while traveling through Grant's Pass in Oregon, the driving had been relatively easy. I had spent Friday night in Wilsonville, just south of Portland, and Saturday in Weed, California. While at the truck stop in Weed, I purchased an "I Love Weed" T-shirt, which I wore as I entered the driver's lounge.

The Super Bowl was playing out the final minutes of the first half in the theater room as I walked in. I spotted Nicole waving at me from her spot close to the front. She had saved a seat for me.

"I love your shirt!" Nicole laughed as I eased into the chair.

"Thanks, I got it in a city named Weed. It's not what you think" I chuckled.

"Philip, did you forget that I grew up in California? I know where Weed is" she retorted sardonically.

"Oh, yeah, sorry" I replied sheepishly.

The first half of the game ended in a 7-7 tie. During half time, most of the drivers got up to go stretch their legs, visit the restroom, smoke cigarettes, or reload on snacks and beverages. Nicole and I stayed seated to enjoy the halftime show featuring

Paul McCartney.

The second half barely interested me enough to keep my eyes open. The game ended in a lackluster fashion. The New England Patriots beat the Philadelphia Eagles 24-21. At the conclusion of the game, Nicole and I purchased beverages and headed out to the patio to enjoy the pleasant evening.

"So how was your first week driving a truck?" Nicole asked while sipping her soft drink.

"It was good. I felt very comfortable with it, as if I had been doing it all my life. I think the trainers here did a great job preparing us."

"That's nice to know." Nicole paused for a moment, continuing on another track.

"Sandra wants to meet with us at eight tomorrow morning to talk about team driving. Have you thought any more about it?"

"Yeah, I just spent the past couple of days thinking it over, Nicole" I sighed, "I really have mixed feelings about it though. On one hand, I can see the benefits of teaming, and I really think that you and I could make good partners… But then, on the other hand…" I paused to gather my thoughts.

"On the other hand what?" Nicole prodded

After a quick glance to the left and right to ensure that nobody was eavesdropping, I looked at Nicole,

"Nicole, exactly 88 days from today I will start presenting as a female. I don't know what the response is going to be when people see me dressed as a female. Frankly, I am scared for my safety. If you were my partner, I would be worried about your safety as well. It could get very ugly."

Nicole laughed loudly, "Eighty-eight days? You're counting days? Why happens in eighty-eight days?"

"Well, May 5th is my target date for coming out as female. Five-Five-Oh Five. It's 88 days from today."

"Dude, you crack me up! You have this all planned out right down to the day?" she laughed.

"Yes, I have everything planned out. I don't do anything

without a plan, which is something you'll soon learn about me."

Nicole nodded, "Can I ask you a question?" She gazed at me quizzically.

"Of course you can." I took a swig from my water bottle.

"Okay, you told me that you were going to get surgery on your face and stuff. If you're so worried about how you're going to look when you start dressing like a girl, why don't you just wait until after you have all that stuff done before you start presenting as a female?"

"I wish it was that easy. There is a requirement in order for anyone seeking to get the surgery called the Real Life Test. It's also known as the Real Life Experience. Whatever you call it, it says that I have to live in the role of a female, full time, for a year, before I can even get GRS. The longer I wait to go full time, the longer I have to wait for the surgery."

"GRS?"

"Gender Reassignment Surgery, sorry" I answered.

Nicole nodded silently as I continued.

"I figure during the next year, I can get my electrolysis done and maybe some minor facial surgery. Meanwhile, I'll save my money, so I can get my GRS on Six-Six-Oh Six" I grinned.

"You and your crazy dates!" She laughed, "What are you going to do on Seven-Seven-Oh-Seven?"

"I don't know right now, but if all goes according to my plan, it will be something other than driving a truck."

The next morning, Sandra ushered Nicole and me into one of the meeting rooms in the administrative area of the operating center. The three of us joined Gregg Sallavolltia, the overseer of the team drivers. Gregg sat at a small table, shuffling through a file folder, as we entered the room to take our seats at the table.

"So, Nicole and Philip, you have decided to become team drivers? Congratulations" Gregg smiled warmly.

I returned the smile. There was something very magical about Gregg. I had a hard time taking my eyes off him.

"I haven't actually made a final decision, Gregg. I think it is something that could work out, but I am still grappling with the whole idea of team driving."

"That's understandable. Just keep in mind though, that if you choose to remain a solo driver you will be limited to west coast regional loads. This pretty much keeps you in California, Oregon, and Washington. The 55 and 60 mph truck speed limits in those states restrict your miles per day and your income."

I glanced at Sandra who was nodding in agreement. Nicole sat listening silently as Gregg continued.

"If you team with Nicole, you will be running coast to coast, be paid more per mile, and have a newer and faster truck. Your income dramatically increases as a team driver. It's definitely worth giving a try."

That finally swayed me, "Okay it's a deal" I smiled.

"Great!" Gregg stood and offered a handshake, which I accepted.

"I have to get back to work. Sandra will take it from here."

After we finished up with Sandra, Nicole and I headed out to the yard. I pulled my tractor next to Nicole's and began the process of moving my personal items over to "our" truck. Nicole and Terry had been assigned a 2005 Freightliner, which was much nicer than my worn out 2003 rig. She chose the upper berth, which was fine with me since I preferred the lower. I moved all of my belongings from my old truck, parked it, and returned the key to the fuel desk.

Nicole drove us in her car to the Wal-Mart in nearby Rancho Cucamonga to stock up on food and personal items for ourselves. After loading our bounty into the truck, we had dinner in the driver's lounge.

"I'm gonna head to Long Beach to spend the night with my girlfriend," Nicole informed me, as she pushed her empty plate aside.

"That's fine with me. I can just call you when we get a load assignment. How long would it take you to get back to the OC from there?"

"It's about 60 miles. It could take two hours in rush hour, or a little over an hour any other time."

"Geez… I cannot believe how spread out everything is in California. I'll call you as soon as we get an assignment."

We received our first load assignments on the Qualcomm that night. In the morning, we were to pick up a load from Kimberly Clark, to bring back to the yard in Fontana to drop it off. After dropping that trailer, we would "dead-head" (take an empty trailer) back to the U.S. Post Office in Fullerton. We would drop the trailer there in Fullerton to pick up a trailer loaded with mail, destined for Chicago. I sent a text message to Nicole informing her of our assignments.

It was 7:30 am as I was finishing my breakfast, when Nicole arrived in the driver's lounge. We went to the truck to do our pre-trip inspection, and prepared to hit the road.

"I hope you enjoyed your evening." I said as we headed off to Fullerton.

"Yes, it was great!" She replied without elaborating. We had agreed that my shift would be from 12:00 am until 12:00 pm, and hers would be from 12:00 pm until 12:00 am. This arrangement worked out perfectly for both of us, as I am an early riser while she was a night owl.

Nicole rested in the berth while I picked up the load from Kimberly Clark, dropped it off in Fontana, and returned to Fullerton to pick up our load of mail bound for Chicago. At 12:00 pm, I pulled into the TA truck stop in Barstow, where I fueled the truck. After parking the rig, we went inside to grab a bite to eat before changing shifts.

I had my road atlas opened as we sat at one of the tables eating our dinner.

"Nicole, how would you feel about altering our route slightly?"

Nichole shrugged while chewing on her chicken fingers.

"Okay, look…" I turned the atlas around so she could follow me, "The recommended route is for us to take Interstate 15 up to Interstate 70, go east through Utah and Colorado, and on to Denver. From there we take Interstate 76 to the 80 and into Chicago, right?" I dragged the handle of my plastic fork along the atlas to show her the route.

Nicole nodded.

"Okay, if we take that route, it's 1,950 miles from where we are to Chicago. If we change our route slightly and take Interstate 40 from here into New Mexico and pick up Interstate 25 north into Colorado, then pick up the 76 to the 80, its 2,042 miles. That's only a difference of 92 miles." I showed her the altered route, again using my plastic fork.

Nicole stared at me blankly, "Why would we want to add 92 miles to our route? I'm confused"

"Because this route takes us through Colorado Springs."

"So you want us to go through Colorado Springs?"

"Nicole, there are some things that I would like to pick up at my house. My ex, Laura and my two boys live in Colorado Springs. You'd be doing me a huge favor if you go along with this. I 'll owe you in a big way."

Nicole laughed "Okay dude, so you owe me. Big time."

I smiled to express my relief at her accommodating my wishes and to show her my appreciation. I felt that teaming with Nicole now seemed like a good idea after all.

It was 4:30 pm the next day, when Nicole parked the big orange truck in front of my house on Holt Drive in Colorado Springs. Steven was outside riding his skateboard as we pulled up, which he immediately abandoned as he ran to the door to yell for Greg to come outside.

Laura was standing in the doorway as Nicole and I climbed down from the truck and walked toward the house. Both of my boys ran up to me, greeting me with hugs and kisses. Laura smiled genuinely, as she opened the door and we all gathered around the kitchen table. I introduced Nicole as my driving partner.

After serving refreshments, Laura handed me a large stack of envelopes held together by two fat rubber bands.

"Here's your mail. There's something in there from the FBI?" she said suspiciously.

"Ah, good, thank you." I knew what the FBI had sent me, but there was no reason to get into it right now.

"Laura, do you mind if I take a quick shower?" Nicole asked.

"Oh, sure! You can use the one in the hallway. Come with me, I'll show you where it is." Laura led Nicole out to the hallway toward the guest bathroom.

"Hey Dad, can Steven and I play in the truck?" Gregory asked.

"Sure, just don't drive it away…" I laughed.

The five of us headed out to the truck. After a brief tour, Nicole grabbed her shower bag and went back into the house with Laura. After explaining all the knobs, levers, and controls to the boys, I left them to explore, heading back to the house, where I joined Laura at the kitchen table. Nicole was in the shower.

"She's kind of young for you, isn't she?" Laura quipped with a wry smile.

"Laura, first of all, she is just my driving partner. Secondly, she is a lesbian." I replied, careful to be not overly curt with my response.

"Oh, that's just great. So in addition to you having a sex change, you're hanging out with lesbians now?"

"Laura, please… She's just a driving partner, that's all. Why are you making a big deal out of it?"

Laura smiled and changed the subject,

"I listed the house with a real estate broker. We're moving back to Dallas, so I can be closer to Mom and Dad."

"That makes sense. It's actually better for me, I can get to Dallas to visit the boys a lot easier than I can get to Colorado Springs. We're still getting our divorce in Colorado Springs though, right?"

"Yeah, I doubt that the house will sell and close before April nineteenth. Don't worry, I'll still be here for our court date. Will you?"

"Yeah, no worries. I'll make sure we get a load coming through here on that date so I can be in divorce court." There was no point in mentioning the additional plans I had for court on that day.

Nicole emerged from the shower wearing a clean T-shirt and jeans. Her long hair hung down across her shoulders, glistening with beads of water.

I went through the house gathering my pillows, blankets, additional clothing, laptop, and some personal items. Nicole was kind enough to help me load them onto the truck. I said my goodbyes, hugged the boys, and Nicole and I climbed into the truck.

Even though Laura had expressed some confusion, she was quite cordial, making it a much better experience than I had envisioned it might be. Once again, it was great to see my boys. It was a brief visit, but gave us the opportunity to have a little bit of time together.

With my direction, Nicole guided the truck back onto Interstate 25, headed north toward Denver. I sat in the jump seat poring over my mail.

"So… what did you get from the FBI? Your paycheck from the Witness Protection Program?" Nicole laughed.

"Nah, it's even better than that… It's the report from my criminal background check stating that I am not a fugitive." I replied.

Nicole glanced at me quickly, and attentively set her eyes back on the road, without saying a word.

I continued, "In order to get your name changed in Colorado, you have to send an application for a criminal background check to the FBI along with a set of fingerprints. The FBI report states to the court that you are not a wanted fugitive. Or from Mars or the future…" I added with a chuckle.

Nicole laughed, "Okay that's a relief. Now I know for sure that you're not a fugitive, a Russian spy, a Martian, or a visitor from the future."

"None of the above." I smiled.

"So, when are you getting your name changed?"

"Well, you heard Laura talk about our date in divorce court on April nineteenth? Right after my divorce is final; I am going over to district court to get my name changed. Everything is in place now that I have my report from the feds."

"So, what is your new name going to be?"

"My new legal name will be Pamela. But I'll just go by Pam."

"That's a cool name! So, when do you want me to start calling you Pam?"

"Anytime you want!" I smiled, as I headed to the back and climbed into my berth to get some sleep.

We made our mail delivery in Chicago on time, and from there we delivered a load of spices in Maine, picking up a trailer full of paper destined for Syracuse, New York. From Syracuse, we headed to Dover, Delaware hauling a load of small appliances.

Our delivery in Dover was a live unload at a warehouse overlooking Dover Air Force base. It was 11:50 am when I backed the trailer into the dock and set the brake. Nicole had just awakened from her sleep, and climbed down from her berth to join me in the cab. I was in a near hypnotic trance, with my eyes fixed on the Air Force base on the other side of the freeway, a fact that did not escape Nicole's notice.

"Dude, you look like you're under a spell, what are you staring at?"

I answered as a gigantic cargo plane came in for a landing, "Nicole, have you ever wanted to be dead? I don't mean suicidal. I just mean not wanting to be alive anymore. Hoping that death would come?"

"Wow, you are freaking me out. No, I've never felt that way.

Why would you even ask me that?"

"Well, I was at Dover Air Force Base almost 40 years ago. This is my first time back. I came back from Vietnam in one of those huge cargo planes."

"Why were you on a cargo plane and not on a passenger plane?"

I broke away from my fixation with the airfield and looked at Nicole.

"I was in the eleventh month of a one year tour of duty in Vietnam. I had volunteered to serve in the infantry in Vietnam, because I didn't want to be alive anymore. Yet, all those months had gone by with people being killed all around me, yet I was still breathing.

One day, while our unit was being resuplied in the field, my company commander approached me to tell me that the Red Cross had put in a request for "compassionate reassignment" because my mother was in the hospital, days away from dying. I boarded one of the supply choppers heading back to the air base in Da Nang to catch the first available aircraft back to the states. As it turned out, one of those gigantic cargo planes brought me to Dover Air Force Base."

Nicole remained silent, patiently waiting for me to continue.

"It was a long plane ride, with only one stop at Elmendorf Air Base in Alaska. I sat on a cot in the front of the cargo hold near the cockpit. I slept when I could and ate the occasional boxed lunches provided by the crew. The rear of the cargo hold held stacks and stacks, and rows upon rows of large boxes. Curiosity and boredom finally got the best of me, and I ventured back there to see what they were."

"What were they?" she asked quietly.

"Well, what I didn't know at the time is that Dover Air Force Base is home to the military mortuary, and is used to process the bodies of military personnel. The boxes had labels on them, each with the name of service members stating "Human Remains." Many boxes filled the plane, rows upon rows, of large boxes, containing bodies of the dead. I was the one who wanted to die, and here I was, the only one alive in the belly of a plane filled with dead bodies."

"Why did you want to die?" Nicole asked.

"You have no idea what it was like living in the wrong body. I was miserable for so many years feeling like a boy trapped inside a girl's body, with no ideas of any kind of solution. I had given up hope. I didn't want to go on, yet I didn't want to commit suicide. Vietnam was a place where I could go and gallantly find an end to my life, but I failed. Now, here I was on a plane full of people who had everything to live for, yet had lost their lives. How ironic."

"Wow, I don't know what to say dude. How old were you?"

I laughed, "I was twenty. I got back to my neighborhood in Chicago, and the bartenders couldn't even serve me a beer. I had endured hell in Vietnam for nearly a year, yet was not old enough to buy a beer."

"I'm so sorry Philip…" Nicole leaned over and gave me a hug.

"Thank you Nicole. Actually, I'm glad we came to Dover. This is just one of the many fragments of my life scattered about. I just need to gather them up one at a time and put the pieces together. There are many fragments remaining. In time I will find them all, so I can try to put them back together."

Chaper Eight
The Girl's Club

Nicole and I logged over 36,000 miles in February and March, hauling toilet paper, beer, tires, appliances, cereal and just about every commodity imaginable. Our travels took us to all four corners of the continental United States, and we touched just about every state at one time or another.

We synchronized well, rarely had a disagreement, and received accolades for our on-time performance. Our truck was now equipped with a CB, satellite radio, thermoelectric food cooler and crock-pot. Thanks to the marvels of wireless internet and my laptop computer, I was able to stay in touch with my friends and family just about everywhere we went.

On the morning of April 1st, while hauling a load of general merchandise from Los Angeles to St. George, Utah, I pulled into the Pilot in North Las Vegas to purchase fuel, refill my coffee mug, and take a nature break. After re-fueling, I backed into a parking spot and set the brake. Nicole was in the sleeper berth, but awoke to go into the truck stop for a potty visit. I refilled my coffee and met Nicole back at the truck. She sat in the jump seat sipping on a bottle of water with a sleepy look on her face as I climbed into the driver's seat.

"Wanna have some fun?" I asked as I pulled the door shut.

Nichole shrugged sluggishly, "Sure."

I typed a message on the Qualcomm and showed it to Nicole before hitting the send button. Nicole came to life and burst into laughter.

'Nicole and I have decided to stay in Vegas for a few days and get married.'

It took less than a minute for Sandra's reply to appear on the screen.

"WHAT?"

I showed Sandra's response to Nicole, "Let's see how long it takes for my phone to ring."

I laughed and sipped my coffee, waiting for my cell phone to ring. It rang before I could set down my coffee mug.

"Philip, you have got to be kidding me. You and Nicole are getting married?"

"Happy April Fools' Day, Sandra." Nicole and I laughed.

"You Brats! Just for that, you two are getting every load I can find to New York City!" Sandra giggled.

"Oh no, not that… I'm sorry." I laughed.

"Thanks for the laugh. You guys be safe out there." Sandra hung up. Nicole climbed into the sleeper berth and went back to sleep.

After unloading in St. George, we drove to nearby Cedar City to pick up a load of cardboard boxes destined for Los Angeles. From there we would head back to the Fontana OC for a couple of days off.

After we picked up our load, I pulled into the Wal-Mart on Interstate 15, to pick up food and supplies for the truck. I also needed to refill my prescriptions. Nicole popped her head out from behind the curtains after I had parked the truck.

"What time is it?" She asked sleepily.

"It's eleven. It's almost time for your shift to start. We're at a Super Wal-Mart in Cedar City, Utah to do some grocery shopping."

I heard Nicole getting dressed. I completed my logbook for the day, just as the curtain flew open allowing her to emerge.

"I'm starving. It's not a good idea to go grocery shopping when you're hungry," She whined.

"Grab a banana and let's go." I chuckled while climbing down from the cab.

I dropped off my prescription refills at the pharmacy then headed over to the grocery section to meet up with Nicole, who had already managed to fill a cart nearly to the top. Our normal staples for the truck consisted of canned soups, fruit, cans of tuna, jerky, cookies, bottled water, etc.

"I'll meet you at the checkout as soon as I pick up my prescriptions," I said while heading towards the pharmacy.

I was delighted that this would be the last time I would have to endure the sideways looks from pharmacy technicians as they filled an estrogen prescription for a male customer.

I paid for my prescriptions, and started walking back to the front of the store. I scoured the checkout lanes, unsuccessfully, to locate Nicole. My cell phone buzzed in my pocket. I glanced at the screen. It was a text message from Nicole.

"Meet me in the women's clothing department."

Nicole was inspecting a cranberry colored top when I found her, which she immediately held up to my chest.

"It's a size twelve; I think that's what you are. Go try it on!"

"Are you crazy? You actually want me to go into the ladies fitting room and try this on?"

"Dude, do you honestly believe these Wal-Mart people have never seen a male trying on women's clothing? Besides, you have long hair and nails, and soft skin. I doubt they will even notice."

"This is Utah, Nicole. They shoot men for wearing pink shirts here," I laughed.

"No, that's Wyoming," she snapped sternly, "Dude, you may be the boss on the truck, but here in the women's clothing department, I am in charge. Now get your ass in that fitting room!"

I laughed while heading over to the attendant's counter.

Nicole was right. The fitting room attendant barely gave me a second look as she directed me to an empty stall. The top fit perfectly, and I was beaming with excitement as I exited the fitting room. Nicole helped me pick out three tops, two pair of Capri pants, and a pair of women sandals. From there we headed to the nearby lingerie department.

"I'm guessing you're a 40B. You can try this on in the truck, and if it doesn't fit, you can always exchange it." She tossed an inexpensive white bra in the cart, followed by a package of six pairs of panties.

"Off to the cosmetics department!" she shouted gleefully while pushing the cart. I followed obediently.

Nicole was blessed with flawless skin and full pink lips, which gave her a naturally beautiful face without ever wearing makeup. Regardless, she was proficient in the cosmetics department, as she picked a foundation and concealer that matched my skin. To the cart, she added mascara, eye shadow, lip liner, and lipstick.

"These are all cheap products, but they will help you to get started. You will eventually want to go to one of the makeup counters in the mall to really get dolled up," she smiled while gently tossing a hand mirror into the cart.

The cashier rang up my personal items separately from the food, for which we split the cost. My first female shopping foray ended up costing me just over $160.00, but it felt great.

"Can I ask you a sort of personal question?" Nicole asked once we were back on the road. I was in the jump seat winding down before bunking down for the night.

"Sure."

"Okay you have been taking those three pills every day to turn you into a girl... I don't even know what the hell they are?" She paused with curiosity.

"Estrodial, Progesterone, and Spironolacton," I smiled.

"Geez, you sound like a walking pharmacy" she laughed, "Anyway, you're doing all these things to become a girl, but you don't seem to care about wearing women's clothes. That seems kind of weird to me."

"Weird in what way?" I took another sip from my water bottle, and gazed at her curiously.

"It just seems like, well someone likes you, um…… " she stammered while trying to find the words.

"…. would enjoy dressing in female attire?" I finished her sentence for her.

"Yeah, that" she laughed.

I turned down the volume on the radio, and stared through the windshield for a minute to give me time to form a lucid response.

"Nicole, look at you. You wear jeans, work boots, denim shirts, men's T-shirts, no jewelry, and no makeup. Does that make you any less a woman?"

Nicole glanced at me for a second before turning her eyes back on the road. Her non-response affirmed my theory.

"To answer your question, I do enjoy wearing female clothing. But for now, I prefer to wait until the time is right."

"So you've never crossed dressed?"

"Well, I wouldn't say that" I laughed, "When I was young I used to sneak my mother's clothes into my bedroom when she wasn't home, and try them on."

Nicole nodded silently as I continued.

"I soon discovered that this was not enough. Simply putting on women's clothing for a couple of hours behind closed doors did nothing for me. I knew that underneath it all, I was still male. It just left me with an empty feeling because I had to put my guy clothing back on. What I came to realize is, I was supposed to have been born a girl. What I wanted was to be regarded as a girl, every single day, regardless of how I was dressed."

"That's messed up, dude. Being born the wrong sex."

"Yeah" I nodded while staring through the windshield at the road ahead, "Very messed up."

"Did your mom ever catch you?" Nicole glanced over at me and grinned.

"No, she had no idea until one Halloween when I went to school in drag."

"Awesome! How did it go?"

I stared through the side window for a few minutes watching the scenery, as we passed through St. George for the second time that day. I took another long drink from my water bottle before turning back to face Nicole,

"It could have gone better. My classmates thought it was funny, but my teachers weren't very pleased about it. The following day they called me into the office to meet with the Principal and the School Counselor. My mother was there too."

"Uh-oh. So what happened?"

"They told my mom that my 'deviant' behavior resulted from the lack of a father figure at home. They suggested I needed to go into extensive therapy in order to 'cure' me. Mom flipped out. Her boyfriend broke up with her right after that, and she never stopped blaming me. Things were never the same with my mom. She kicked me out of the house when I was sixteen and we didn't see or speak to each other after that until she was on her deathbed."

"Did you make up before she died?" Nicole asked softly.

I could barely hear her above the roar of the diesel engine, but I knew what she was asking. I stared at my water bottle as I twirled it around in my hands. This was a painful memory.

I stole a glance over at Nicole through blurry vision, as my eyes watered.

"When I was brought home from Vietnam I went to visit her in the hospital. She knew she was dying, and asked me to hold her one last time. I could not get past my hurt and anger, and I refused. That night, they called and told me she was dead. I left the cemetery after they buried her, and never went back. As hard as I tried, I couldn't shed a single tear over her death."

"Wow, I don't even know what to say" Nicole whispered.

I rose from the jump seat and headed to the sleeper berth to catch a few hours of sleep before our arrival back at the OC.

"There is nothing anyone can say. I have had to carry this guilt in my heart for most of my life. I should have hugged her when I had the chance. Now, I'll never have another chance."

We arrived at the OC at ten that night. Nicole packed her overnight bag, and after a friendly hug, she left to spend two days with her girlfriend in Long Beach. I enjoyed a light snack, checked email, and called my kids before settling in for the night. It always felt good occasionally to sleep in a stationary bed, rather than one that was hurtling across the Interstate. I slept like a rock, and did not arise until 8:30 the next morning.

The driver's lounge was abuzz with activity when I walked in. There were students and trainers engaged in conversations, as well as seasoned drivers who were busy chatting among themselves about one thing or another. I was finishing my breakfast when Gennipher walked in from the office and joined a group of her fellow trainers at a table in the back. I took my tray to the bussing station where I deposited the trash, laid it on the stack of other dirty trays, and walked over to say hello.

"Good morning everyone!" I said cheerily.

"Good morning. How are you and Nicole doing out there?" asked Brandon.

"We are doing great. I'm actually enjoying it a lot more than I thought I would. And Nicole has turned out to be a great driving partner!"

Gennipher piped in, "They are both great drivers. Give credit to their trainer!" She laughed.

"You can yourself on the back, Gennipher," Brandon

kidded.

"Gennipher, when you have a minute, can we talk privately?" I asked.

"How about right now? I'm ready for a smoke break. Wanna go outside?"

"Sure, let's go."

Gennipher and I walked outside to the smoking area, where several people were gathered around in conversation, enjoying their cigarettes.

"Can we go for a walk to get away from the crowd? I really have something very private to discuss with you," I asked.

"Yeah, sure. Are you okay?" She asked while lighting up.

"Yeah, I'm fine. Let's go for a stroll." I began walking toward the yard. Gennipher fell into step beside me. Once we were far enough away from any eavesdropping ears, I began.

"Gennipher, in a few weeks something very shocking is going to happen with me that will have the entire place buzzing. I want you to have a heads up before it happens."

"Okay…" She peered at me curiously while taking a drag on her cigarette.

"Nicole is the only other person who knows this, you are the second."

I paused for a moment while we circled around a row of trucks, in the back of the yard, and headed back toward the driver's lounge.

"For the past year I have been in the very slow process of a sex change. On May 5th I am going to officially begin my life as a female." I turned and studied Gennipher's face for a look of shock. There was none.

"So on May 5th you are going to become female? What's your name going to be?"

"Pam" I answered.

I continued to study her face searching for some sort of reaction to my revelation. She took a drag from her cigarette tossing it to the ground in front of her foot, where she demolished it with a grinding motion.

"That's a pretty name." she paused for a few seconds before asking, "So, what's the shocking part?"

I laughed, "You don't think my becoming 'Pam' is shocking?"

"I'm sure it will shock a few people, but to be honest I'm not the least bit surprised. Quite a few of us have noticed how feminine you appear, with your long fingernails, earrings, soft skin, and long hair. This just answers the question that a few people have asked, are you a boy who looks like a girl, or a girl who looks like a boy?" she laughed.

"Wow Gennipher, you have no idea how relieved I am."

"So, why May 5th? What's so special about that day?"

"On April 19th I have my divorce hearing, and my divorce will be final. On that same day, I will be in court to get my name changed. That gives me about two weeks to get my driver's license and social security card changed so I can take care of the paperwork with Schneider human resources. I chose May 5th as my coming out day because I want it to be a memorable date."

"What's so memorable about May 5th? Cinco De Mayo?" She looked at me curiously.

"Five Five Oh Five" I grinned.

"Ah, okay. Yes, that is a very cool date" she laughed.

I was close to the building when I noticed that Gennipher was no longer beside me. I stopped and turned around. She was standing about ten paces behind me with her hands on her hips. I walked back toward her.

"That's no fair!" She exclaimed incredulously, "You get to be a girl, but never have to have a period?"

We both burst into laughter and hugged each other.

On April 19, Nicole and I headed to Fort Collins, Colorado to pick up a load of beer at the Anheuser Busch facility. I had informed Sandra of my date in divorce court, and she had made sure we had a load scheduled for Colorado on that day.

I was dressed in a pair of jeans, with androgynous top and black loafers. Nicole had helped me put on some light makeup. She dropped me off in downtown Colorado Springs, and headed to Fort Collins. We decided she would rendezvous with me after picking up the load, and I was finished with my divorce and name change.

I arrived at the courthouse at 8:55 am and found Laura outside the courtroom for our 9:00 am hearing. We were assigned to Courtroom X, a fitting location for the dissolution of our marriage. The judge called us first, and simply asked a few questions before announcing our marriage dissolved. Laura and I said our goodbyes, and I headed over to civil court for my name change hearing.

The procedure for obtaining a name change is to attach the FBI report indicating there are no outstanding warrants to the name change petition, and present it to the clerk of the court, who in turn schedules a hearing.

Once I had submitted all of my paperwork and fees, the clerk set my appearance before the judge for 1:00. I called Nicole.

"Well, I'm officially divorced. Now I'm just waiting to get my name changed. My hearing is at one."

"Okay I have our load and am heading back south. I'll just park at a truck stop until I hear from you, and come pick you up."

"Sounds good. I'll call you as soon as I'm finished."

I arrived in the courtroom at 12:30 and stared nervously through the windows at the city below, while waiting for court to begin. In time, other people began to filter into the courtroom. I felt self-conscious as they looked across the room at me. I was sure they were trying to figure out whether I was male or female.

At exactly 1:00 pm, the bailiff announced 'All Rise' as the judge entered the courtroom. He was a middle-aged man with a salt and pepper handlebar mustache, a warm smile and twinkling eyes. Much to my delight, they called my case first.

"Pamela Anders" the judge called out. I shuddered with excitement upon hearing my new name called as I stepped up to the podium.

"Are you petitioning for a name change in order to avoid creditors?" he asked in a perfunctory manner.

"No, Your Honor."

"Are you changing your name for any illegal purpose?"

"No, Your Honor."

"Okay then, I don't see any reason to deny this name change" He signed my petition and handed it to the bailiff.

I let out a huge sigh of relief, resisting the urge to run up to the bench to hug him.

The judge looked at me with his twinkling eyes and smiled, "You are all set Ms. Anders. Go see the clerk of the court. He will tell you what to do next."

"Thank you, your Honor!" I beamed as I stepped away from the podium and exited the courtroom. The sound of his voice saying, 'Ms. Anders' reverberated in my ears.

At the clerk's desk, they gave me instructions for publishing my name change in the paper. It was to run for three days in order for the judge to sign off on the decree. In other words, until then it would not be official. I made a beeline to the Denver Post and paid the fee to have the notice published immediately. I called Nicole.

"Don't call me Philip anymore, my name is Pam!" I exclaimed. She was delighted at the news.

"I'm on my way Ms. Pam," she exclaimed.

On May 4, just before 9:00 am, we pulled into the Fontana operating center. Nicole let me borrow her car, with whicy I spent the morning running errands while she dozed in the truck. My first stop was at a private postal center near the OC, where I obtained a post office box and an official California address.

The next stop brought me to the social security office on Sierra Avenue, where I submitted a form to change my name, along with my court ordered name change. Within an hour, a printout declared my new name, and a promise that the card would be in my mailbox in a couple of weeks.

I was doing well as I headed to the California DMV office down the street on Merrill Avenue. After a simple eye exam and a photograph, I secured a California commercial driver license with my new name. Much to my chagrin however, it stated that I was male; a problem that I would have to solve later. For now though, I was pleased by the fact that I had a driver license with my new name. I arrived back at the OC by lunchtime.

I had arranged a 1:00 pm meeting with Sandra to discuss some 'personal matters'. Sandra and I sat in one of the small conference rooms.

"So what's up Philip? Is everything okay?"

"Everything is fine," I smiled, "I just need to inform you that I have had a name change."

I handed Sandra my name change decree, temporary California CDL, and the printout from the social security office. I smiled, studying her face, as she examined the documents. Her eyebrows rose to look at me.

"Your name is Pamela now? Does this mean what I think it means?"

"Yes, I am undergoing a sex change, and my new name is Pamela."

"Should I call you Pam?" She smiled.

"Yes, please" I replied enthusiastically.

"Okay Pam," she smiled while emphasizing my name, "I just have to call Human Resources to see what steps we need to take to make this official. When do you plan on making your debut?"

"Tomorrow morning!" I beamed.

"Okay, this should be interesting…" She laughed.

Before dawn the next morning, I roused Nicole out of a deep sleep. She was not happy.

"What the fuck? It's still dark outside!"

"It's almost time Nicole. You've got to get up and help me get ready!"

Nicole looked at her watch and growled, "Its 5:00 am, dude!"

"Yeah, in five minutes it's going to be time. You need to get up!"

Nicole sat up, and slithered sleepily down from her berth, "Time for what? What happens in five minutes?" She stood on rubbery legs while rubbing the sleep from her eyes.

"Five Oh Five on Five Five Oh Five!" I chuckled.

"Geez Pam, you are fucking insane," she grumbled.

After taking our showers, and returning to the truck, Nicole assisted me in putting on my makeup and styling my hair in a feminine style. I had decided to wear the cranberry top that she had selected for me at the Wal-Mart in Cedar City, along with a pair of black cropped Capri pants and sandals.

As a finishing touch, I wore a pair of dangly earrings and a pearl necklace. Once satisfied with my look, we walked toward the driver's lounge. I felt as though I was walking to the executioner's chamber as I trembled with fear at what the reaction would be.

The driver's lounge was a flurry of activity when Nicole and I walked in at 7:00 am. The drivers, students, trainers, and staff members were either taking care of business, or eating breakfast. We passed through the doorway and let the glass door close, as we surveyed the scene before us. All conversation had suddenly come to an abrupt halt when we entered, creating a nearly deafening silence. After a few seconds of silence, the room resounded with the earsplitting symphony of forks dropping onto plates, as all eyes locked on the bizarre sight at the entranceway.

Nicole and I made our way to a table toward the back and demurely sat down. Many of the trainers sat at their usual table in the corner staring in astonishment at my new appearance. At this point, most of the people in the lounge had gone back to whatever they were doing, although many remained fixated on me.

Seconds after taking our seats, Brandon, Pat, Amy, and Gennipher were standing next to our table smiling.

"So, what's your new name?" Brandon asked.

"My name is Pam" I smiled.

Gennipher stood behind me gently squeezing my shoulders.

"Welcome to the girl's club, Pam."

Chapter Nine
Cryptic Messages

After finishing our breakfast, Nicole and I headed to the Phoenix yard with a trailer load of appliances we were to drop off, then pick up an empty to bring back to Fontana. Nicole was having ongoing problems with her girlfriend Rachael and had requested a few days off, so that she could sort things out. After three weeks on the road without a break, I was in need of a few days of rest myself.

After picking up the empty, I pulled into the Pilot to grab a quick bite to eat and change shifts. After a quick potty break, we purchased sandwiches at Wendy's and began heading westward on Interstate 10 toward Fontana, now with Nicole at the helm. I completed the driving portion of my log for that day and proudly signed my new name officially for the first time. I sat in the jump seat quietly gazing out the window at the scenery on Interstate 10.

Nicole had spent the better part of the morning on the phone arguing with Rachael and had not gotten much sleep. After driving sulkily for an hour, she finally broke the silence.

"I guess your debut as Pam went well," she said without smiling.

"It went a lot better than I had expected" I replied, "I'm relieved that this part is over and now I can move forward. Although, I think there are still a lot of challenges ahead."

"How do you feel, now that you have come out as Pam?"

"I'm a bit uneasy about my presentation as a female, but I'm sure in time I'll become more comfortable with myself. I think the girl at Wendy's noticed it. She was staring at me rather curiously."

Nicole replied curtly, "Dude, you don't exactly look like Lady Godiva ya know. As long as you have those male features to your face and that five o'clock shadow under your makeup, yer gonna get stared at. Get over it."

I reached behind my seat and pulled the hand mirror out of the pouch, studying my face in the magnifying side of the mirror for a moment, before replying, "Yeah, you're right; I need to work on those things. It's all a matter of time. Once I have saved enough money, I will find a plastic surgeon to feminize my face. In the meantime, I'm going to look for an electrolysis place in LA so I can resume that process."

"Good plan" she replied quietly.

After a few minutes of silence, I decided to broach a touchy subject.

"So, what's going on between you and Rachael? If you don't mind my asking."

Nicole sighed, "Rachael has this idea in her head that while I'm out gallivanting around the country; she has the right to mess around with other women. Do you think that's right?"

"First of all, I would hardly call this gallivanting," I said sarcastically.

"Yeah, I kinda said the same thing to her, but I don't think she gets it."

I turned in my seat and looked at Nicole, "What's your relationship with her? Have you two made any kind of commitment, to be exclusive to each other?"

"Well, we've only been together for about six months. I started seeing her right before I started truck-driving school. We never made any kind of agreement not to see other people, but I thought it was sort of understood that we wouldn't."

"So, she seems to be using the fact that you are away for weeks at a time, as her justification to step in and out of your relationship?"

"Yeah, I guess" Nicole shrugged her shoulders.

"Relationships are hard enough in themselves, without creating, the additional challenge of being apart for weeks at a time. Have you taken that into consideration?"

"I hadn't really thought about it much until she brought it up, but I think you're right."

"Well, this is something that you two need to talk about during the next couple of days that you're together."

We arrived at the OC at 6:30 that evening. I gave Nicole a hug, along with my best wishes for her time with Rachael; she packed her bag, and headed off to Long Beach. I went into the driver's lounge to grab dinner.

Russ, the food concession manager was behind the counter. I slid my tray along the track, ordering the pot roast dinner.

"Congratulations on the new you," he smiled, "Your name is Pam now, right?"

"Yup, my name is Pam," I proclaimed proudly.

There was only a smattering of men and women in the driver's lounge. I found a seat at an empty table. The television played CNN, with many of the drivers watching the flickering screen. I ate my dinner, casually glancing around the room. I caught eyes staring at me, which quickly darted away the moment I made eye contact.

I was simply a novelty item now, as most assuredly word had spread quickly throughout the company of my grand entrance earlier that morning. I gazed at the faces in the lounge in an attempt to gauge their thoughts. Their inaudible whispered conversations reverberated throughout the room. What were they thinking? What were they saying? How were they reacting to me?

I finished my dinner and took the tray to the bussing station to clean it off and stack it with the other soiled trays. I then headed to the women's room to freshen up and brush my teeth before heading to the truck for the night.

The Fontana operating center had two men's rooms and one women's room. The women's room had three stalls, a vanity with two sinks, and a large wall-to-wall mirror. After visiting one of the stalls, I washed my hands and face. I removed the small tube of toothpaste from my purse to brush my teeth with my travel toothbrush.

While I was rinsing my mouth, a woman emerged from one of the stalls to the sound of a flushing toilet, and stood next to me at the vanity to wash her hands. I glanced at her reflection in the mirror. She was one of the women I noticed whispering with some of the men in the driver's lounge. Her slight build, jet-black hair, deep-set dark eyes, and a hard chiseled face betrayed a tough life.

She dried her hands with one of the paper towels from the dispenser, glaring at me, as she spoke in a heavy accent that I was unable to identify.

"I think you are in the wrong restroom."

I immediately felt my face flush, but before I could react, she had disappeared through the door. It took me a few minutes to regain my composure. I slowly opened the door. My hands trembled, as I did my best to walk casually back into the driver's lounge. The woman and the group of men with whom she had been talking had already departed. I walked back to the truck with a knot in my stomach.

I awoke just after 7:00 the next morning after the first twenty-four hours of my life as a female. It had been a fitful night, with visions of that threatening woman churning in my mind. As I dressed, I vowed not to let this one unpleasant experience discourage me in my quest. Once I was dressed, I slid the privacy curtains open to let the sunlight in, and climbed down out of the cab into the cool fresh morning air. As I closed the door, I noticed a folded piece of paper tucked into the window frame. I unfolded the paper and read the note, refolded it, and placed it in my purse. This was not how I wanted to start my second day as a female.

I entered the driver's lounge and made my way over to the food line. I scanned the room looking for the dark haired woman that I had encountered in the women's room the previous night, but she was not there. Purchasing a cup of coffee and a plate of scrambled eggs, I found a vacant chair and sat down by myself to eat my breakfast.

There were a couple of dozen drivers in the lounge, both male and female, with none of them giving me a second look. Two men at the end of my table glanced at me briefly and exchanged greetings with me before resuming their conversation. All in all, there was nothing out of the ordinary in the driver's lounge, and had it not been for the encounter in the ladies room, followed by the note on the truck, I would not have been experiencing the uneasiness that I now felt firmly lodged in the pit of my stomach.

Gennipher walked into the lounge with another woman, and I called to her,

"Hey Gennipher, good morning!"

She turned and walked over to my table smiling "Hey There Ms. Pamela. How are you?" She emphasized the *Ms.*

"I'm good. Thanks for the encouragement." I paused for a few seconds, "Can I ask you a question?"

"Sure, what's up?" She sat down in the chair across the table from me.

"Do you know a female driver about five foot six with black hair? She is on the thin side and speaks with an accent?"

Gennipher thought for a moment before replying, "That doesn't sound familiar. I can't think of anyone like that at this OC, Why do you ask?"

"Well, last night she was in here talking with a group of drivers. I went into the women's room to wash up and brush my teeth and she was in there. She just glared at me and told me I was in the wrong restroom. That was it, and then she walked out.

When I came out a minute later she was gone and so was the group she was with."

Just as Gennipher started to speak, another voice interrupted,

"Can I join you guys, or is this a private conversation?" The woman that Gennipher had walked in with now stood at our table holding a tray full of food.

"Of course you can, sit down." Gennipher patted the chair next to her and made the introductions.

"Alice, this is Pam. Pam, this is Alice. She's an owner operator." My trainer friend made waving gestures at each of us. Alice was a somewhat plain looking woman with medium length dishwater blonde hair that was not styled in any particular way.

Alice reached across the table in offer of a handshake, which I gratefully accepted,

"Nice to meet you Pam. I've seen you around the OC but haven't had the chance to meet you. I must say, you look a bit different now," she laughed.

"Nice to meet you too, Alice. Thanks" I smiled.

"Alice, Pam was just telling me about an encounter she had in the ladies room last night," Gennipher said.

"Oh yeah? What happened?" Alice looked at Gennipher, while chewing on a piece of bacon.

"Some woman told Pam she was 'in the wrong room'" Gennipher replied.

"Geez…. What? Is she afraid Pam might have heard her fart in the toilet?" Alice laughed and turned to me.

"Did you tell her to kiss your sweet ass?"

"Well, no. I was taken a bit by surprise and didn't really know what to say," I answered sheepishly.

"Girl, you need to grow a set of balls. Oh wait, you already have those!" she chortled.

Gennipher laughed, patting my arm. "Alice is an acquired taste. She takes some getting used to."

Alice laughed, "Fuck you too, Gennipher!"

"It's okay," I smiled.

Gennipher continued, "Don't worry about it Pam. Some women will have a problem with it for a while, but they all need to just get over it."

I nodded, "There's one more thing."

I reached into my purse and pulled out the note that I had found on the truck this morning, which I unfolded onto the table. This was the first of many notes I would find on my truck during my transition, all with the same cryptic message at the bottom.

Alice and Gennipher took turns reading it, and tossed it back onto the table. I picked it up and read it one more time.

'You have embarked upon a very dangerous and risky endeavor. Be warned, there is danger ahead. Be careful who you trust. călătorie în siguranță, dar ai grija de pericol'

"I don't interpret this as a threatening note, do you?" Gennipher asked.

"I'm not sure how to take it," I responded. "The words don't come across as a threat, but more like a warning. When I first read it, I thought someone was threatening me, but after reading it a few times… I don't think so.

"What's that gibberish on the bottom?" Alice pointed at the paper.

"That's a good question," I replied. "I don't even recognize what language that is."

"Do you think that bitch from the bathroom wrote it?" asked Alice.

"I don't know. She came across as mean and threatening. This note seems almost protective."

"So, do you want to report this?" Gennipher asked.

"No, I don't think so. I don't want to stir up a hornet's nest over it."

"Good idea. Like I said, I'm sure in time all of this will blow over," Gennipher said as she looked up at the clock on the wall.

"Well, I'd better get going, I have work to do. You guys enjoy your day."

"Thanks girlfriend, I'll see you around." I waved as she walked away.

"Later Gennipher," said Alice.

"So, are you waiting for a load or what?" Alice asked me.

"No, I'm off for the next two days. My partner went home, and I'm just hanging out here."

"Ah, so you're a team driver. Who's your partner?"

"Her name is Nicole. She and I went through training together."

"Don't know her." Alice quickly shifted gears "You doing anything today? Wanna go see a movie?"

"Yeah, that sounds…" Alice interrupted me before I could finish.

"Have you seen 'History of Violence'?" she asked.

"No, actually I've never heard…"

Alice interrupted again, "Good! We'll go see that and grab something to eat and go party!"

"That sounds …"

"Hey Mikey!" Alice was yelling across the room at a man who had just entered the driver's lounge "Come here!"

"Have you met Mikey?" Alice asked.

"No I don't think…"

"Mikey, Pam and I are going to Loretta's tonight. Wanna join us?"

I looked at Alice "Loretta's?"

Mikey was now standing next to the table looking at me curiously.

"Oh, Mikey, this is Pam. Pam this is Mikey. He's going to party with us tonight."

"I am?" Mikey raised his eyebrows at Alice.

"Loretta's?" I asked

"Nice to meet you Pam," Mikey said as he extended his hand to me.

"So, we'll see you later on over at Loretta's?" Alice said to Mikey.

"Nice meeting you Mikey" I shook his hand.

"Okay Alice. I'll see you over there."

Alice drove us over to the Ontario Mills Mall, where we parked in front of the Dave & Busters located right next to the theater. After the movie, we walked over to D&B, where we had hamburgers and beers at the bar. While we were there, Alice managed to flirt with every man that walked in.

"Pretty good movie, huh?" She asked while sipping on a mug of beer.

"Yes. Very violent, but well done. I really like Viggo Morten…"

"You need to do your hair differently" Alice interrupted me. She reached over to push my hair behind my ears,

"There, that's better!"

"Thank you" I smiled while sipping on my beer.

"Your lip color is all wrong for your skin color too. Who picked that out for you? Oh, never mind. We need to go shopping together. Not tomorrow though, I'm gonna be hung-over tomorrow."

I laughed, "You have a hangover planned for tomorrow?"

"Yeah I do" She drank a swig of her beer and wiped the foam from her upper lip,

"Give me your phone number. We can stay in touch and next time we're together we can go shopping."

I recited my phone number, which she immediately dialed from her cell phone.

My phone rang, but I didn't answer. "There, now you can save my number. We can call each other."

After we left Dave & Busters, Alice parked her car in the employee's lot at the OC, and we walked over to Loretta's together.

If you look up the term Honky Tonk, it is very likely that you will find a picture of Loretta's Lounge. Located within walking distance of the Fontana OC, and only a short distance from most of the trucking companies in the area, it has established itself as a favorite hangout for truck drivers.

The front of the building is painted flat black, including the windows and the entrance door. The inside is not much different, with acoustic ceiling tiles and black walls adorned with neon beer signs. The brightest light in the bar comes from the jukebox and the hanging tiffany lamps over the pool table. A menacing looking bouncer attended the entrance.

Within ten minutes, Alice had taken me around the bar and introduced me to all the regulars, including the bartenders, waitresses, and that bouncer, all of whom made me feel surprisingly comfortable. Mikey was there. He introduced me to a female driver named Sandy and a few of the other drivers from the OC.

Alice and I claimed a table near the dance floor where we enjoyed an endless supply of drinks sent to us by patrons. We played pool and danced until closing time. Alice and I staggered back to our trucks, high fived one another, before going our separate ways. She had taken me under her wing and undoubtedly, we would be good friends from here on.

I crawled into my sleeper berth without bothering to take off my clothes. My head was spinning, partly from the alcohol, but mostly from the crazy events of the day. My second day as a female had begun with a strange note on my truck, and ended with newfound friendships, trust, and a feeling approaching that of euphoria. Could my transition possibly be this easy? Perhaps the hardest part was yet to come.

Chapter Ten
Sisters

Nicole returned to the truck on Monday with two plastic grocery bags, a tray of brownies, and a container of home baked chicken. She looked rested, refreshed, and happy as we put the food in the truck. We loaded her overnight bag into her sleeper berth.

"How was your time with Rachael?" I asked while wedging the container of chicken into our miniature refrigerator.

"It was awesome!" she answered cheerfully. I could tell she meant it.

"You can tell me all about it on our way to Dallas. Right now we have to head to Fullerton to pick up a load at Kimberly Clark to take to the Dallas OC"

The drive from the Fontana OC to Fullerton was only thirty-five miles, but it took nearly an hour in the heavy LA morning traffic. Nicole climbed into her sleeper berth to get some rest. For a change, she slept serenely rather than on the phone arguing with Rachel. This pleased me immensely, and I was eager to hear how things had been resolved between the two of them.

After hooking up to the loaded trailer at the Kimberly Clark distribution center, I guided the truck onto State Highway 91, which led to State Highway 60 and onto Interstate 10, East toward

Dallas.

The trip from Fullerton to Dallas would be 1,450 miles, and our load was not due at the Dallas OC until Wednesday; giving us plenty of time. I would make it to Phoenix by noon, in time to buy fuel and change drivers.

It was a beautiful Southern California day, featuring a crystal clear blue sky, studded with several puffs of small white clouds. The drive along I-10 is normally quite pleasant, particularly east of Palm Springs where the traffic tends to lighten up.

I have always enjoyed driving, and had made the round trip from Dallas to Southern California often during family motor home trips to destinations such as Disneyland, Knott's Berry Farm, Sea World, and Lego Land. Our final motor home trip was in the spring of 2001, when the family proudly traveled to San Marcos, California to see my daughter Cheryl graduate from college. Just a few short months later however, the horrific events of 9/11 changed our lives forever.

Shortly after 9/11, we sold our home in suburban Dallas and moved to Colorado Springs where we purchased another home. Laura immediately secured a job as a schoolteacher, and I launched my magazine publishing business. Laura and I projected the outward appearance of a happy couple, although a variety of internal issues began to cause the wheels to fall off our marriage.

In the spring of 2004, Laura announced that she wanted a divorce. Shortly thereafter, I made the decision, long overdue, to begin my hormone therapy.

As I pulled into the Pilot truck stop in Phoenix several hours later, I could hear Nicole stirring behind the curtain. After our lunch break, Nicole would take over at the wheel.

"Where are we?" Nicole's sleepy face popped through the part of the curtains.

"We just pulled into a Pilot in Phoenix," I said, while guiding the truck into one of the fuel lanes. I killed the engine,

"Gonna get some fuel and take a break before we change shifts."

"Gawd, is it noon already?" Nicole yawned before vanishing behind the curtains to get dressed.

"Its 11:45," I replied while opening the door to climb down to the pavement, "We have time to grab a bite to eat before your shift starts."

I slid my Comdata Fuel Card through the card reader on the fuel pump, followed by my Pilot card; thus ensuring that I would earn another free shower. I inserted the nozzle into the driver's side tank and plunged the trigger to start the flow of fuel. I then walked around to the passenger side to repeat the process in that tank.

While the tanks filled, I washed the windshield and side windows with the sponge and squeegee attached to a long pole. The fuel gauge displayed at the 1/8 mark when we pulled in, so it required 170 gallons of diesel fuel to fill both tanks.

The pump nozzles shut off with a loud snapping sound, and I removed them from the tanks, replacing them onto the pumps.

Nicole sat in the jump seat sipping on a small bottle of coke as I climbed back into the cab and started the engine. After releasing the air brakes, I guided the truck to the parking area, and backed it into an open slot. I changed my status from driving to off duty. Nicole and I climbed down and we headed into the truck stop.

Nicole had packed several pieces of chicken from our refrigerator into a small plastic container. She used the truck stop's microwave to heat the chicken, while I purchased drinks and potato chips for both of us.

I paid the cashier, while Nicole set up a table with plastic utensils, paper plates, and napkins, secured from the food station.

"This chicken is good," I said while taking a bite from a thigh,. "Did you make it?"

Nicole laughed, "Are you kidding? I can just barely cook a hot dog. My mom made a nice dinner yesterday for my birthday. She gave me a bunch of leftover chicken for the truck."

"Yesterday was your birthday?" I raised my eyebrows.

"No, it's actually Thursday, but she wanted to do something since I would be on the road. Rachael came over too. She gave me this."

Nicole pulled a gold heart pendant, attached to a gold chain from under her shirt, and grinned proudly, as she dangled it in front of my face for me to examine.

"Very nice," I smiled. "I guess I'll save my birthday greeting for Thursday. This will make you 25, right?"

"Yup, I'll be the big Two-Five in a couple of days." She ate a bite of chicken, washing it down with a sip of her soft drink."

"So your mom lives in Norco right? And you live in Long Beach with Rachael?"

"Actually I officially live in Norco with my mom. That's what my driver's license says, and it's where I get my mail, but I've been spending a lot of time at Rachael's apartment in Long Beach. I don't think we're ready for me to move in with her yet."

"That's good thinking. Did you and Rachael work things out while you were together during the past few days?" I finished the last of my chicken and wiped my fingers with one of the napkins.

"Yeah, I think so, at least for now. She's not happy with the idea of having a partner who's gone for three weeks at a time., and she can only be with for a couple of days a month," Nicole said, as we walked to the exit, stopping at the trashcan to dump our debris.

"So what did Rachael and you decide to do to make your relationship work?" I asked while we strode across the lot toward the truck.

"We're going to see how things go during the next few weeks, and we'll take it from there. She made me promise that if she absolutely could not handle me being gone, I would look into getting a job as a local driver." Nicole replied ruefully while unlocking the drivers' side door, climbing into the cab.

"You must really care a lot about her to even consider taking such a drastic step to save the relationship," I said while climbing into the passenger seat.

"I do" Nicole said, then turned the key and started the engine with a roar.

"So what did you do on your days off?" Nicole asked while merging with the traffic on I-10.

"I just hung out at the OC mainly. I did some laundry, caught up on email, placed some phone calls, and picked up my mail. Oh, and guess what I got in the mail" I said excitedly.

Nicole shrugged while I reached into my purse and extracted my CDL from my wallet.

"I got my California CDL!" I beamed proudly, holding it out for her to see.

Nicole snatched the laminated ID out of my fingers and examined it, her eyes oscillating between the road, and my commercial driver's license.

"Nice picture!" Her smile quickly transformed to a frown as she took a second look. "Dude! It says you're a male! That's messed up!" She exclaimed while handing the license back to me.

"Yeah, it sucks, but there's nothing I can do about it until I have my surgery. For now, I'm just happy that is has my new name on it" I responded, replacing the license in my wallet.

I decided to change the subject,

"While I was at the OC, I met a driver named Alice; do you know who she is?"

"No, I don't think so."

"She's an owner operator Gennipher introduced to me. She and I went to see a movie on Saturday, and then went to a bar called Loretta's down the street from the OC."

"On Valley? Yeah, I know that place. I've never been in there but it looks like a real dive from the outside!"

"It's not much different on the inside, but it was fun," I laughed. "I met a lot of nice people."

"Did anybody say anything to you?" Nicole glanced at me briefly before quickly shifting her sights back onto the road.

"Say anything to me about what?"

"You know, the way you look"

"Not really. I got a few stares, but nobody actually said anything negative to me. This is actually going a lot better than I had thought it would; I was actually expecting a lot more confrontation than what I've had."

"What you've had? What confrontation have you had?" Nicole asked with a sideways glance.

"On Friday night after you dropped me off, I was in the ladies room at the OC. Some woman made a snide remark about me being in the wrong restroom, or something like that. It was no big deal." I refrained from telling her about the note I found on Saturday morning.

I stared out the window, mindlessly watching the scenery along Interstate 10. We were on the outskirts of Tucson as the automobile traffic built up on the freeway. I let my mind go blank.

"So, what made you wait so long?" Nicole asked after several minutes of silence.

"Wait so long for what?" I snapped out of my trance and looked over at her.

"To do what you're doing. The sex change thing. You're like forty-something now. Why did you wait this long?"

"Well actually, I'm fifty-six" I smiled

"Oh, wow! I thought you were a lot younger!" She looked at me astonished.

"Thank you, I'll take that as a compliment" I smiled.

"So why did you wait? Why didn't you do it when you were younger?" she pressed.

I returned my gaze to the passing scenery as I gathered my thoughts. This was a question I asked myself many times, and really did not know the answer. After a few moments, I turned back to Nicole.

"Most of my life was spent believing there was no solution to my dilemna. I knew that I was supposed to have been born a girl, but there was a mess up somewhere. I didn't know what to do about it. I felt very alone because I didn't think there was anyone else in the world who felt the way I did."

"Okay…" Nicole gave the standard 'I'm listening' response.

"I finally discovered that there are tens of thousands of

people who were born this way, and I was not alone. So, when I was thirty I made a feeble attempt to do something about it. I went to see a therapist that specialized in gender issues, and joined her group sessions. I started hanging out with the cross dressers and transvestites from her group, but I quickly discovered they were nothing like me. To them, it was a fetish. To me, it was a sense of identity. I felt out of place in that group. Does that make sense?"

"Yeah, I guess..." Nicole responded tentatively.

"Anyway, it just wasn't the right time for me. I ended up meeting Laura several years later, and she became my wife. I have two wonderful boys, which I wouldn't have now had I proceeded with transition. All in all, it's a blessing that I waited this long."

"Life must have been very hard for you, Pam." I could sense sincere compassion in Nicole's voice.

I turned in my seat and looked directly at my driving partner, "Nicole, there are many challenges dealing with this, but for the most part, life has been very good to me. I have three wonderful children, I have traveled around the country, and to many parts of the world. I have enjoyed success, money, and luxury... you name it. The one thing that has always been missing from my life is to be in harmony with who I really am. That is what I am working on now, and when I am finished I will have truly achieved happiness."

"That is awesome, dude!" Nicole turned to me and smiled.

"Now dear, I need some much needed beauty sleep." I stood and walked to the back of the truck.

"Goodnight, Pam."

The next thing I knew, I was jolted out of my sleep by the rocking and swaying of the truck, followed by the inertia of coming to a stop and the sound of the air brakes.

My legs swung to the floor, as I poked my head through the curtains. The clock on the dashboard informed me that it was 11:55 pm Nicole was seated in the driver's seat writing in her logbook.

"Where are we?" I yawned.

"We're at the Pilot in Van Horn, Texas. I'm gonna take a shower before I go to bed."

"Good idea" I exclaimed while opening the curtain.

Nicole and I packed our shower bags with clean clothing and underwear, and headed across the parking lot toward the travel center.

"We have a slight problem," Nicole said as we entered the building and headed to the beverage station.

"Uh-oh what's wrong?" I asked while filling a Styrofoam cup from one of the coffee urns.

"It's the Qualcomm. It's completely dead. At first it was just flashing a bunch of gobbledy-goop, and then it just went completely dead."

"Ah… so they can't communicate with us. I wonder if the GPS is even working. They may not even know where we are," I laughed as we walked to the counter to pay for our drinks and sign up for showers.

"Now's our big chance!" Nicole giggled, "Let's head to Mexico. We can make a fortune from our truck load of tampons and retire !"

"Yeah, really" I laughed, "Seriously, though, I think we should shut down when we get to Dallas and get it fixed. I'll call Sandra as soon as the OC opens and let her know."

"Spoil sport!" Nicole stuck her tongue out at me and laughed as we headed off to our showers.

It was 9:45 am Texas time when I guided the truck off Interstate 20, at exit 242 in Sweetwater, and pulled into the TA truck stop. Nicole had been sleeping peacefully ever since we left Van Horn, but had awoke as I backed into the parking spot, and was ready to head inside for a potty break.

It was a beautiful morning in Texas with a crystal clear sky, and a brilliant sun, which shone most of the morning on my face as I drove eastward. The bright sun sat almost directly above us now as we headed into the building. Tumbleweed of all shapes and sizes scampered past us in the gentle breeze, a clear reminder that we were in West Texas.

We made a beeline to the women's room, and over to the snack bar. After filling a large plastic cup full of soda, Nicole fixed herself a cardboard container of nacho chips smothered in melted cheese and jalapenos. I plopped a hot dog onto a bun from the steamer, and we both headed to the counter to pay for our nutritious breakfasts.

"Are you going to be able to go back to sleep after you eat that?" I laughed.

"Oh yeah, spicy food doesn't bother me when I sleep, not even these jalapenos" she said smugly while popping one of the potent pepper slices into her mouth.

I rolled my eyes and laughed, "Oh, to be 25 again."

"Why are there pictures of rattlesnakes all over this place?" Nicole asked after we had seated ourselves at one of the tables. "They even have rattlesnake pictures in the bathroom."

I laughed, "Nicole, this is Sweetwater, Texas; home of the largest rattlesnake roundup in the world!"

"Rattlesnake roundup? What the hell is that?"

"Every March, I think it's the first or second week, they have the Annual Rattlesnake Roundup right here in Sweetwater, Texas. It's sort of a snake rodeo for crazy men who have way too much testosterone," I laughed while taking a bite of my hotdog.

Nicole stared at me while holding a chip in her hand. Cheese dripped onto her plate as she held it motionless in front of her mouth, seemingly mesmerized by the thought of a snake rodeo.

I continued.

"From what I have been told, it started out as a way of controlling the rattlesnake population and has somehow evolved into this annual event. Men actually jump into a pit of snakes and compete to see who can capture the most."

I took a bite of my hotdog and watched Nicole for a reaction. She sat motionless as I chewed my food, so I went on.

"I went to it once while I lived in Dallas…. it's quite a

spectacle. There are vendors selling snakeskin items, belts, boots, snakeheads, rattles, and just about anything, rattlesnake related you could imagine. You can even buy an order of fried rattlesnake nuggets with French fries!" I laughed.

"Have you ever eaten rattlesnake?" Nicole asked as she emerged from her daze. Her hand remained suspended in front of her mouth despite the fact that the chip had fallen from her fingers, leaving behind a glob of coagulated cheese.

"Yeah I had to try it. It was only like three bucks for an order, so I figured what the hell. To be honest, it's not that tasty, and it's a pain to eat because the ribs and spine of the snake are included. By the time you pick the meat off, there really isn't that much to it."

"Okay that would keep me awake if I ate it." Nicole laughed.

After we returned to the truck, Nicole sat in the jump seat sipping her soft drink while I occupied the driver's seat updating my logbook. I called Sandra to inform her of the problem with the Qualcomm. She confirmed that we should get it fixed or replaced when we arrived at the OC in Dallas.

Sandra also informed me of a load of boat parts to pick up from a distribution center in Dallas to take to New Orleans. We had plenty of time in Dallas to get the Qualcomm fixed first.

"Sandra said to pick up a load in Dallas for New Orleans." I said while pulling back onto the freeway.

"Awesome!" Nicole exclaimed jubilantly. "I've never been to New Orleans."

"Well, don't get too excited" I laughed, "It's not like we can park our truck in front of Pat O'Brien's to go in for a hurricane."

Nicole gazed at me quizzically. It was not difficult to read her mind.

"Pat O'Brien's is a well-known bar in the French Quarter. It's mainly a tourist bar, but also very popular with the locals. They invented a world famous, signature rum drink they call The Hurricane."

"It sure sounds like fun" Nicole got up to head to the back

of the truck. She spoke so quietly I could barely hear her above the roar of the engine,

”I'm going back to sleep.”

“Okay. We'll be in Dallas before your shift starts so you can sleep in. Sleep tight.”

“Thanks” Nicole said glumly as she pulled the curtains shut.

I estimated that we would arrive at the Dallas OC around 4:00 pm Central time. I needed to check the truck in at the shop to get the Qualcomm replaced, which meant Nicole and I would have to hang out in the driver's lounge for as long as it took the shop to perform the work. Perhaps I could conjure up an alternative plan for tonight. I grabbed my cell phone from my purse and dialed my sister's number.

Candy rarely answers her phone, so I was not surprised when I heard her voicemail greeting. I left her a message, letting her know that I was on my way to Dallas, and would like to get together with her tonight. I put my cell phone back in my purse.

I had moved from Chicago to Dallas in 1979. Less than two years later, Candy moved to Dallas, not because I was there, but because her best friend Debbie and her husband had relocated to Dallas. I had never been very close with my sister, most likely due to the fact that we'd had so many philosophical differences, but we have always had a cordial relationship. We had somehow always managed the occasional get together; sometimes even succeeding in avoiding an argument.

I hadn't seen my sister in quite a while, ever since Laura and I had moved to Colorado in 2001. Tonight would be a good chance for us to get together, since Nicole and I would be idle while our truck was in the shop.

I heard the ringing of my cell phone, and reached into my purse to grab it. Candy's phone number was on the caller ID.

“Hello!” I said cheerfully.

“Hey it's me. So you're going to be in Dallas tonight?”

“Yeah, our truck is going to be in the shop for a couple of hours, I thought it would be a good time for us to get together.

Plus you can meet my driving partner, Nicole."

"Kind of short notice, don't you think?" She said curtly. I knew that one was coming.

"Well that's the way it is now. I don't really get much notice in regard to where I'm going. I just figured you might want to get together while we have the chance."

"I already have plans for tonight. Debbie and I were going to do something together."

"That's great…. I would love to see Debbie too. Why don't you and Debbie have dinner with me and Nicole?"

Candy sighed, "Okay, what time do you want to meet us?"

"Well actually, I need you to come pick us up at the Dallas Operating Center in South Dallas."

Candy lived in the northeast suburbs of Dallas, so I knew this would not go over well, but my sister can sometimes surprise me.

"No problem. Give me the address and I'll pick out a restaurant nearby. Debbie and I will come by and pick you up, how does six thirty sound?"

"Six thirty sounds great. Can I ask you one more favor?"

"What?" She asked sarcastically. I could almost hear her eyes roll.

"Tomorrow is Nicole's birthday. Would you mind picking up a small cake? I'll reimburse you for it."

"Sure, no problem. If you'd have given me more notice I could have baked one for her."

I gav e Candy the address and general directions to the Dallas OC, we said our goodbyes, and hung-up. I was happy that I would be seeing my sister tonight. Despite the fact that we have always disagreed on so many things, she was supportive of my transition. I hoped to be able to develop a "little sister" relationship with her. In only a few hours, Candy would be meeting her sister for the first time.

Chapter Eleven
Gator Tails

It was slightly after 1:30 PM when I pulled the truck into the Dallas Operating Center. Although my shift ended at noon, I had decided to drive the remaining 60 miles and let Nicole sleep.

After topping off the tanks at the fuel lane, I pulled into the yard and backed into an empty slot. Once I had cranked down the landing gear and disconnected the hoses and electrical cables, I pulled the pin on the fifth wheel and hopped back into the tractor.

A yawning Nicole sat in the jump seat sipping on soda and rubbing the sleep out of her eyes as I pulled the tractor away from the trailer with a thud, and headed over to the bobtail parking area. All the operating centers had designated parking for bobtails, which are considerably shorter than the ones in the yard.

I found an empty spot close to the service center and backed the tractor into it. Without a trailer, I had to quickly re-think the maneuver required to back in, since now it was as simple as backing a very large car into a parking spot at the mall.

"Egad, what's that mess all over the windshield?" Nicole exclaimed, while opening her door and climbing down from the cab.

"That, my dear, is the carnage of West Texas," I laughed while we walked over to the service desk. What she was referring to were the splattered bugs of all sizes that covered every square inch of the windshield; with the exception of the semi-circle shaped paths of the windshield wipers.

"Geez, they sure do have some huge bugs in Texas," she laughed.

There was a short waiting line at the service desk, on which Nicole and I took turns standing while each of us visited the restroom. While I was washing my hands, another woman emerged from a stall and stared at me for a moment before quickly exiting without washing her hands. As I departed the restroom and walked through the drivers' lounge, I spotted her seated at one of the tables with a group of drivers, all of which stared at me intensely as I headed back to the service desk. 'Here we go again', I said to myself.

By the time I returned to the service desk to rejoin Nicole, the line ahead of us had dissipated and it was our turn. Nicole was standing slightly behind me as I stepped up to the counter and faced a grease-covered mechanic with the name 'James' stitched on his shirt. He stared at me curiously.

"What can I help you with, sir?" James asked gruffly.

"Well first of all, you can call me ma'am, not sir." I was wearing a peach colored sleeveless top, tan capris, and sandals; an outfit that screamed female. Nicole, who was now standing at my side, glared at James. She was dressed in a man's work shirt and baggie jeans.

James glanced briefly at Nicole while shaking his head in disgust, and then turned his attention back to me.

"Okay, whatever" he retorted sarcastically. "What can I do for you, *driver?*"

I did not want to argue any further about my gender, so I got right to the point. "Our Qualcomm is dead. We need to get a new one installed."

"We're extremely busy and won't be able to get to it for a few hours," James replied arrogantly.

"That's okay, as long as we can get it fixed sometime tonight.

We have a load that has to be delivered tomorrow," I feigned a smile.

James reached under the counter and retrieved a work order form. "Fill this out and park your rig outside the shop. We'll get to it as soon as we can, but don't expect it to be ready until around 10:00 tonight."

"So what was all that about?" Nicole asked as we walked back to the truck.

"You mean that 'sir' comment? I'm sure I'm going to get that a lot until I get my electrolysis finished and I get facial surgery. As much as I hate to admit it, I think I pretty much look like a guy in women's clothing right now."

"Yeah you do" Nicole replied pointedly. "But that doesn't give people the right to be rude to you."

"Well, I knew this would be part of the deal when I started this. I warned you about it too, remember?"

"Yeah, I remember. So, is this what you were talking about when you said I would have to deal with a lot of shit?"

"It will probably get a lot worse, Nicole. People calling me sir is just a minor thing compared to what could happen."

"You mean, like violence?"

"Violence is unlikely; more likely threats and verbal attacks."

"Well like I said, I can take a lot of shit. I just don't know how much," She replied cautiously. She then changed the subject.

"So, what are we going to do for the next five hours while we're waiting for our truck to be ready? Hang out in the drivers' lounge?"

"Oh, I forgot to tell you, Nicole. I have plans for us," I grinned.

"Plans? What kind of plans?" She asked.

"My sister and her friend are coming by to take us out to dinner to celebrate your birthday. Let's get back to the truck and get dressed up!"

Nicole and I took showers, and I spent nearly an hour

primping for my debut with my sister and her friend. Nicole waited in the drivers lounge. When I finally emerged and entered the lounge, I spotted Nicole standing outside the glass doors chatting with a woman who I recognized as the one who had glared at me in the ladies room earlier. When Nicole spotted me, she entered the lounge and joined me at a table.

"You look nice" she smiled warmly.

"Thank you. This will be the first time my sister will be seeing me as Pam, so I wanted to make a good first impression."

"I'm sure you will," she replied.

"Who was that woman you were talking to outside?"

"I just met her. Her name is Marylou and she is out of the Indianapolis OC," Nicole paused for a moment before continuing.

"She was asking about you."

"Oh? And what was she asking about me?"

"She asked if you were a male or female. I told her you were in the middle of transitioning from male to female" Her voice trailed off as she finished the sentence. I knew there was more.

"Go on…"

Nicole fidgeted in her seat and wrung her hands. I knew she was about to say something that made her feel uneasy.

"She said that you made her feel uncomfortable when she saw you in the ladies restroom. She thinks you should be using the men's bathroom" she replied in a soft voice.

"Oh, well that's just wonderful" I replied sarcastically.

Candy called at 6:20 to tell me that she and Debbie were five minutes away. Nicole and I left the drivers' lounge and waited outside near the entrance to the visitor's parking lot. Within a few minutes, Candy's blue Nissan pulled in. After hugs and introductions, Nicole and I took Candy and Debbie on a tour of the operating center and a visit to our truck. They were both in awe at the sight the sea of orange trucks, and impressed by the size of our truck. Afterward, we all headed back to the visitor lot and piled into Candy's car.

"You sure look different from the last time I saw you" Debbie turned around in the passenger seat and addressed me, as Candy guided the car out of the parking lot.

I laughed "Yes, this is the new me." I did not know what else to say.

"Well, don't expect everyone to just automatically accept you. It's going to take some getting used to. I'm having a hard time even calling you 'Pam'. I'm just going to call you 'P' for now until I get used to the 'new you'" Debbie said brusquely before turning back to face forward.

"I have something for you, Pam," Candy said as she reached back and handed me a small gift bag.

"Wow… thank you, Candy. I wasn't expecting you to bring me a gift!" I said while taking the bag from her.

"It's just a little something to help you get started." Candy glanced back at me briefly, and then turned her attention back to the road. "Take a look."

I reached into the bag and pulled out what appeared to be a miniature metal briefcase with a small handle and a latch. I unlatched the case and opened it to find a treasure trove of make-up brushes, eye shadows, blushes, lip colors, and glosses. The inside of the lid had a small mirror with which one could easily apply make-up.

"Candy, this is great! Thank you so much!" I exclaimed while handing the case to Nicole for her inspection.

"I figured you could use this while travelling around in the truck."

"Just don't overdo the makeup," Debbie interjected with a laugh.

"I'll make sure she doesn't," Nicole laughed while handing the case back to me.

Candy drove us to a nearby national chain restaurant where we had a brief wait for a table; enough time for Candy to smuggle in Nicole's birthday cake and give it to the hostess, with instructions to bring it to our table after we had finished dinner. Once we were seated, our server appeared and took our appetizer and drink orders, then disappeared into the kitchen.

"So Candy, are you shocked about all this?" I asked.

"No, I'm not in the least bit surprised. The only surprise is the name you chose. Why did you choose Pam?"

"Those were my initials when mom was married to John, but I've always thought of myself as Pam."

"Ah, okay. Very clever!" Candy smiled.

Debbie looked perplexed.

I turned to Debbie and answered her unasked question. "Our mother was married to a man name John Mair and we took his last name. During that time, my name was Philip Andrew Mair."

"Ah yes, that is clever" Debbie laughed.

I turned back to my sister, "Candy, you said you weren't surprised. Why not?"

"Have you forgotten that you wrote me a letter telling me about it right after you moved to Dallas twenty years ago? Remember, you said that part of your reason for leaving Chicago was as an attempt to escape those feelings?"

"Yes, I do remember that letter now. I had forgotten about it though."

"It's not just that though… Even as kids you were doing some things that made me wonder about you."

"Like what?"

"Like you sitting around gazing at the women's clothing section in the Sears catalog. Or all those times I saw you dressing in mom's clothes when she was at work."

"You noticed that?"

"Yes. And you always wanted to be the 'mom' when we played house," Candy laughed. "And don't think I didn't know about you playing with my dolls and stuffed animals."

The entire table had erupted in laughter by the time our drinks and appetizers arrived. Debbie, Candy, and I had each ordered a glass of wine, and Nicole had ordered a coke. I nodded approvingly at her, since she would be taking the first driving shift when we returned to our truck.

After we had all placed our dinner orders, Nicole rose from her seat.

"I need to go the bathroom."

"Me too, I'll go with you," Candy stood and joined her.

After Candy and Nicole had departed, Debbie spoke to me.

"I'm glad you have at least taken the first steps. Candy has been concerned about this since you first told her about it."

"So you knew about this?"

"Oh yeah, she first told me years ago. It's a hard concept for me to imagine, but I'm sure I'll get over it. Just don't go crazy with it and go get gigantic boobs or anything like that," she laughed.

A few minutes later, Candy and Nicole returned from the restroom, and soon afterward, our entrees arrived.

Debbie broke the silence while we all enjoyed our dinners.

"Did Candy tell you that Bob and Jessica and I went to Bogota Columbia for Christmas to visit my cousin and her family?"

"I think she mentioned that you were going to Columbia, but I didn't know you had a cousin there."

"Yeah, they have lived there for about 18 years. My cousin is a teacher and she was off from work all the way until the middle of January, so we had a personal tour guide the whole time we were there," she laughed.

"That sounds wonderful," Nicole said.

"Yes it was, it's very beautiful there. But, they still have problems, so you have to be careful. Having a family member as a tour guide really helps."

"So where are you two heading from here?" Candy asked.

"We have a load of boat parts that we have to take to New Orleans. It's due tomorrow," I replied.

"Yay, Nicole! You get to spend your birthday in New Orleans!" Debbie exclaimed.

Nicole frowned "Yeah and all I get to see of it is some stupid loading dock."

"At least you can say you went to New Orleans for your birthday," Candy laughed.

After we had finished our dinners, and the server had cleared our table, a cadre of staff members appeared, singing happy birthday to Nicole. The flaming, candle covered cake was placed on our table, which Nicole quickly extinguished with a puff of breath.

Candy drove us back the OC and we chatted for a few minutes before exchanging goodbye hugs. Candy and Debbie wished Nicole and I best wishes on our journeys before departing. Nicole thanked them for a wonderful birthday dinner and cake.

When we returned to the yard, our truck was ready and waiting for us in a parking spot outside of the service center. Nicole and I had decided that we would both catch some sleep before heading out. After stopping in the drivers' lounge for one last potty break and to brush our teeth, we climbed into our sleeper berths. I set my alarm for midnight and went to sleep.

Despite the fact that my alarm went off at 12:00 am, it was 3:00 by the time I hooked up to our trailer load of boat parts, and rolled out of the OC to head east on Interstate 20. The trip from the Dallas OC to our destination in New Orleans was 538 miles, which I could easily make in nine hours. Our load was not due until 3:00 pm, which gave me plenty of time for stops along the way.

Nicole was sleeping soundly, unaware of the birthday plan that was now incubating in my mind.

After brief stops in Shreveport and Alexandria for coffee, I pulled into the Love's Truck Stop in Baton Rouge to top off the fuel tanks. While I was busy re-fueling and washing the windshield, Nicole emerged from the truck and padded into the building without uttering a word. A few moments later; just as I was finishing at the fuel pumps, she reappeared with a large soft drink cup in her hand, and climbed back into the cab.

"Where are we?" Nicole asked as I climbed back into the cab and started the engine. She sat in the jump seat sipping on her drink. Her long mane of hair, tangled in every possible direction, made her resemble Medusa.

"Red Stick," I replied with a grin as I finished updating my log. I put the truck in gear and pulled out of the truck stop and back onto Interstate 10.

"Red Stick?" Nicole looked at me quizzically. Her bare feet were on the dashboard as she leaned back in her seat and took another sip of her drink.

"Baton Rouge. It's French for Red Stick," I replied.

"Ah, okay" she replied while gazing out of the side window at the passing scenery. "How much further to New Orleans?"

"It's about 80 miles from here. We should be there in about an hour and a half" I looked at her and smiled. "Happy birthday!"

"Thanks" She replied flatly.

"Are you feeling ok? You look awful."

Nicole made a feeble attempt to smooth down her out of control hair as she replied. "I feel fine, just sleepy is all."

"I think you may have a fever. Your skin is very pale looking. You probably have stomach cramps too?"

Nicole glared at me. "Pam, I feel fine. I don't feel like I have a fever and I don't have stomach cramps. I don't know what you are talking about."

"I think something you ate for dinner last night is disagreeing with you. You probably have a mild touch of food poisoning, which is why you have a fever and stomach cramps. It also explains why you have been up all night vomiting."

"Pam, have you completely lost your mind? I was not up all night vomiting. And I don't have a fever or stomach cramps. Why are you talking so crazy?"

I ignored her protestations. "Nicole, you should not be driving in your condition. The best thing for you right now is rest. I think a day of rest will help break the fever; and hopefully your stomach cramps and vomiting will go away also."

Nicole was speechless as she simply stared at me in astonishment. I continued.

"I'm going to call Sandra and tell her how sick you are. I'm sure she will agree that we need to shut down in New Orleans for a day or two until your fever breaks and you are able to hold down your food."

I glanced over at Nicole. A slight smile was beginning to replace the confused expression she had on her face just a moment ago.

"Now that you mention it, I am feeling kind of sick," she grinned.

"This is payback for Colorado Springs, Okay?"

"Absolutely" She exclaimed. She leaned over toward the driver's seat with her right hand in the air. I gave her the high five.

After delivering our load of boat parts, I sent an 'empty' message on the Qualcomm and then immediately called Sandra.

"Hi, Sandra. We just delivered in New Orleans, but Nicole is really sick. I think she needs to just sleep for a while."

"What's wrong with her?" Sandra asked.

"She ate some seafood for dinner last night. I think it may be a touch of food poisoning. She's been throwing up all night. Today she has a fever and stomach cramps."

"Okay, well I have you guys on a load of coffee that has to go to Boston, but we have four days. Can you pick it up tomorrow and get it up there after Nicole has had a chance to recuperate?"

"Yeah, no problem," I replied.

"Isn't today Nicole's birthday?" Sandra asked.

"Yes it is."

"Tell her happy birthday for me. What a shame to be stuck in New Orleans on her birthday!" I could sense the facetious tone to her voice.

"Thank you Sandra. I'll tell her."

The Mardi Gras Truck stop is located on Elysian Fields Avenue, just a few miles from Bourbon Street. Most truck stops make their profit from diesel fuel, food, and supplies, and therefore do not charge truckers to park. The Mardi Gras does not sell fuel, and therefore charges $20 per 24 hour period to park, which Nicole gladly paid. Once we had parked the truck, we grabbed our shower gear and headed into the building to take showers, for which we also had to pay. After our showers, we returned to the truck to devise a game plan for the evening.

Nicole and I were each dressed in tee shirts, shorts, and sandals. In my usual effort to cover the shadow of my facial hair, I was wearing my heavy coat of makeup. Nicole was without makeup and as always, looked ravishing. I was envious of her, not just for her beauty, but also for her youth, and the many opportunities that awaited such a beautiful woman.

We walked out to Elysian Fields Avenue to catch a cab. There was another female driver waiting when we got there, and she offered to share a cab with us. After the taxi dropped us off at the French Quarter, we split the fare and went our separate ways.

Our first stop was Pier 424 restaurant for dinner. We grabbed a couple of beers at the bar, and then headed for a table where I ordered for both of us since Nicole had never been in a Cajun restaurant before this.

"We'll have two cups of gumbo and an order of gator tails to start, followed by crawfish etouffee for two," I said to the waiter.

"Gator tails?" Nicole asked after the waiter had departed.

"Yes Nicole. It's exactly what you think. It's meat taken from the tail of an alligator, breaded and fried. It is very lean and healthy and tender, and has a wonderful flavor!"

"This sounds like that rattlesnake meat you were telling me about. I hope this isn't going to give me nightmares," she said.

After we stuffed ourselves at Pier 424, we went bar hopping along Bourbon Street. We hit Pat O'Brien's for their famous hurricanes, then we were off to Lafitte's, then Yo-Mama's and then Cooter Brown's. We walked down Bourbon Street and enjoyed the street theatre. We shopped at many of the quaint little stores and purchased souvenirs and visors with 'New Orleans" emblazoned on them. As we walked past the hotels, Men on balconies tossed beads at us, imploring us to "*Show us your tits!*" Nicole and I just laughed.

We were both having the time of our lives.

We ended up later in the night at 'Rubyfruit Jungle', the only lesbian bar in all of New Orleans.

Nicole and I were both amused and surprised when we ran into the same woman that we had shared the cab with earlier. She introduced herself to Nicole and me as Tammy. Tammy and Nicole immediately hit it off, but Tammy took an immediate disliking to me. I did my best to simply brush off her outward animosity toward me, but throughout the rest of the night Tammy continued to make several snide remarks about me and even directly to me.

Nicole was pretty lit by now, and was so busy kissing and dancing with her newfound friend that she did not even seem to notice the rotten treatment that I was getting from Tammy. It was her birthday celebration after all, so I did my best to ignore it, or at least try to take it in stride, but it made for a horrible night for me from then on.

Tammy was full of herself, full of booze and I guess the fact that she was now semi-attached at the lips to my friend that it must have emboldened her even further in her attacks against me. On several occasions, she referred to me as a transvestite. She was relentless as she slammed me with insults about my "gender confusion" constantly referring to me as 'him' and 'he'.

When I could not take it anymore I decided to find a lonely spot away from the dance floor and spent the remainder of the evening drinking alone, watching Nicole and Tammy dance and make out.

After last call at Rubyfruit's, the three of us caught a cab back to the truck stop. Nicole and Tammy took off to Tammy's Black Peterbilt to spend the night together. I'm sure Nicole would have a memorable birthday now, even if most of it would only be recalled as a semi-lucid memory.

I took off to the other edge of the lot to find our truck. As I wearily climbed aboard, the hostilities that Tammy had shown me replayed themselves throughout my mind. I did not want to dwell on these things, but it was like a bad dream that you've just awakened from. These become etched in your memory, and you just can't seem to brush them off.

I tossed and turned for a while as I tried to let it all go, but to no avail. After the night I had just had I finally decided that it would be worth paying for another shower, so I grabbed my gear, and walked back to the building. I then took one of the longest, hottest showers I had taken in a very long time. I do not know if the ritualistic actions of washing my body helped much to rid me psychologically of the night's trials or if the hot water simply allowed me to relax enough to release some of my physical tensions.

I dried off, dressed and made my way back to my berth where, eventually, but alone, I was able to drift away into a relatively peaceful slumber.

Chapter Twelve
It Ain't Workin'

"Nicole, wake up!" It had been nearly a full five minutes now that I had been pounding on the door of Tammy's truck trying to rouse her and Nicole.

The curtain flew open and Tammy glared venomously at me through the window. With a whirring sound the driver's window slowly slid down.

"WHAT THE HELL? We're sleeping dammit! What time is it?" Tammy spat at me.

"It's ten-thirty in the morning. Please tell Nicole she needs to get up. We have to get on the road soon."

Nicole's face suddenly appeared behind Tammy. "I'm up!" She yelled.

"Nicole, we need to pick up that load of coffee and head to Boston. I can go pick it up by myself, but I need you to be ready to start driving when I get back, ok?"

"Okay." She said sounding somewhat apologetic. "I just need to get a coke and take a shower. I promise I'll be ready," Nicole said as the window began to close again with that whirring sound. Tammy continued to glare at me through the glass.

Our trailer of coffee was at a distribution center in Hammond, which is 78 miles north from the Mardi Gras Truck Stop. Fortunately, it was already pre-loaded. It would have been much more efficient if we would have simply picked it up and headed north to Boston, rather than me backtracking to pick up Nicole, but you have to roll with the punches. It took me an hour and a half to drive to Hammond, then fifteen minutes to locate the trailer and couple to it. I still had another hour and a half drive to get back to the truck stop to pick up Nicole. By the time I finally pulled into the parking area, it was already 1:50. Nicole was leaning against the front of the black Peterbilt when I arrived, holding hands with Tammy who was smoking a cigar.

"Come on Nicole, we've got to roll!" I shouted to Nicole as I set the brake.

"Oh, great! He's a freakin' poet!" snorted Tammy.

I ignored Tammy's deliberate gender slur. I was not in the mood to argue, I was running out of time and patience and just wanted to be rid of her. I hopped over to the jump seat as the two girls kissed one more time before Nicole climbed into the driver's seat. After starting a new log for the day, she buckled up and put the truck in gear. Finally, we were on our way to Boston.

Our trip began on Interstate 10 east. As Nicole drove, I sat quietly in the jump seat and gazed at the unusual landscape of New Orleans; including the many voodoo temples and the ancient cemeteries with their above ground crypts. New Orleans is a fascinating city to visit, and had always been a favorite of mine. Little did I know that the next time I drove through this city, it would be devastated by hurricane Katrina.

Nicole was also glancing at the cemeteries as we passed. "Why are people buried above the ground in all these cemeteries?" she asked.

I hid my anger at Nicole and simply explained without smiling. "It's because of all the rain they get here. New Orleans is mostly swampland, and when it floods, anything buried beneath the ground tends to float to the surface; including bodies. Back in the 1700's they decided it would be best to bury the dead above ground, so they started building a number of these 'cities of the dead'."

"They do look like miniature cities," Nicole observed.

"Remember the cemetery scene in the movie, Easy Rider? It was filmed in one of these cemeteries."

"Yeah, I loved that movie," Nicole exclaimed.

I changed the subject "So, did you enjoy your birthday?" Despite my fury at Nicole and Tammy, I tried my best to be cordial and not let my anger show. I guess I did a fairly convincing job of it as Nicole showed no sign that she felt my inner rage.

"Yeah, the parts I remember," she laughed. "Actually, it was really a lot of fun. Thank you for making my birthday special!"

I felt my animosity waning. "You're welcome." I smiled weakly.

"What about Tammy? Are you going to see her again?" I asked while gazing out of the side window. I was slightly terrified that I would hear an affirmative response and I deliberately avoided any eye contact with her.

"We exchanged phone numbers, but I doubt that we'll call each other. She lives with her partner in Cleveland."

My internal relief was nearly audible. "So this was just gallivanting for each of you?" I asked pointedly.

"What's that supposed to mean?" Nicole quipped.

I turned back from the window to face her.

"Rachael made that reference about you 'gallivanting around the country'. Is this what she meant?"

"Pam, don't try to be my mother!" She snapped.

"I'm not trying to be your mother! Nicole. I'm just asking…"

"Well it sure sounds like you are scolding me, or giving me a lecture or something."

I turned and resumed gazing out the window for a moment as we crossed the long bridge over Lake Pontchartrain. Once we crossed the lake, we would be in Slidell, where we would pick up Interstate 59 north into Mississippi.

I turned back to Nicole. "Nicole, I'm sorry if I seemed to be lecturing you. Sometimes I just feel like you are my daughter and I have to look out for you."

"Well, I'm not your daughter and you're not my mother. I'm a big girl. I can take care of my own life and you don't need to be looking out for me," she replied tersely.

"Okay Nicole, you're right," I said resignedly. "I'll stay out of your personal life. You do whatever you want." With that, I rose from the jump seat and headed to the sleeper berth.

Forty-eight miles from the Mardi Gras Truck Stop, and a mile and a half across the Mississippi state line on Interstate 59 is a weigh station. Thanks to our trucking company, our rig was equipped with a PrePass, which is basically a transponder that is attached to the windshield. As a truck equipped with one of these approaches a weigh station, a 'reader', attached to a boom over the freeway, interacts with the PrePass to validate the truck's credentials. If everything checks out okay and there are no further actions necessary a green light blinks on the Transponder, indicating that it is all right to bypass the weigh station. In the event that a truck is required to pull into the station for scaling, a red light would blink instead. It would then be necessary to pull into the station along with the trucks that are not equipped with PrePass. Under normal circumstances the only two reasons a truck would get the red light is if it had an unacceptable safety record, or if it had simply been chosen at random.

On any other day, our PrePass would have given us the green light to bypass the station, but this time we caught the random red light, indicating that we had to pull through the scales. We were already behind schedule now, and as if having to stop for a random weight check wasn't enough to slow us down; as Nicole eased the truck across the scales… another act of randomness. The LED sign over the scales began flashing a message, instructing us to park and bring our log books and bills of lading into the scale house. This is a chance occurrence that only happens to approximately one out of one hundred trucks that go through the scales, and today seemed to be our lucky day.

Nicole parked the truck and headed into the scale house with our log books and bills of lading. There was no reason for me to go in since I was off duty, so I lied back in my berth and let myself doze off. I had only slept for what seemed like a few seconds, when Nicole reentered the cab and climbed back in, slamming the door behind her.

"Fuck! They want to inspect the truck," she grumbled as she started the truck and put it into gear.

I poked my head out of the sleeper berth and watched as she maneuvered the truck toward one of the giant inspection bays. A uniformed woman stood in front of the truck guiding us in, and then crossed her arms signaling Nicole to stop. Once we had come to a complete stop and Nicole had set the brake, the woman climbed onto the running board and peered into the truck.

"Ms. Nicole, We're going to perform a Level One inspection. It shouldn't take more than 30 minutes and you'll be on your way." She smiled apologetically at Nicole, and then at me. "Sorry to disturb your rest Ms. Pam. You'll be snoozing away in no time."

"No problem" I smiled. She had obviously already inspected our logs and knew our names.

"My name is Nancy, by the way. Your logs and bills of lading checked out, and your weight is just fine." She handed the log books and bills back to Nicole. "Feel free to get out and stretch your legs or use the restroom if you want. I won't need you at the controls for about 10 minutes."

"I could use a potty break," I said to Nicole as I emerged from the berth. "You want to go with me?"

"No, I'm good" Nicole said sulkily. She had obviously not recovered from her foul mood, and this inspection was not improving it any.

"Where are the restrooms?" I asked Nancy after I had climbed down from the cab. She held a clipboard in her hand as she crouched down to speak to a technician under our truck. When she finished her sentence, she stood up and smiled at me, "You have to go back out into the parking lot area and walk around to the front entrance of the building. The restrooms are to your right as soon as you walk through the front door."

"Thank you Nancy," I replied with a smile. She had a charming southern accent and was a very pleasant woman.

As I walked around to the entrance, I passed two Mississippi State Trooper cruisers parked on the side of the building; one with the K-9 insignia on the doors, and a large dog seated on the rear seat. When I entered the building, I saw the two troopers seated at a small table, a few yards away. They were sipping coffee and conversing as I entered, but their conversation ended abruptly as I passed them and headed into the ladies room. From my peripheral vision, I could see them eyeing me suspiciously.

A little rattled by their suspicious looks, I remained in the restroom long after I had finished washing my hands. I freshened my makeup as best I could, but was unable to cover the shadow of facial hair that had grown since I had shaved earlier this morning. It now seemed intent on betraying me from beneath my foundation. No longer able to look at my hideous face in the mirror, I turned and stared at the faded blue and white tiles on the walls instead. I began counting each color in each diagonal row, seeing how many different ways I could divide the sums of each row. I mentally checked to make sure every row had the same amount of each color tile. I was intentionally stalling for time, in the hopes that the two troopers would be on the Interstate, trapping unsuspecting speeders by the time I finally emerged.

No such luck. I knew without a doubt at this very moment that had I bought a lottery ticket this day that it would have been the same as flushing my money down the toilet of the ladies room from which I just vacated. As I opened the door to exit the restroom, my breath caught in my throat. The troopers were now standing near the small table at which they had been seated previously, staring in my direction, as if waiting for me. The DOT officer behind the counter was also staring at me as I tried to walk casually and confidently by them to make my way to the exit. Before I could touch the handle on the glass door, I heard the sound that I had been dreading.

"Sir!... Can we have a word with you please?" I cringed at the sound of them addressing me as, 'sir', and for the briefest flash of a moment, I actually considered ignoring them. However, I knew this was not going to be a pleasant experience and ignoring them would inevitably only make it worse.

"Are you talking to me?" I said in my most feminine manner as I turned to face them while trying to project a sincere smile.

They both approached me menacingly as one of them spoke in a macho voice. "Let's see some ID." His name badge said McMartin.

I reached into my purse and pulled out my wallet, then handed my CDL to McMartin. He looked at it for a moment, made an almost imperceptibly sour face and then handed it to his comrade. The other trooper glanced at it briefly, gave me a much more obvious look of disapproval, and then slid it into his shirt pocket. His name was "Buford"

"Is there something wrong?" I asked innocently.

These were Mississippi State Troopers after all, and I certainly was not looking the part of 'Damsel in Distress'.

"Sir... that was the ladies room you just came out of. You need to be using the men's room." Like Nancy, they had southern accents, but there was nothing charming or pleasant about these two.

"Officers, with all due respect I wish you wouldn't address me as 'sir'. I am a female and I normally use the ladies room." I smiled weakly as I looked each trooper in the eye.

Buford reached into his pocket and gazed at my CDL for a moment, then looked at me. "It says here on your CDL that you are a male Mister Anders."

"Yes, I know it says that. It's only a technicality. You see... I am transitioning from male to female and part of the process is that I am required to live as a female for a full year before I can get the surgery. After I get my surgery, my license will be changed to female." I pointed to my CDL.

"Well, until that day happens… you'd better use the men's room," McMartin barked.

I reached into my purse and extracted the two letters that I carried, but had hoped never to have to use. They are appropriately called 'carry letters', which are simply letters written by medical professionals explaining to any interested party that the person in question is in the process of transitioning from one gender to the other. My therapist in Colorado Springs wrote one of the letters, and my hormone doctor wrote the other. I handed the letters to McMartin. I was hoping his level of distaste for me would be more accepting of my current situation than I already knew Buford's would be.

McMartin quickly scanned the letters, and then handed them to Buford, who in turn briefly scanned them before handing them back to me with a sneer.

"These letters say you're presenting as a female…" He grinned wickedly at me while handing me my CDL. "It ain't workin' buddy!"

They both shared a couple of good-old-boy, "Ain't we funny!" looks before turning away from me as if to dismiss my existence as they headed outside.

I could only stand there shocked and stunned for a moment. I felt paralyzed by the shock of this sudden and unexpected exchange I had just experienced. It had left me feeling humiliated and empty, no… almost nauseous actually, as the two troopers exited the building and got into their cruisers. 'Is this what I am to expect to have to endure for the next eleven months until I can get my surgery?', I asked myself, astonished.

I felt violated, enraged and persecuted, saddened, maddened and hurt that this had been at the whims of officers of the law who had sworn an oath 'To Serve And Protect'!

Fuming to myself now, I went back out to the truck and found Nicole and Nancy standing near the rear end of the trailer where the inspector was completing his report. My hands were shaking as I joined them.

"Ms. Nicole, Ms. Pam. Everything looks fine." Nancy said with a sweet smile as she began signing off on the inspection report. "I just need one of you to sign here…" She held out the clipboard and a pen toward me. My hands were shaking so badly from the encounter with Buford and McMartin that I was barely able to function, let alone sign my name, so I handed them off to Nicole.

Nicole took them from me and signed her name. While she was signing, I glanced toward the tractor and was suddenly surprised to find the two state troopers and the dog standing next to our driver's side door. They called out to Nancy, and she walked over to chat with them. A few minutes later, she came back to the end of the trailer where Nicole and I stood.

"Do you ever party in your truck?" She asked.

"Party? In what way?" I asked.

"The dog hit on your truck. If you have anything in there… please tell me. The troopers want to do a search of your cab. If there's anything in there it would really be in your best interest for you to cooperate with them now."

"The dog hit on our truck?" Nicole asked incredulously. "You mean like they smelled drugs? No way!"

"Yeah, that's pretty much what they're saying" Nancy replied, indicating the two troopers as we followed her to the cab.

"Neither of us does drugs, Nancy." I said numbly. "Nicole's previous partner had a container of drugs that he had brought into the truck, but Nicole found them and turned him in. It really freaked her out and she was even required to take a drug test to prove her innocence. But that was removed long ago. The only "drugs" that I take are my prescriptions, none of which is narcotic and I have the documentation for all of them. I think the dog is mistaken." I protested.

Our protestations were of no avail. Buford and the dog were now inside the cab where I could hear him thrashing around and encouraging the dog, while McMartin stood next to the door intent on peering under the seats with his flashlight.

"Don't they have to have a warrant or something to do this?" Nicole asked angrily.

"You're operating a commercial motor vehicle Ms. Nicole. That gives any officer of the law implied consent to search the truck." Nancy was sincerely apologetic. She was even blushing a little. It was obvious to me that she believed us, but had no authority to stop their tirade.

After what seemed like hours, but was in fact merely a matter of twenty minutes, Buford and the dog climbed down from the tractor. Without saying a word, they walked back to their cruisers, which were parked next to the inspection bay.

"It looks like you are free to go…" Nancy smiled. As she headed back into the building, she stopped and offered what felt like a sincere apology. "I'm so very sorry for the inconvenience ladies."

"No apologies from those guys?" Nicole pointed to the two cruisers.

"Let's just get out of here and back on the road Nicole. Those guys have the power to make our lives hell." I said as I began to walk around to the passenger side of the truck.

Nicole was in before I even got close to the door. "OH DEAR GOD! Look at this truck! Look what those two assholes did to our truck!" Nicole was standing between the driver's seat and the jump seat as I climbed into the cab. "They didn't even bother to try to put things back the way they were. Not even an apology for tearing up our truck!"

I looked at the back of the truck at the horrific sight, and was nearly speechless. "Geez what a mess…" was all I could manage to say.

Our clothes, once neatly folded and stacked, were now strewn all over the cab and sleeper berths. Our mattresses, now stripped of their sheets, lay tossed atop the piles of clothing. Food from the refrigerator was scattered everywhere haphazardly. The contents from each of our shower bags now covered the floor, as each piece had been investigated, before being tossed aside. Papers from the desk drawer were everywhere. It looked as if a cyclone had visited our truck.

"Don't worry about it! I'll put this place back together while you drive, Nicole. Let's get the hell out of here. NOW, please!" I stepped over the rubble as I headed into the back of the truck.

Nicole grudgingly acquiesced before settling into the driver's seat, updated her log, and started the engine. After fastening her seat belt and putting the truck in gear, she cautiously eased our way out of the scale station and back onto Interstate 59 careful to observe the speed limit and observant of anything that might possibly delay our 'escape'.

We had left New Orleans three hours ago, and had traveled less than 50 miles. With Nicole back at the wheel, we were once again on Interstate 59 heading north.

"I can't believe that stupid dog smelled Terry's drugs after all this time, Pam! This truck has been swept and cleaned and vacuumed several times since that stupid box of his was removed!" Nicole shouted over her shoulder as I began putting our food back into the refrigerator.

"The dog didn't smell any drugs, Nicole." I said calmly as I closed the refrigerator and began separating Nicole's shower items from mine, returning them to their bags.

"They told that lady that the dog smelled something. Why else would they want to search the truck?"

I plopped the mattresses back onto our berths and began re-dressing them. "They did it to assert their power. There is no other reason than that."

"Assert what power? Why? We didn't do anything to them!" she said in confusion.

I finished gathering up the pile of unfolded clothing, went to the cab of the truck, and sat in the jump seat. As I began re-folding the tee shirts, shorts, and slacks, I answered.

"Nicole, they were asserting their power over me. It had nothing to do with the truck... or with you."

"You? Why did they want to assert their power over you?"

Nicole peeked sideways at me with a befuddled expression.

"When I went inside to use the restroom, they were sitting there drinking coffee. When I came out, they questioned me about using the ladies room and not the men's. They seemed to have a problem with me from the moment I walked into the building." I continued folding the clothes without looking at Nicole.

"What? Why the fuck didn't you tell me about this?"

"Nicole, I'm telling you now. This is the first chance I have had to say anything to you about it…"

"So these two morons ravaged our truck just because they didn't like you? What did you say to them that pissed them off?" she asked with an accusatory tone.

"I didn't say anything to them Nicole. But, when they questioned me about being in the ladies room I had to explain that I am in transition and have a right to use the women's restroom. I had no idea it was going to lead to this mess." I waved my arm at the chaos in the back.

"Geez, Pam," she mumbled.

After restoring order back to the truck and restoring both sleeper berths, I said goodnight to Nicole and closed the curtain. She seemed to be deep in thought, was apparently still angry about the incident at the weigh station, and did not respond. Exhausted from the events of the day, I quickly fell asleep.

We made our delivery in Boston, and from there we went to Richmond, Virginia. During the next week, we picked up and delivered in Charlotte, St. Paul, and Montgomery. After unloading in Montgomery, our Qualcomm announced that we had a load back to Fontana. We had been on the road for two weeks, had covered over 12,000 miles, and we were both desperately in need of a break.

On the way from Montgomery to Fontana, I pulled the truck into the Pilot truck stop in Deming, New Mexico. It was 11:30 AM and I had been driving steadily since midnight when I had taken over the driving in Abilene, Texas.

I fueled up the truck, found an empty slot in the parking lot, and got us backed in. As I set the brakes, Nicole opened the curtains and looked at me sleepily.

Before she could ask, I said, "We're at the Pilot in Deming, new Mexico. It's 11:30 and I need a shower and some food."

"Good idea." Nicole closed the curtain. I could tell by the rustling behind the curtain that she was preparing for a shower too.

Once we were ready to go, we climbed down from the truck and headed off to get our showers. As we were walking past the other trucks in the lot toward the building, we came upon two redneck looking men who stood smoking cigarettes and talking in front of one of the nearby trucks. As we approached, they ceased their conversation and stared at us in the quietness of the afternoon as we passed. Just as we were walking by, the strap on one of my sandal broke, and it fell off my foot, leaving me teetering on my one still sandal clad foot. I stopped, attempting to retrieve my other sandal from the ground, and one of the men sniped "Oh look, it's Cinderella…"

As I struggled to put the now damaged sandal back on my bare foot, the other man said, "No, it's *Cinderfella*." at which they both burst out in laughter.

Nicole spun without stopping and gave them the finger with both hands, as we continued on our way to the building.

When we got inside, we put our names on the list for a shower. There was a thirty-minute wait, so we went to the Subway counter to order lunch. While we sat at a table eating, the two men, who had laughed at me about my sandal, came in and ambled up to the Subway counter to order sandwiches. While they were waiting for their sandwiches, they glared coldly at Nicole and me while whispering and snickering. Much to my relief, they did not stick around when their food was ready, but headed back outside almost immediately. I didn't think I could handle a second episode with the same two goons on the same day.

"This is crazy!" Nicole said while chewing on her sandwich.

"Everywhere we go… people are either staring at us or making some sort of smartass remark. You have no idea how many places we have been where someone has asked me if you are male or female and I have to defend you!"

"Nicole, I told you…"

Nicole interrupted me. "Yeah… you told me a million times. But this shit is getting old. Every time we're in a truck stop I hear people calling you sir and you arguing with them. Then this crap with the Mississippi state troopers. Dammit! It's stressing me out Pam!"

Before I could respond, our numbers were called on the PA system letting us know that our showers were now available. After obtaining our keys, we each went into our respective shower stalls without speaking a word to one another.

After my shower, I headed back to the truck. Nicole was there waiting for me. She started the engine as soon as I closed the door and without speaking a word, pulled out of the truck stop. She began the final leg of our trip to Fontana, and I went to the sleeper berth to get some much-needed sleep in my sleeper berth.

It was 11:00 pm when we arrived at the Fontana OC. I woke up and joined Nicole in the cab while she backed the trailer into a slot.

"So what are you going to do with your two days off?" I asked.

"Rachael and I are going to Lake Mead for a few days. I'm taking four days off" Nicole replied while packing her bag.

"Four days? Nicole, I can't afford to sit here for four days." I said in astonishment. She had just dropped a bombshell on me with no advance warning of any kind. "I have bills to pay, child support. Plus I need to save money for my transition!" I said, sounding more pleading than I meant to.

"I'm sorry Pam, but I'm very stressed out and I need the time off. Plus, I need to smooth things out with Rachael. Things are very tense between us right now." She opened her door and climbed down. I did the same and walked with her toward the employee parking lot.

"So you're not coming back until when? Tuesday?"

"Yeah, that's the plan. See you then." She opened her car door, tossed her bag in, and then slid into the driver's seat.

Quietly, and close to tears at this sudden revelation that I would now be stuck for an extra two days with no income, all I could manage to say was, "Have fun Nicole."

With no response and not even a glance back at me, she closed her door and drove away.

For the first time since we had become a team, it felt like we had parted on bad terms. No hug for each other as had become our sisterly custom, and not another word spoken between us as we went our separate ways.

I was beginning to feel that this was going to seem like a very, very long four days.

Chapter Thirteen
Dangerous

I spent the first day at the Fontana OC, trying to be as productive as possible while mixing in some personal enjoyment. First, I picked up my mail and was pleasantly surprised to find my paystub from Schneider with my new name on it. Next, I went to a salon in Rancho Cucamonga where I got my hair and nails done. Then I was off to do some clothes shopping at Ontario Mills Mall.

Rather than spend four days sitting idle in my truck, I had asked Sandra if I could get some local runs and at least earn some money while I was here. As it turned out there was plenty of work for me. For the next three days, I kept busy picking up loaded trailers at the rail yards and delivering them to various locations in and around Los Angeles and the surrounding areas.

Alice was in Fontana on Sunday to pick up a load, so we went to Loretta's that night, where once again I had the time of my life. Alice was her usual self, filled with laughter and cattiness. Mikey was also there, and he joined us at our table.

Alice was shooting pool for drinks against a male driver, so Mikey and I took the opportunity to sit near the pool table sipping beers, catching up on company events, and listening to the jukebox.

"Can I ask you a personal question?" Mikey slurred his words. I could tell this was going to be his beer talking.

I laughed, "Whenever someone prefaces a question with 'Can I ask you a personal question', I know it's going to be a real zinger. Okay, go ahead."

Mikey smiled and leaned closer to me. "Are you attracted to women or men?"

"You mean sexually?" I asked as I took a sip of my beer.

"Yeah, sexually I guess?"

I looked at Mikey and smiled tentatively. "Mikey, do you really think what I am doing has anything to do with sexual preference?

Because, if you do, it most certainly does not."

"I'm not sure… I've never met anyone like you before, so I don't know. I'm just curious I guess." He took a swig of beer, and then wiped foam from his upper lip as he set the mug on the table with a thud.

"Okay… I think women are incredibly beautiful creatures, and I admire them for that. But in some ways I am sort of attracted to men."

"So you're gay, then?"

"What would make you think that?"

"If you are attracted to men… that would make you gay, right?"

"No, I'm a woman." I said. Being attracted to men would make me heterosexual."

"But you were married to a woman. You had sex with women, right?"

"Yes lots of women. In my previous life…"

"So, you're a lesbian?"

"Mikey, let's go dance!" I laughed as I dragged him out to the dance floor.

On Monday morning, I joined Gennipher, Pat, Mary, and Amy at their table for breakfast. Nicole was scheduled to return to work on Tuesday, and I still hadn't heard anything from her. I had talked to Gennipher on Saturday about the search of our truck during our escapade at the weigh station in Mississippi. I had also mentioned the friction between Nicole and me, and the disagreement that we had had before she left regarding the time she was taking off.

"Have you and Nicole patched things up?" Gennipher asked.

"I haven't been able to reach her since she left here on Friday. I've tried to call her, but she doesn't answer her phone. She hasn't returned any of my messages either. I hope she's not so angry with me that she won't even talk to me."

"Didn't you say she was going up to Lake Mead for the weekend? Maybe she is out of range for her cell phone service…" Amy speculated.

"All I know is that when she left on Friday she said she was going away for the weekend and would be back on Sunday. I tried calling her this morning and left her another voice mail message and sent her a text message" I replied.

"When are you guys going back on duty?" asked Pat.

"Tomorrow"

"I'm sure she'll be here tomorrow and you guys will be best friends again."

"Yeah, I'm sure we will make up. I feel kind of bad about the way we left things when we parted."

Amy changed the subject. "By the way Pam, I meant to tell you Saturday when I saw you, your hair looks great!"

"Yes! And her nails too! Show them your nails Pam!" Gennipher grabbed one of my hands and held it up for them all to examine.

"Very nice! That's a sexy color on you!"

"Yes… very sexy."

The voice of Gregg Sallavolltia, who had suddenly appeared at our table, interrupted our girl chat. "Good morning ladies" he smiled.

"Good morning Gregg," we all chirped in unison.

"Pam, when you're finished with your breakfast could you come by my cubicle please?"

"Sure Gregg" I replied. My stomach suddenly knotted up with anxiety.

"Great. See you in a bit. Have a great day everyone," Gregg said, as he headed toward the offices.

Gennipher waited until Gregg was out of earshot and then asked, "What's that all about, Pam?"

"I have no idea. Maybe he wants to tell me how much he's attracted to me and that he wants to marry me!" I smiled impishly in an attempt to conceal my anxiety.

"I hate to burst your bubble Ms. Pam, but Gregg is happily married with kids," Mary pointed out with a laugh.

"Oh come on you guys. Let the girl enjoy her fantasy!" Gennipher chortled.

The office setup at all of the operating centers consisted of a simple series of cubicles, in which personnel from the various departments went about their daily tasks. Nobody, regardless of their position or stature within the company, had a closed office. In the event that closed doors should be necessary, the only suitable place for a private meeting would be in one of the many small conference rooms. Nicole and I had previously met with Greg and Sandra in one of them.

As I approached Gregg's cubicle, I found him studying a report. As soon as he spotted me, he stood and walked over to greet me.

"Pam, we're going to meet in one of the conference rooms," he said as he started walking toward the row of small rooms. I followed. Falling silently into step with us was a semi-bald, grey haired man with whom I was not familiar. He opened the door to a room and ushered us in. I had seen this man around the OC several times, but had no idea who he was or what his function at Schneider might be. I was soon to find out. We all at the small round table, and Gregg made the introductions.

"Pam, this is Ed Paul. Ed is in charge of loss prevention. Ed, I believe you know Pam?"

"Yes, I am very familiar with who Pamela is." He made it sound as if I were an infamous criminal. He handed me a business card.

I studied the card for a moment before glancing briefly at Gregg and then locking eyes with Ed Paul. His dark stare exuded an aura of contempt for me.

"Loss prevention huh?" I laid the card down on the table. "What's up?"

Ed Paul answered with an accusatory tone "We need to talk to you about your visits to the women's restrooms."

"Why? Is there a roll of toilet paper missing?" I asked sarcastically.

Gregg smiled wryly "I'm afraid it's a bit more serious than that, Pam"

Ed continued gruffly, never breaking even the slightest smile. "We have received various complaints from female employees about your presence in the women's restroom; one here in Fontana, and one from the Dallas OC. I need to make it exceptionally clear to you that we take these complaints very seriously."

"What are the complaints about? I go in, lock myself in a stall and do my business, come out, wash my hands, and leave. They do the same thing. It's not like we're all running around naked in there."

He bristled at this and tersely replied, "They just don't like the idea of a man being in the ladies room, and I can certainly understand their concern."

"A man in the ladies room? Look at me. Do I look like a man?" I asked him angrily.

Ed reached into a manila folder and produced a copy of my CDL.

"It says right here on your CDL Pamela... You... are a male!"

I did my level best to hold my temper, but after the recent events in Mississippi, I was still a little raw. I took a deep breath and inwardly started to count to ten before I responded to his ludicrous statement. I made it to 'seven'.

"Mr. Paul, the fact that my CDL states that I am a male is irrelevant. The only reason that it doesn't say that I am a female is because I haven't had my surgery… yet. I am presenting as female and therefore should be entitled to use the restroom that conforms to my presentation."

For the second time now, and both within less than a week, I was compelled to use my carry letters. I pulled the two letters out of my purse and laid them on the table.

Ed picked them up and quickly read each one, then proceeded to speak again. "According to our human resource department in Green Bay, you are to use the restroom that corresponds to the gender on your license, not how you are dressed, or what some shrink says." His face, becoming a rashy red now, he continued. "The bottom line here is this… as long as you are legally a male; you are not to use the ladies restroom." With that, he arrogantly tossed my documents toward the table where they fluttered to the surface.

I slowly picked up my papers and quietly folded them back into my purse. I proceeded to speak calmly now, but still defended my plight. "But I have no choice. I am presenting as a female and there is no way I can use the men's room. If there was a unisex restroom, I would gladly use it, but since there isn't, my only option is to use the ladies room."

Ed was not going to budge. "You are a male as far as Schneider is concerned. You either use the men's room or you don't use any of the facilities."

"So… are you suggesting that I go into the men's bathroom looking like this?" I made a waving motion with both hands from my head down.

"What I'm telling you Pamela is: don't go into the women's bathrooms. There are plenty of fast food restaurants and gas stations within walking distance of our OCs. You can use their restrooms," Ed responded curtly as he started to rise from his seat.

Gregg spoke up. "Ed… I'm sure we can work out a solution to all of this. After all, she does have to go somewhere…" He emphasized the word 'somewhere'.

"Thank you Gregg." I smiled. I was pleased to hear him stand up for me, and even more pleased to hear him refer to me with a female pronoun.

"Well, you two work it out. I just don't want to hear any more complaints about him using the ladies room," Ed said as he abruptly stood and exited the room. My skin crawled at the sound of him referring to me as 'him'.

After the door had closed behind 'Mr. Loss Prevention', Gregg spoke to me in an apologetic manner.

"Pam, I can understand your frustration, but we have to go by whatever Human Resources says. I'll call them today and see if we can't come up with some sort of work around for this."

"Thanks Gregg, I really appreciate your support on this." I resisted the urge to give him a hug.

"The big problem right now is that your CDL does say that you are a male. What we're up against here is that this is what HR is going to stand on. How soon before you can get female on your license?"

"As far as I know I can't get that until after my surgery, but I can't have the surgery until I live as a female for a full year."

"Rest assured Pam, I will do whatever I can to resolve this."

"I appreciate it Gregg. What do you want me to do in the meantime; just hold it?" I laughed.

He smiled. "When are you going back on the road?"

"Nicole is due back tomorrow. We should have a load out by then."

"Okay, just try to keep a low profile until then. Is there any way you can go into the ladies restroom and make sure nobody goes in while you are in there?"

"You mean like one of those "Closed for Cleaning" signs?"

"Maybe you could have someone stand guard outside the door to make sure nobody goes in."

I laughed. "This is making going to the bathroom a clandestine operation."

Gregg laughed. "Just try your best to do what Ed says until we come up with something from HR. If you come up with any ideas, let me know."

I didn't tell him that an idea was already hatching in my mind.

After the meeting with Gregg and Ed Paul, I headed to my truck to check the Qualcomm. There were five load assignments waiting for me, which I was expected to complete by the end of the day. They were mainly pickups from the rail yards, with deliveries at various locations throughout the greater Los Angeles area. I would have ample opportunity to stop at a truck stop along the way to pick up the supplies I needed to execute my bathroom plan.

By noon, I had completed all but one of my runs. My last assignment was to pick up a trailer at the Union Pacific yard and take it to a distribution center in Shafter, 125 miles north on Interstate 5. I dropped the loaded trailer at the distribution center, picked up an empty, and headed back toward Fontana.

On the way back, I took exit 219 off Interstate 5 and pulled into the Petro truck stop to pick up the supplies I would need, and to take a quick potty break. While I was in the ladies room, I couldn't help but inwardly chuckle as I envisioned what Gregg's reaction might be to the solution I had concocted.

My first stop in the travel center was the aisle that displayed various office supplies for truckers. There were log books, tape, pens, staplers, notepads, and paper clips. After scanning the shelves for a few minutes, I found the items I needed: A suction cup attached to an alligator clip, and a black Sharpie marker.

My next stop was at the rear of the travel center where I found a display rack of various types of HazMat placards. There are dozens of different HazMat placards, which are required by the DOT to be displayed on trailers containing materials which could pose a public health or safety hazard. I flipped though the placards for 'Explosive', 'Corrosive', 'Flammable', 'Radioactive', 'Combustible', and 'Poison' before I finally found the one I was looking for. Normally, a trailer loaded with hazardous materials would need three placards; one on each side and one on the rear; but for my purposes, one was all that was necessary.

After stopping off at the Subway counter for a sandwich, I grabbed a bottle of water from the cooler and headed to the cashier counter to pay for my items. I was so filled with elation at my idea that I barely even noticed when the clerk addressed me as 'sir'. For now, I had to focus on the problem at hand, which was the restroom issue. With new feeling of purpose and a schoolgirl's grin on my face, I headed out the door to the parking lot, hopped in my truck and headed back south to the Fontana OC.

I arrived back at the OC at 6:15 and quickly dropped my empty trailer into one of the available slots. I then drove the tractor over to the bobtail parking area where I would park for the night. I ate my sandwich, grabbed my shower kit and headed into the drivers' lounge. I made a beeline for the fuel desk.

I was glad to see that Glenda was working behind the counter. She greeted me with a smile, "Hello Pam, how are you tonight?"

"I'm good Glenda, how are you?"

"I'm just great. What can I do for you?"

"Can you give me the key to one of the showers? I'm not going to take a shower or use any of the towels; I just need to go potty and brush my teeth."

Glenda looked at me quizzically, "Why don't you just go to the restroom?"

"I was told this morning that I am not allowed to use the ladies room, and I am certainly not going into the men's room."

"What? Are they crazy? What do they expect you do to do, pee out in the yard like a dog?" Glenda was incredulous.

"I'm not sure what they expect me to do. All I know is that I am not allowed to use the ladies room. Gregg is working on a possible solution, but for now I was told to stay out."

"I don't know why they even care. You've been using the ladies room all this time… why is it suddenly a big deal about you going in there now?"

"Well, apparently one of the women complained about me going in there. Their reaction to that is to ban me from the ladies room rather than trying to educate the woman who complained."

"Who complained? Everyone here seems to be fine with you using the ladies room. You are a female now, after all," Glenda smiled.

"I don't know who complained, they didn't tell me and I doubt that I'll ever know who it was."

Glenda shook her head in bewilderment and handed me a key "When do you go back on the road?"

"Tomorrow. That gives me a few weeks to get things worked out before I have to worry about it again. At least I know Schneider can't prevent me from using the restrooms in the truck stops," I laughed.

After I finished in the shower, I returned the key to the fuel desk and headed back to the truck to work on my project.

I first removed the HazMat placard from its plastic wrapper and laid it on the slide out writing table that was part of the desk. I then pulled out the Sharpie, and began carefully writing on the white space beneath the warning words of the placard. I took my time, meticulously crafting each letter so that the sign would be legible, and my message would be clearly conveyed.

Once I had finished, I held the placard up with my arms outstretched so that I could admire my handiwork. I was pleased, and looked forward to presenting my idea to Gregg tomorrow morning.

Although I was certain that there was no way this would ever be implemented as a solution to the bathroom issue, I hoped that this bit of sarcastic humor would get my point across, and perhaps get a good chuckle out of Gregg. With a devilish grin, I placed it inside a plastic shopping bag, folded the bag neatly around my handiwork, and placed it on the console.

I pulled the curtains shut around the windshield and side windows, then changed into my pajamas. Before sliding into my berth, I dialed Nicole's number one more time in the hope that she might answer. Unsurprisingly, I heard several rings before her voicemail greeting began. I did not bother leaving another message.

The next morning I awoke to the chirp of my Qualcomm. Before checking it, I glanced at my cell phone to see if I had missed any calls from Nicole during the night, but there were none. I swung my feet down onto the floor and padded to the front of the truck to grab the Qualcomm, where I discovered that we had a load to pick up in Compton and take to Omaha that was due in three days. I dialed Nicole's number again, this time leaving her a voicemail telling her that she needed to get back to the OC so we could get on the road.

After a quick shower, I went back to the truck to drop off my shower bag and take my meds. I then grabbed the plastic bag containing my modified HazMat sign, and headed back to the drivers' lounge to have breakfast while I waited for Gregg to arrive. I was anxious to discuss my solution with him.

Gennipher walked by as I finished the last bite of my eggs. She stopped at my table and held up her arms in a questioning gesture.

"Still no Nicole?" There was concern in her voice.

"No, not a word from her. I've lost count of how many messages I've left for her. I'm actually kind of worried now."

Gennipher slid into an empty chair beside me.

"Is that what Gregg wanted to talk to you about yesterday? Was it something to do with Nicole?"

"No, it had nothing to do with her. It was something else entirely. Something pretty nasty actually." I took a sip of my coffee

"Really? Is it something you can talk about?"

"Yeah I guess, just don't make a big deal out of it okay? We're trying to work out a solution right now."

"Sure."

"Do you know who Ed Paul is?"

"Yeah, he's the loss prevention dude."

"Yeah, well apparently, according to the loss prevention dude, a couple of the women complained about me using the ladies room. I was told that I can no longer use the ladies room at the OC."

"Someone from here complained?"

"Yeah. He said someone from here complained and also someone at the Dallas OC."

"That's nuts! Everyone here seems to be okay with you. You haven't done anything crazy in the ladies room have you? Like run around naked?" Gennipher laughed

"Of course not," I smiled. "I just do what everyone does, go into a stall, do my business, wash up and leave. I don't feel that I've done anything to give anyone reason to feel uncomfortable."

"Do you think it was that lady that gave you shit in there a few weeks ago?"

"No, I don't think so. I got the impression from Gregg and Ed that it was someone who works here at the OC. You said you didn't think that woman was from here."

"Well, I'll keep my eyes and ears open. What are you going to do in the meantime?"

"Gregg said he's going to talk to human resources and see if we can't get this resolved. For the time being he told me to try to only go in there when it's empty, and try to keep anyone from going in while I'm in there."

"Oh… wonderful! And how, may I ask, are you supposed to keep women from going in there?" Gennipher asked sarcastically.

"Well, I came up with an idea that I am going to present to Gregg when he comes in. I doubt that I'll get to actually use it, but it gets my point across about how ludicrous this whole thing is. Want to see it?" I grinned with a mischievous twinkle in my eye.

She grinned back at me. "Sure!"

I reached into the plastic bag and pulled out my placard, now attached to the alligator clip on the suction cup. "All I have to do is hang this on the door while I am in the restroom, to warn unsuspecting women not to enter."

Gennipher gazed at the placard for a moment before bursting into laughter. "Oh my god Pam! You are insane!"

"Yes, I guess I am" I laughed.

Gennipher stood up. "I've got to get to work. That is too funny, Pam. I love you!"

When the big clock on the drivers' lounge wall said it was 8:00 am, I headed into the administrative area and waded through the sea of cubicles to find Gregg. Sure enough, he was sitting at his desk sipping on a cup of Starbucks coffee, staring at his monitor as the computer booted up.

"Morning Pam," he greeted me cheerfully.

"Morning Gregg. Have you got a sec?"

"Sure, do we need a conference room, or is it something we can discuss right here?"

"Right here is fine, I just want to show you what I came up with as a solution to the bathroom issue," I smiled as I plopped down onto the plastic chair next to his desk.

"Good, what did you come up with?"

"Do you remember saying that I should make sure no other women go into the ladies room while I am in there?"

"Well, yeah, that is just a temporary solution though."

"I know; I know… Until HR can come up with a resolution for this issue or until I am "officially" a female, documented and in writing… Only God knows which might happen sooner. Anyway, in order to try to find a reasonable temporary fix I had to do some creative thinking about the whole situation. This is what I came up with. I made this myself last night."

With that, I pulled my placard out of the plastic bag with a flourish and laid it on his desk, in front of him. "PRESTO! All I have to do is stick this on the door when I go in!"

DANGEROUS
Transsexual woman inside
Enter at your own risk

Gregg's face immediately broke into an incredulous smile as he held up the red and black placard with my added artwork. It was one of the most wonderful smiles I had ever seen in my life. Especially since I had elicited the desired response to my "solution".

"Pam, this is quite amusing," he said, still smiling, "but I don't think it will fly with human resources," he laughed.

"I know, but I really just wanted to use a bit of my acerbic humor to point out how ridiculous this whole thing is."

"I totally understand. I'm still working with human resources to try and figure out what we can do about it. Meanwhile… just stay out on the road for a couple of weeks and try to avoid using the ladies room at the OCs until we get it resolved."

"Will do." I said and rose to make my way back through the maze of cubicles surrounding me and into the relative comfort of the drivers' lounge.

I tried calling Nicole once more, but once again was only successful in reaching her voicemail. I left her another message to call me, but was by now certain that it would go unreturned just as the previous ones had. After waiting two hours in the drivers' lounge for her to return, I finally decided it was time to discuss the situation with Sandra.

I have always found the Service Team Leaders' area to be rather fascinating, with each of them busy studying their computer monitors in the never-ending attempt to keep up with the GPS location of each of their assigned drivers. Sandra was busy talking on the phone to a driver, and simultaneously typing a message to be sent to someone's Qualcomm, as I approached her workstation. She smiled as she raised an index finger in my direction, silently asking me to "wait a minute." I nodded affirmatively.

"Hey, what's up Ms. Pam?" Sandra smiled as she hung up the phone. As usual, she radiated warmth and beauty, and I couldn't help but smile back.

"Hey Sandra, I was wondering if you had heard from

Nicole?"

Sandra frowned "No I haven't. Is she not in the truck? You guys have a load to Omaha."

"No, I have not heard one word from her since she left here on Friday. I have left message after message on her voicemail, sent her… I don't know how many text messages, and she has not called me back. We left on what I felt were bad terms on Friday so I thought that she might be angry with me. She was supposed to be back here today so we could get back out on the road, but she still isn't here. I need to get back on the road and make some money. Plus… there is this bathroom issue going on. I need to get out of this place for now."

"Yeah, Gregg briefed me on that whole bathroom complaint thing." Sandra patted my hand gently, and then got back to the topic of Nicole. "What were you guys fighting about?"

"We weren't really fighting, not in the yelling and screaming sense. There was just some friction between us. Mainly because of that incident in Mississippi, and there were a couple of other incidental things…" I purposely didn't mention the spat that we had regarding Tammy in New Orleans.

"Yeah, that search of your truck in Mississippi must have been awful. Why would it cause friction between you and Nicole though?"

"That's the thing… I think she blames me because she feels that it only happened because of who I am. She's probably right."

"Who knows? Anyway, why don't you scoot over to Compton and pick up the load you have scheduled. Meanwhile, I'll call around and see if I can locate Nicole. If we can get her here, you can swing back by here and pick her up on your way to Omaha."

"Alright." I said. "That sounds like a plan."

Our load was 56 miles away in Compton, and with the late morning traffic, it took me a little over an hour to get there. Once I had coupled and completed a pre-trip inspection of the trailer, I called Sandra.

"Any word from Nicole?"

"Nope, nothing. I called her mom and she hasn't heard from her for about a week. At this point we are considering her AWOL." My heart sank a little at that.

"So… what do you want me to do with this load?"

"Well, I don't have another truck available to take it. The only option I have is you. You're just going to have to solo it to Omaha. You have three days, so you should be able to get it there on time even with your breaks. We'll still pay you the same rate you would have gotten as a team driver though. That sound okay to you?"

"Okay, yeah… that'll work… and what happens after that?" I asked.

"Well, that's going to depend on what the situation is with Nicole. If she does show up, we will just put her on suspension until we can get you back here to Fontana. We can't tolerate drivers not showing up for work." I knew she regretted having to penalize Nicole, but she had her job to do.

"Okay, I'll hit the road for Omaha now. I'll talk to you later." I hung up the phone with the beginnings of a sick feeling in my stomach.

Had I upset Nicole so much that she was willing to risk her job as a driver with Schneider? Those feelings continued to evolve and mutate into something looming near depression and despair. As I entered Interstate 710 to begin the 1,560-mile trek to Omaha, it was starting to feel as if I were embarking on a journey to the end of the world.

Chapter Fourteen
Marla

By the time I made my way through the maze of highways in LA and finally got on Interstate 15 en route to Omaha, it was nearly noon. The first leg of the trip got me as far as the Pilot truck stop just outside Las Vegas, at four in the afternoon, where I shut down for my obligatory ten-hour rest. At 2:00 the next morning, after re-fueling, showering and grabbing a quick bite, I was back on the road.

From Las Vegas, I continued north on Interstate 15 into Utah, where I passed through St. George and then Cedar City. The sight of the Wal-Mart on the side of the highway in Cedar City reminded me of that day back in April that Nicole had taken me shopping for clothes and cosmetics. She had been so helpful in showing me what to wear and, more importantly, what not to wear. She also helped show me the best way to put on makeup without overdoing it. Despite the fact that I was old enough to be her mother, she had still been a mentor to me. I was discovering more and more that I missed her terribly, and found myself occasionally glancing over my shoulder toward her sleeper berth, expecting to see her head pop out from behind the curtain. Each time that happened brought a sharp pang of regret.

I had continued to leave voice and text messages for her, but still had not heard back. Sandra had not heard from her either. In fact, no one had heard a word from her since that Friday when she left the OC in Fontana. Word on the grapevine was that she was on the verge of termination. I cared for her a great deal, not only as my co-driver, but also as my friend. I wanted desperately to reach out to help her.

The second leg of my trip concluded in Frisco, Colorado where I took my ten-hour break, and once again was on the road at 2:00 Thursday morning. By 6:30 am, I had travelled 260 miles and now found myself on Interstate 80 in Big Spring, Nebraska. I pulled into the Pilot truck stop, and after refueling, I parked the truck and went into the travel center for coffee and a bathroom break.

As I washed my hands, I glanced up to find my reflection watching me in the mirror. I studied that person in the mirror before me for a moment, surprised by a revelation that forced me to admit that, intentionally or not… I had been lying to myself. The face that gazed back at me was grizzled, hard, with the chiseled features of a male. In the well-lit bathroom, I could clearly see the shadow of a beard bleeding through the caked on makeup.

This was definitely not the soft and feminine woman that my delusional mind had led me to believe that I now was. This warranted further inspection. I glanced downward to appraise the attire of the person in the mirror. Although I was wearing feminine khaki shorts and a pink sleeveless top, I looked every bit like a man dressed as a woman. Perhaps Buford had been right after all when he had told me '*It ain't working*'.

Movement in the mirror interrupted my self-assessment. A woman had emerged from one of the stalls and now stood beside me as she washed her hands. Before I could escape her gaze in the reflection, she looked up, and for a moment we locked eyes with each other right there in the mirror. I tried my best to avoid eye contact with her, but she continued to stare at my reflection with an obvious look of disdain. It was easy to surmise that she had come to the same conclusion as I just had in my self-evaluation; I was a man dressed as a woman.

I could not tell if she was more surprised, scared, or angry that this anomaly was standing here alongside her, invading the sanctity of what I am sure she believed to be a safe and private haven. I was not about to stick around to find out which it was, so I hastily and silently took my leave.

I quickly headed over to the food service area, purchased a cup of coffee and a sandwich and trudged unenthusiastically back out to the truck. The zest that I once had was now waning and I was beginning to have second thoughts about going forward with my transition. I turned the CB radio on as I ate my sandwich, so the unintelligible chatter of truckers on the Interstate served as a backdrop for my deep thoughts. Suddenly my meditation was interrupted, as the sound of faint voices was broken in on by the crystal clear sound of a female voice, addressing nobody in particular. Judging by the volume and clarity of her voice, I knew she was right here in the truck stop.

"I can't believe this! I just saw a friggin' transvestite in the ladies room!"

"What? You mean a guy was in the women's bathroom?" A male voice responded.

"It was a guy dressed up like a girl. He was wearing makeup and earrings and girls shorts. He was standing right next to me when I was washing my hands," The female responded.

"Tell me where that fuckin' faggot is parked. I'll go kick his ass!" It was a different male voice.

The severity of these caustic comments seemed amplified by the confines of the cab of my truck. My 'home'... my safe haven. My chest began to tighten up and I could feel my hands beginning to tremble with fear and shame. My stomach knotted up and I was unable to finish my sandwich. I couldn't stand listening to anymore of this, so I lashed out with my hand, almost knocking over the rest of my coffee and snapped off the CB.

The abrupt silence was nearly deafening.

Then inner voices began rapidly assaulting me from every direction.

'Why am I doing this to myself?'

'Is becoming who I really am worth all of this torment?'

'Should I just give up and quietly go back to my former self?'

'Do I honestly believe that anyone's ever going to take me seriously as a female?

'End this charade now, before it's too late!'

But wait! This is what I have always truly wanted… NO, needed! To surrender now would only lead to a continuation of all of the unhappiness that I had endured throughout my entire life. Isn't there a price to be paid for every victory? I would not let these minor defeats keep me from reaching my goal.

I recalled the words of young 'Hafid' in the book, 'The Greatest Salesman in the World'… Words that had inspired me throughout my life and have led me to many a triumph:

"Failure will never overtake me, if my determination to succeed is strong enough."

My determination to succeed was indeed strong, stronger even than my sudden fear of failure, and I was not about to let this series of minor setbacks overtake me. In order to find success, I had to take massive action, and that meant I had to do something about my appearance…. and soon.

I hopped into the back of the truck and booted up my laptop. As soon as it was up, running, and had connected to the internet, I logged onto Genderlife, an online informational forum for transsexual women.

My first goal would be to get the facial hair removed from my face as soon as possible. The beard removal process is slow and tedious, requiring multiple sessions leading up to hundreds of hours of electrolysis to kill the thousands of follicles found on the typical male face. However, I recalled seeing some information about a place in Dallas that offered complete facial hair clearing in one sitting rather than one hour at a time dispersed over a period of years. Within minutes, I had found what I was looking for.

A transsexual dentist by the name of Bren, had founded Electrology 2000, commonly known as E2000. E2000 specializes in having the client sit for several hours as two technicians simultaneously work on her face, while Bren continuously injects local anesthesia to offset the pain. I had already endured several one-hour sessions of electrolysis and can personally attest that it is a very painful experience. The idea of going back to have a tiny needle inserted into each and every single hair follicle to cauterize them was not high on my personal list of "Things I'd Like To Do Today". There are several thousand hair follicles on the typical male face, and the process of eliminating them all is a long and tedious one. I wrote down the phone number for E2000, so that I could call them later in the day to set up an appointment.

As I continued through the Genderlife site, I also found some discussion on a plastic surgeon in Dallas whose specialty was facial surgery for transsexuals. Within minutes, I had found the information I was looking for, and jotted down his phone number as well.

It was time to schedule a trip to Dallas.

My delivery in Omaha was a live unload, which gave me the time needed to call and make my appointments in Dallas. My first call was to E2000.

"E2000, this is Bren…" a pleasant voice answered the phone. I was happy to hear that I was speaking directly to the owner.

"Hi, my name is Pam Anders and I would like to make an appointment for a facial clearing."

"Are you full time now or just getting started?"

"I'm full time. I am an over the road truck driver and need to get this done as soon as possible. I just overheard someone on the

CB refer to me as a transvestite."

"Oh, you poor dear. When would you like to come in?"

"I'm thinking the first week of July, right after the holiday."

"How about July 6th?"

We set up an appointment for 8:00 am for a six hour session, with two girls working on me at the same time. This would be the equivalent of a twelve-hour session. The rate was $105 per hour for each girl, totaling $1,260.00. I had just enough in savings, which I had earmarked toward my facial surgery, but this was important enough to prioritize.

My next call was to Dr. Raphael.

After speaking briefly with the receptionist about my situation and needs, I was transferred to his assistant.

A pleasant voice picked up the phone. "Hello. This is Katherine."

"Hi, my name is Pam Anders and I would like to schedule a date to come in for a consultation for some facial feminization surgery."

"Sure, when would you like to come in?"

"I'm planning on being in Dallas July 6th. Can I come in around 4:00 pm?

"We are completely booked up at that time. Can you come at 2:00?"

"Actually, I am scheduled for 6 hours of electrolysis at 8:00 that morning. The earliest I think I could get there would be 3:00.

"You going to E2000?"

"Yes," I replied, pleased that she was familiar with E2000. It was a short-lived elation.

"That won't work, Pam. When E2000 finishes with you, your face is going to swell like a pumpkin for several days. Dr. Raphael won't be able to evaluate what needs to be done if your face is distorted. Can you come here first thing in the morning and then go to them after your consultation?"

"But I'm going to have five days of growth on my face for

my session with E2000. I don't want to come in to see Dr. Raphael with all that stubble on my face!"

"Don't worry about the stubble. We can work with that a lot better than if you have a swollen face."

After calling E2000 back and rescheduling for 11:00, I called Katherine back and scheduled my consultation for 8:00 am. I was very happy to be finally taking the first steps toward improving my appearance.

It took less than an hour for the forklift operator to unload my trailer, and then I was on my way to the Pilot in nearby Council Bluffs, Iowa where I would shut down for the night. My next assignment was to deadhead to the Des Moines OC, drop off my empty trailer, and pick up a loaded trailer to take to Sacramento. I would call Sandra when I got to the truck stop and tell her that I needed to be in Dallas July 6th. At this point, my relationship with Nicole as a driving partner was uncertain, but whatever the situation was at that time, I would have to deal with it.

After a two-hour drive on Friday morning from Council Bluffs, I arrived at 8:00 at the Des Moines OC. After dropping the trailer, I discovered that my loaded trailer had not yet arrived, because the driver who was bringing it from Philadelphia was running several hours behind. They were now expecting the drop off at noon. I spent the morning at the Des Moines OC waiting for the trailer where I enjoyed an early lunch in the drivers' lounge. The staff at Des Moines was extremely friendly, as were most of the drivers that I met there. Aside from the few stares of wonderment that I received from the occasional stranger, this looked like it was going to be quite a pleasant day.

After finishing lunch, I headed into the ladies room. I knew that I really should not be using the women's restroom, but I really had to go. It was here, once again that I experienced a horrible feeling of Déjà vu. It could almost have been the exact same encounter that I had had while in the ladies room during my unexpected self-realization about my manly appearance. The only noticeable difference was the woman's clothing and body type. This time, however I was less distressed, armed with the knowledge that my appearance would soon be blessed with the marvels of modern medical alteration.

At 11:40 am the driver with the relay to Sacramento finally arrived at the OC. After a few minutes of small talk with him while he disconnected from the trailer, I hooked it up to my truck and performed my pre-trip inspection. It wasn't long before I was happily headed west on Interstate 80 to Sacramento. It was noon by the time I left the OC, which was a very late start for me. I would only drive for a few hours from here before shutting down so that I could get my usual early start in the morning.

Five hours and 316 miles later, I pulled into the Pilot truck stop in Kearny, Nebraska to shut down. It was a small truck stop with limited parking, and was characteristically full for this time of the day. Fortunately, there were two empty spots right next to one another, and I swiftly backed into one of them.

Within seconds after setting my brakes and completing my log for the day, another Schneider truck rolled into the truck stop and backed into the spot next to me. The truck stop was now completely full.

After the other truck had finished backing in, I heard the loud hiss of the air brakes. I glanced over briefly toward the driver. It was a woman with long blond hair covering most of her face, her head down as she wrote in her log book. After a few moments, she looked over at me, caught me looking at her and waved. I returned the wave and opened the door to climb down from the truck. As I began walking toward the truck stop, the other driver and I intersected at the front of our trucks. She was about an inch shorter than me, and stunningly beautiful. I could barely contain my envy.

"It looks like you and I got the last two spots," she laughed. I detected a slight southern accent.

"Yeah, it looks that way" I smiled.

"My name is Marla. I was heading in to grab a bite to eat,

care to join me?"

"Sure I'd love to. I'm Pam, by the way." We shook hands as we walked into the building and headed toward the Subway counter.

"What OC are you out of?" she asked, as we stood in line waiting to order our food.

"I'm out of Fontana, how about you?"

"Me too!" She paused for a moment and looked at me. "You must be the Pam that Jeff told me about…"

"What Pam? Who's Jeff?" I was confused.

"Jeff Mullen, he's one of the service techs at the Fontana OC. He said you had brought your truck in one day for service." She reached into her wallet and pulled out a photo. "This is him."

"Oh yes. I vaguely remember him. Why do you have a picture of a service tech in your wallet?" I laughed.

"Because Jeff and I are engaged to be married," she smiled.

"Ah… okay." I paused for a moment and looked at her curiously. "You said he 'told you about me' What did he say about me?"

"Just that there was a driver named Pam who was a man going through a sex change."

I cringed at the thought of that description of me, but bit my tongue.

"Did he seem negative about it?"

"He just acted like a man. He said he can't understand why anyone would want to have their dick cut off. That is sooo typical of men. They're very protective of their penises," she laughed.

"How do you feel about it?" I asked tentatively.

"It's fine as far as I'm concerned. I look at it as though you're coming over from the dark side to the bright side of humanity."

I laughed. I was rapidly growing fond of Marla.

"Where are you from Marla? You sound like you're from the South."

"Covington LOO – EEESY --ANNA." She laughed while emphasizing the state.

"Ah, that makes sense. You do have a bit of Cajun in your

accent . I was just in New Orleans a week ago. We shut down for a day and went bar hopping in the French Quarter.”

“We?”

“Well, actually I’m a team driver. It was my partner’s birthday and she had never been to New Orleans before. So we took some time off so she could see what it’s like there.”

“So is she in the truck sleeping?”

“No… she’s currently AWOL. Nobody has heard from her since our last time off in Fontana. They sent me out with a solo load and now I’m headed to Sacramento. Then probably back to Fontana to hook up with her.”

Marla and I ate our dinner together, talked about everything under the sun including Nicole and Tammy, the encounter in Mississippi, my restroom issue, and the “transvestite incident.” She was an attentive listener, very understanding, accepting and compassionate. Marla was genuinely one of the nicest people I had met in a long time. I knew then and there that we would become great friends.

It was close to 10:00 pm by the time we walked back to our trucks to bed down for the night. We exchanged phone numbers and took pictures of each other with our cell phones. After hugging my new friend, I climbed into my berth and went to sleep in a swirl of mixed emotions. Anxiety came from thoughts of the horrible incident in Big Spring, excitement from the fact that I had finally taken some steps to improve my appearance, and elation came from having just made a new friend.

I slept until 5:00 on Saturday morning, and after a quick shower, I was on the road by 6:00. Marla’s curtains were still drawn, so I didn’t bother waking her to say goodbye. I had awakened in a state of euphoria. Now as I drove westward, on Interstate 80, in spite of the negative events of the previous few days, I felt as though I was on top of the world. It was wonderful knowing that in a few short weeks I would be in Dallas and on my way to obtaining a more feminine appearance. Only yesterday, I had been ready to give up. Today I felt that victory was at hand.

Four hours later, as I was crossing the state line into Wyoming, my Qualcomm chirped. Darting my eyes quickly between the road ahead and the digital display on the device, I was able to read the message. It was from Sandra asking me to call her as soon as possible. I pulled into the TA truck stop in Cheyenne, twenty-five miles west of the state line.

"Hi Sandra, its Pam. What's up?"

"Hey Pam. I talked to Nicole this morning. She actually called yesterday and we had a meeting today."

"Oh, I'm glad she's alright. I was getting really worried about her."

"Yeah, I was too, but yes… she is just fine."

"Good! So we're going to hook up again in Fontana, right?"

"Well, actually no." She hesitated for a moment. "She says she doesn't want to team with you anymore."

It took me a minute to digest this. "Did she say why?"

"Pam… I would really rather be able to sit down face to face with you to discuss this…"

"I understand Sandra, but I'm a big girl now and besides… having to wait until I can get there to find out will just drive me right out of my mind, so please… just come out and tell me."

"She says that all of the complications that have arisen for you and the trouble that you've attracted are just too stressful for her. She said that she just doesn't feel that she can handle it any more."

"I understand" I lied. I felt as though I had just been punched in the gut.

"Pam, I know this must be very difficult for you. Especially coming at you all at once like this over the phone…"

"I'll be okay Sandra. I promise. I'm just grateful that I know she's physically alright and not dead in a ditch on the side of the road somewhere. I'll be okay."

She sighed, "Well… You just get yourself safely back here to

Fontana and we'll hook you up with a new partner."

"Sounds like a plan" I said, although I was tempted to tell her that I would prefer to go back to solo driving.

"See you then" she said as she hung up the phone.

Continuing west across Wyoming, I was deep in thought as I watched the swirling snow dance across the highway and along the roadside. Snowdrifts covered most of the plains on both sides of the Interstate. I had slowly grown to despise Wyoming, and wondered how anyone could live in a state that is still enduring these deep freeze winter conditions in June.

I felt sad about losing Nicole as a partner, and a bit hurt that I had to find out from Sandra and not from her. Even so, Nicole had seemed like a daughter or kid sister to me and I had never realized that a lot of that was resultant from her immaturity. She was a kid emotionally if not mentally. At the same time, I was almost surprised to find that I was happy to be solo again. I did not want a new partner. Nicole had not worked out for the very reasons that I had chosen to drive solo in the first place. Now that she was gone, there really was no reason for me to get another partner, and have to start all over again with the explanations. I would discuss this with Sandra when I got back to Fontana.

At 1:00 pm, while crossing through Evanston, Wyoming my phone rang. A glance at the caller ID informed me that it was from the Fontana OC

"Hello?"

Hello Pam, this is Gregg Sallavolltia. Are you somewhere where you can pull over for a minute?"

"Sure, give me a minute." I put the phone in my lap.

I was on a stretch of Interstate 80 that had ample shoulders on which to park. I flipped on my right turn signal and began to slow down as I gradually guided the truck onto the shoulder. When I finally came to a stop, I set the brake, turned on the hazard lights, and killed the engine.

This was unusual… Gregg never called me while I was out

on the road, and I had never been asked to pull off the road before. With a slowly building feeling of dread for who in my life I might be about to find out was sick or dead or dying, my fingers trembling, I picked up the phone. "Ok Gregg, I'm parked."

"Pam, I have Mike Leary from human resources on conference with us. He wants to talk to you." My inner self whined:

'Oh, Dear God… Who is it?…' 'What has happened to whom?…' 'Are my kids okay!?'

"Pamela, this is Mike Leary. I am the Manager of Human Resources in Green Bay. I need to talk to you about these complaints regarding your use of the women's restrooms. We have received complaints from Fontana, Dallas, and another one yesterday from the Des Moines OC"

"Okay?" it was all I could manage to say. Relief coursed through me only to begin to slowly be replaced by portents of impending doom.

"The bottom line is this. You are not to use the women's restroom at the Fontana OC or in any other OC in the country. Regardless of what kind of clothes you wear, or what gender you imagine yourself to be. You are considered to be a male. You are not allowed in any of the ladies restrooms. DO I MAKE MYSELF CLEAR?"

"Where am I supposed to go? None of the OCs have a unisex bathroom."

"I have no problem with you using the men's room. If you don't feel comfortable with that, there are Porta-Potties in the yards. Or, you can go to a local gas station or fast food place."

My throat constricted. Even if I could find the words to say, I was not sure I was capable of speech.

Leary continued. "I'm putting you on official notice Pamela. Should we receive one more report about you using the women's restroom at any of our facilities this will be cause for immediate termination. Is that clear?"

"Yes…" My voice was weak and raspy. I was surprised that he could hear me at all.

"Good! I'm glad that we have an understanding. Have a nice day." I heard the click of his phone disconnecting.

"I'm sorry Pam…" It was Gregg. "I tried my best to work this out…"

"I know you did, Gregg. Goodbye." I pressed the 'end' button on my phone and tossed it listlessly onto the jump seat.

I felt spent. I was physically and emotionally devastated. If I had thought that the past two weeks had been a drain on my spirit, the past two days had been a roller coaster ride through hell and back. I had been totally caught off guard by this turn of events and was completely blindsided by this conversation. I sat zombified in my seat and stared blankly through the windshield. What I thought had been going so well had become a train wreck. Tears streamed down my cheeks as I simply stared mindlessly at the nothingness of the world before my face and began to sob uncontrollably. I had no comprehension of time or space or even that the world still existed around me at all.

My phone rang, snapping me out of my trance.

Apparently, the ever-diligent Sandra had been tracking my truck, along with the rest of her charges, and had discovered that my truck had been sitting on the side of the road for what turned out to be nearly an hour.

"Hello?" I answered weakly.

"Are you okay?" Sandra asked in a compassionate voice.

"No" My voice quivered. I was sobbing again.

"Well, Pam… it's been a rough day for you. Hang in there, okay? Everything will be just fine… You just keep ahold of that, you hear?"

"Okay Sandra, thank you."

I regained as much of my composure as I was currently capable. I rinsed out my mouth with toothpaste and water, dabbed at my tear stained face with a clean wet washcloth, then I started the engine and flipped on my left turn signal. As soon as I had a clear lane, I accelerated and merged back onto the Interstate. Ten minutes later, my Qualcomm chirped with one last message from

Sandra before she left for the weekend:

The phone call from Mike Leary had so traumatized me, that I lost track of time and distance. By the time I finally pulled into the Flying J truck stop in Elko, Nevada, I had covered 982 miles in sixteen hours. I didn't bother attempting to eat dinner; I knew that it would be nothing more than an exercise in futility. Even had I had the strength to go to the facilities inside, that was the very last place on Earth that I even wanted to think about, let alone visit.

I had nothing left inside of me now. I felt hollowed out and empty. There was nothing of me but a shell within which now were cradled the husks of despair, defeat and sadness. It felt as if it took every remaining ounce of my being to just be able to crawl into my sleeper berth where I cried myself to sleep.

Chapter Fifteen
All She Needs is a Little TLC

The world came crashing back into existence for me on Saturday morning by the ringing of my cell phone. I groped around the desk and found the phone, answering without opening my eyes.

"Hello?" I answered sleepily.

"Hey it's me. You're not sleeping are you?" It was my sister Candy's voice on the other end of the line.

I opened my eyes and slowly raised myself up to a sitting position on the bed before gingerly lifting the slightest corner of the curtain from the side window. I winced as I was nearly blinded by the intensity of the laser like sliver of light that beamed in from the bright sun outside. I was only barely successful at suppressing the involuntary audible gasp invoked by the sudden pain in my eyes.

"Yeah, I was sleeping. What time is it?" I asked.

"Its 10:30 am Dallas time, I figured you would be on the road right now. Don't you normally start driving early in the morning?"

"Yeah, I usually start before dawn. But I had a rough night and didn't get much sleep, and I'm not in the best frame of mind right now. I've got problems with work."

"What kind of problems? What's going on?" There was sincere concern in her voice.

I told her the entire story regarding the bathrooms at work, the complaints, and all the way up to the call that I had received from Leary yesterday.

"Transition would be so much easier if I didn't have to go to the bathroom" I quipped.

"I don't think they can prevent you from going to the bathroom. Isn't there a law that says you have a right to use the bathroom appropriate to your presentation?"

"I'm not sure Candy. I haven't even had the time to look into it. Plus I don't have the money to go hire a lawyer to fight them on this."

"I vaguely remember reading about a non-profit law firm that specializes in transgender issues," she said. "Hold on while I dig around and try to find it."

This was a total surprise for me coming from Candy. Everything had happened so fast that I hadn't even considered my legal rights in this whole ordeal.

"Candy, I need to take a shower and get some coffee. Can I call you back in 30 minutes?"

"Sure, I'll have the info for you by then." I ended the call and tossed my cell phone into my purse.

All of the stress of the previous day had resulted in a throbbing in my temples like the booming bass from a bad rap song. I grabbed my bottle of Tylenol and shook out two capsules, popped them into my mouth and washed them down with a long swig from my water bottle. I laid my head back down with my eyes closed for a few minutes to give them a chance to begin their magic journey into my system. I grabbed some clean clothes, stuffed them into my shower bag and climbed down from the truck careful not to jar myself too badly and avoid the risk of aggravating the drum line now residing in my head.

As I trudged across the parking lot, shower bag in hand, I

couldn't help but notice the contrast between this day and previous days when I had taken this same walk toward my morning shower. Unlike the darkness and relative quiet of the pre-dawn hour that was my normal experience as I crossed the parking lot to the building, on this occasion the soothing, early morning dark sky was instead a garish panorama of brilliant blue and nearly blindingly bright sunlight. The stillness of the night to which I had become so accustomed was now replaced by a flurry of activity all around me, along with the rumbling of diesel engines and the odors associated with them.

The parking spots, normally occupied by the dark silhouettes of big rigs gently idling as their drivers slumbered, were mostly emptied now. The benefits of my regular pre-dawn ritual were becoming crystal clear in my mind as I proceeded on my way.

I stood in the shower stall as I sipped on my coffee with a new appreciation for the jets of hot water streaming onto my head and body. The events of the previous days had created a whirlwind of emotions in me, resulting in my spirits going up and down like an express elevator run amok. As the shower worked its fluid charms on my body, my brain slowly began bit by bit to engage. There was no sense spending any more time or energy dwelling on the problems that had been thrust upon me. Instead, I would now attempt to focus on possible solutions.

What could I do about this restroom problem? I knew that I could not go for nearly a year without going to the bathroom, so that notion was not even worthy of thought. The steps that I had embarked upon to improve my female presentation were still a future solution to the problems in the truck stop restrooms. I still faced the immediate problem of my employer telling me that my only options at our OCs were to use the men's room or the outhouse. This was the biggest dilemma of all of them and I still had no idea how I was going to realistically manage the impossible task of performing my body's basic needs while still obeying the dictates of my masters.

When I had returned from my shower, I dialed Candy's

number.

"Hi again," I said after she answered.

"Okay… I found it! Ready?" she asked.

"Shoot" I replied with pen and pad already in hand.

"It's called the Transgender Law Center. They're in San Francisco." She recited the telephone number, which I carefully copied down.

"According to their website they offer legal advice and even representation in certain types of cases. Do you want their web address too?"

"Sure" I replied.

She then rattled off the information, which I added to my list.

"There's lots of information and laws on there that I think you'll find very helpful."

"Thanks for the tip, Candy! I'll give them a call Monday."

"I hope it helps…" She paused for a minute. "Oh, I almost forgot why I called you in the first place. When you come to Dallas to meet with that plastic surgeon, I'm treating you to a haircut and style at the salon that I go to. It will be your birthday present."

"Candy, you are awesome! Thank you!" I exclaimed.

"You're welcome. Let me know how it turns out okay?"

We said our goodbyes and disconnected.

I updated my log, started the truck, and belted myself in. I then pulled out of the truck stop and back onto Interstate 80, off yet again to California. The conversations with my sister and the assistance she had provided had cheered me up considerably. I was well on my way back to the positive state of mind that I was so usually accustomed to. All throughout my life, I had felt that Candy had treated me in a condescending manner. I even got the feeling from her sometimes that she didn't even like me. Yet, now… as I looked back over our history as siblings, I was beginning to realize that whenever I really needed something she had actually always been there for me.

I made my delivery in Sacramento at 3:00 pm on Sunday,

and then drove on to Woodland to pick up a load destined for Portland, Oregon. After picking up my trailer in Woodland, I headed north on Interstate 5. I stopped at the Pilot in Dunnigan, where I refueled and shut down for the night. After grabbing a burger at Wendy's, I felt like I was some kind of secret agent as I cautiously used the ladies room to go potty and brush my teeth. Fortunately, I was able to slink in and out of the restroom this time without any further unsavory encounters.

By 4:00 Monday morning, after a quick shower, I was back on the road headed north toward Oregon. With the 55 mile per hour truck speed limit in California and Oregon, it would take me all of ten hours to cover the 540 miles to my destination in Portland. I had miles and miles ahead of me to find a place to stop somewhere along the way to make my very important phone call.

I crossed the state line into Oregon at 8:30 am. I drove on another 33 miles before pulling into the Pilot truck stop in Medford. After topping off the tanks, I parked the truck, settled inside with a fresh cup of coffee, and called the Transgender Law Center. A friendly receptionist took my personal and contact information and, after taking down a brief outline of my legal issue, they told me that someone would call me back.

After a quick, and thankfully uneventful visit to the ladies room, I decided to grab a bite to eat. This truck stop had both a Subway and a Taco Bell, and I chose the Subway for my breakfast. I had just seated myself at one of the small tables with my sandwich when my phone rang. The caller ID displayed a call from the 415 area code of San Francisco.

"Hello?" I answered the phone hopefully.

"Is this Pamela Anders?" a male voice asked.

"Yes, this is her."

"Hi Pamela, my name is Chris Daley and I am an attorney with the Transgender Law Center. I understand you are having some bathroom issues at work that are related to your transition."

"Hi Mr. Daley, yes, that is true." I responded.

"Please… call me Chris." he said in a kind voice. "The notes that I've received from your intake say that you are a California resident and that your employer is based in Wisconsin. Is your workplace in California?"

"Yes Chris, I am an over the road truck driver, based in Fontana," I replied.

"Good. We only practice law in California, so we will be able to help you. I have the basics here in front of me, but just to make sure that we get all of the pertinent data regarding your case, could I get you to brief me on the details?"

My arms pimpled up with gooseflesh, knowing that I was actually being taken seriously, and that I now had a 'case'.

Before responding, I mentally thanked Sandra for having persuaded me to relocate to California. My scrambled egg and sausage sandwich sat on the table getting cold, but I didn't care. I was experiencing something very near a thrill knowing that I now had an ally that could actually do something to help me on my side. This was a critical phone call.

I told Chris about my meeting with Ed Paul, and the alleged complaints from women in Fontana, Dallas, and Des Moines. I then told him about my more recent phone conversation with Mike Leary.

"Pam, California law is very explicit in this regard. As a transgendered woman, you have every right to go into the ladies room during your transition, no matter what your company's policy might have to say about it. What does your driver's license state as your gender?"

"Well, it has my legal female name on it, but it still states that I am a male. I was told by the California DMV that I couldn't get the 'female' designation until after I had undergone my surgery."

"Someone from the DMV told you that?" he asked with an astonished tone. "They didn't give you a DL 328?"

"What's a DL 328? No, nobody ever mentioned that." I replied. It was now my turn to show astonishment.

"It's a form that any California DMV office should already be aware of. In California, the laws state that if you get your physician to fill out and sign the DL 328 stating that you are identifying and presenting as a female for the purposes of transition, the DMV will then change the gender status on your driver's license to 'female'."

"Oh my god!" I exclaimed. "I wish someone had told me that! How do I get this form, and how do I get someone to sign it for me?"

"Who is your hormone doctor?" he asked calmly.

"I don't really have one right now… Initially, over a year ago I went to a doctor in Colorado Springs. She did all the initial tests on me and wrote me a refillable prescription for Estradiol, Prometrium, and Spiro. I guess I need to find someone in California, huh?"

"That's an easy one. Go see Dr. Horowitz in Beverly Hills. He treats about half the trans community in LA. He is very knowledgeable about the process and once you have become his patient he will take care of all the necessary paperwork to get your driver's license changed. In the meantime, I will write a nice letter to Mr. Leary enlightening him about the law. Would you like me to email a copy of the letter to you?"

"Yes, please!" I said enthusiastically. "What should I do as far as the facilities until then?"

"My suggestion to you Pam would be… even though you are in the right… I would prefer that you don't push too hard on this. I think it would be in your best interest to just keep a low profile until we can get it resolved. These types of cases seldom go to court, but if we should find it necessary to take it to that level, the TLC will be right there with you." I could practically hear him smiling on the other end of the phone.

"TLC, what a great acronym!" I laughed.

After exchanging contact information for Dr. Horowitz and Mike Leary, we said our goodbyes and disconnected.

I laid my phone onto the table, and began eating my cold sandwich. Being so elated by the conversation with Chris, the sandwich could have been frozen solid, and I would not have cared. This was a great day, and I was now inundated with a feeling of Euphoria. I gobbled down the sandwich as quickly as I could, and washed it down with my now lukewarm coffee. I then picked up the phone and dialed the number that Chris had given me for Dr. Horowitz.

"Hello, my name is Pam Anders. Chris Daley at the Transgender Law Center in San Francisco referred me to Dr. Horowitz. I would like to come in for a consultation." I said to the lady that answered the phone.

"Are you currently on hormones?" she asked.

"Yes, I have been on Estradiol, Prometrium, and Spiro for a little over a year now."

"Okay then… The doctor will want to do the standard blood tests, vitals statistics and check your medication dosages, but that is simply standard procedure. When would you be available to come in?"

"Well, I'm an over the road truck driver and I'm heading up to Portland right now, but I'm sure I can get a load from there right back to LA. How about Friday?"

"He has an opening at 1:00 pm on Friday. How does that sound?" she asked sweetly.

"Perfect! I'll be there!" I paused for a moment and then asked, "Chris Daley mentioned something about a form DL 328 that Dr. Horowitz could fill out for me. Do you know anything about that?"

"Oh yes, of course," she laughed. "We fill those things out all the time. Dr. Horowitz will even write you an official letter for you to give to the DMV with your form."

"Excellent!" I beamed.

I gave her my contact information, confirmed my appointment for the following Friday at 1:00 pm, and hung up the phone. This was turning out to be one of the most extraordinarily beautiful days of my life!

My next call was to Sandra, informing her that I needed to get back to Fontana for a doctor's appointment on Friday. She promised me a load back to LA after I made my delivery in Portland.

Following Chris's suggestion to keep a low profile, I resisted the urge to thank Sandra right then and there for urging me to relocate to California. I didn't think having to explain why would help me in my new cause, even if Sandra was my friend.

I made my delivery in Portland and received my next assignment, a load to Fullerton, California. This would get me back to the OC by Thursday. I headed back south on Interstate 5 and stopped at the Wilsonville TA, where I enjoyed a quick bite to eat, while it was still warm this time, and then shut down for the night. Before I went to sleep, I turned on my laptop and checked my email. Amidst the smattering of emails from friends, and buried within dozens of spam messages, I found the one email that now truly made my day complete. The message was from Chris Daley. Attached, was a copy of the letter that he had mailed to Schneider.

Dear Mr. Leary:

My name is Christopher Daley and I am an attorney with the Transgender Law Center of San Francisco, CA.

I was recently contacted by one of your employees, Pamela Anders, about some issues which she is currently facing at work. According to Ms. Anders, she is being denied access by your company to the women's restroom in Schneider National's California Facilities. At the same time, she is being told that the only restrooms that she shall be allowed access to consist solely of the men's restroom, an unhygienic portable restroom located outside of the building, or any off-site restroom.

The goal of this letter is to provide you with basic information on California law, thereby providing you the opportunity to create a restroom access policy for Schneider National that respects Ms. Ander's identity and allowing you to satisfy your legal duty.

I have attached a publication that explains the California state employment law in regards to transgender people. In short it is unlawful in California to discriminate against people based on their gender identity (in the case of Ms. Anders, that is her female identity).Under this law, transgender people shall be provided access to restrooms corresponding to their gender identity (in this case the women's restrooms).

It is my hope that once you have received this basic information, Schneider National will modify its stance accordingly. Ms. Anders has told me that she travels to other Schneider National facilities across the country in the course of her employ with your company. While open legal questions exist at the present in regards to whether or not Ms. Anders, as a California employee, is protected in your non-California facilities, I have also included a publication which lays out current development under the federal employment discrimination law. As you will read, Title VII of the federal law is being interpreted to offer the same protection in other states as California's Fair Employment and Housing Act. Therefore, I would strongly recommend that your company create a national restroom policy that complies with these laws.

I will be more than happy to speak with you or your legal counsel if you have any further questions about this letter. I am optimistic that with this information in hand, Schneider National will be able to meet both your legal and ethical obligations in this matter. Of course, if you are unable to do so, Transgender Law Center will provide Ms. Anders (and any other Schneider employees which may reasonable interest) with the information and assistance necessary to enforce their rights under this law.

Sincerely

Christopher Daley, ESQ

Monday had begun with a treacherous headache from the stress of the previous few days. Then, with something as simple as a supportive phone call from my sister, which led to two other phone calls… My world had drastically taken a turn for the better that would put my transition back on track. This day was now ending with an exceptionally pleasurable reading of a letter that would effectively fly in the faces of Ed Paul and Mike Leary. It suddenly felt as if all of the Angels of Heaven and Earth were smiling down upon me and singing a song of joy specifically for me! I could barely contain my glee as I read the letter over and over again, until finally, I rolled into my berth and with a beatific smile on my face. I drifted away into a wonderfully intoxicating and peaceful sleep.

Chapter Sixteen
Beverly Hills Tuna

I arrived at the Fontana OC on Thursday night. Once I settled in, I called the local Rent a Wreck and arranged for a rental car. They were even courteous enough to deliver the vehicle to me at the OC on Friday morning. It was not the prettiest car in the world, but it served its purpose, and the price was reasonable.

The drive from the Fontana OC to Dr. Horowitz's office was a little over 60 miles, which in most cities would be about a ninety-minute drive at most. This was Los Angeles however, so I allowed for an extra thirty minutes of travel time, and left at 11:00 am. Traffic was surprisingly light on Interstate 10, and I exited at La Cienega Blvd at 11:50. By the time I was able to make my way through the multitude of traffic lights on La Cienega to 3rd Street, it was nearly 12:30. I found a relatively inexpensive (for Beverly Hills) parking place, and walked two blocks to the elegant silver and glass building that housed the doctor's office. I was able to easily locate Dr. Horowitz's office on the eighth floor of the medical building near Cedars Sinai Hospital on 3rd Street in Beverly Hills.

When I exited the elevator on the eighth floor, it was already

12:40. I quickly found my way to the proper suite by

consulting the office listings for this floor posted by the elevator doors, and confidently walked into the office. It was just what I would have expected for a Beverly Hills physician's office.

The first thing that I noticed in the reception area was the lack of carpeting on the floor. In its place was a beautifully finished parquet wood floor, which to my untrained eye, appeared to be made of teakwood. The muted and calming earth tones of the walls played well in the brilliant Beverly Hills sunlight that filtered in from the single smoked plate glass window that ran from wall-to-wall.

The lavish furnishings consisted of a large area rug that I guessed to have been imported from India, upon which stood a low, moderately sized rectangular cocktail table, which appeared to be made of the same wood as the flooring. The table held a beautiful arrangement of about twelve different varieties of freshly cut flowers, flanked on each side by very current and trendy magazines. A long, comfortable looking and inviting sofa was situated behind it. It looked like it was from the seventeenth century, but due to the fact that it seemed to be covered with a rich burgundy suede, I was sure that it had to be twentieth century retro. On either side of the table, were two large chairs, which matched the sofa, and there were live banana palms in enormous fired clay pots in each corner of the room.

Above the table were two identical, lighted ceiling fans with blades made to look like banana palm leaves which lazily spun in tandem, creating a gentle breeze in the room. The tastefully appointed remaining three walls held incredible renditions of the Hollywood hills and various area landmarks painted in acrylics and oils. I was not familiar with any of the artists' names, but the quality of the work told me that even if they were not famous artists yet… they were still fabulously costly pieces. To my left, between two of the largest paintings, seated upon a small ledge, was a medium sized sliding window through which a beautiful, petite woman was now looking up at me.

"Hi, you must be Pamela," the lady behind the counter said

with a smile.

"Yes, I got here a little early, I hope it's okay?"

"That's fine. Dr. Horowitz is running about fifteen minutes behind schedule though. There's a deli two floors down if you'd like to go down and grab a bite to eat while you wait. I need you to fill out these papers for me, and you can do it over a sandwich." She handed me a sheaf of forms attached to a clipboard, which I quickly assumed to be the standard medical questions.

"Okay, I am a bit hungry. What time do you want me to come back?"

"Come back at 1:30. He should be ready for you by then." She smiled.

I went back out to the elevators, rode down the two floors to the sixth floor, and then followed the signs to the deli. It was identical in appearance to most any other deli I had ever been to, with very similar items listed on a menu board, attached high on the wall behind the counter. The price of the food seemed to be the only thing that set this deli apart from all of the others I had ever been to. I ordered the cheapest item I could find on the menu: the tuna salad sandwich for only $14.25. Well, it DID come with potato chips and a soft drink.

'I'm sure the tuna is much better in Beverly Hills than it is anywhere else in the country,' I reassured myself as I paid the cashier with a twenty, and stuffed a dollar from the change into the tip jar.

I slowly savored every bite of my fourteen-dollar tuna sandwich, while filling out the paperwork that the receptionist had given me. It was nothing more than the standard health questionnaire, as I had assumed. I had become so adept at responding to the answers on these types of required paperwork, that I was able to complete the entire form before I even took the third bite of my sandwich. After finishing my sandwich and chips, I took a sip of my drink and glanced up at the clock on the wall. It was only 1:10, so I had time to make a phone call before heading back up to the eighth floor.

It was just after 3:00 pm in Dallas, and Candy was at her desk. She answered on the first ring.

"Hey Candy, it's me" I said cheerfully.

"Hey, what's up?" she asked. I could tell by her pithy greeting that she was busy with her work, and had little time for chit chat.

"I know you're busy, I just wanted to bring you up to date on things. I talked to the TLC on Monday."

"TLC?" Candy asked quizzically.

"Oh, I'm sorry. The Transgender Law Center. Remember you gave me their number?"

"Oh, yeah Okay… TLC. Cute acronym. So, what did they say?"

"I talked to one of their attorneys and told him the whole story about the loss prevention guy and the phone call from the guy in human resources. He basically told me that the laws would protect me and that Schneider had to allow me to use the ladies room."

"So are they going to help you file a lawsuit against them?"

"He wrote them a letter pretty much laying down the law to them as far as what their legal responsibilities are. He said in the letter that if they were not willing to provide me with a bathroom facility, the TLC would assist me in whatever needed to be done. I took that to mean that they would represent me in a lawsuit. Hopefully it won't come to that, but if it does…"

The beep-beep sound, indicating that I had another call, interrupted me. My caller ID said it was Alice. I had left her a message earlier and really wanted to talk to her.

"Candy, I have another call coming in. I'll give you a call later." I disconnected with Candy and switched over to Alice.

"Hey Alice" I answered.

"Hey, what are you doing?"

"I'm at the doctor's office, I can't talk long." I looked at the clock. It was 1:20.

"What's up? Why are you at the doctor? You sick?"

"No, it's just a routine visit about my hormones." I didn't

want to get into details with her on the phone. I would fill her in the next time I saw her in person.

"Ah, getting your girly pills huh?" She laughed.

"Hey Alice, thanks for returning my call. I have a question for you."

"Yeah? Okay… what?"

"I'm thinking of leasing a truck like you do. On paper it seems to be a lot more money, but since you already lease your own truck, I wanted to ask you what you think about it."

"You're thinking about becoming an owner operator? That's a big step you know. Once you sign up for that lease payment, you gotta keep that truck rolling; otherwise you can go down the drain fast. Those lease payments and insurance payments don't stop when the truck is parked."

"Well, I drive a lot of miles. According to the math I think it could work."

"Why do you want to be an owner operator? Aren't you happy being a company driver?"

"Well, I've been looking at my finances and I'm just barely making ends meet. I'm barely able to save anything for my surgeries that I need and I just can't meet my goals at twenty six cents per mile."

"I hear ya. How long you been driving now?"

"I got my first load the end of January, so almost five months. Why?"

"They won't let you lease a truck and become an owner operator until after you've been driving for at least six months. Plus you have to have a perfect record."

"Okay, that means I would have to wait until the end of July. That's fine, gives me plenty of time to do my homework." I looked at the clock. It was 1:27. "Alice I gotta go. I'll call you later." I hung up the phone and dashed out to the hallway to catch the elevator.

I had just barely seated myself on one of the plush chairs of the reception area when a nurse appeared in the waiting room.

"Pamela?" She looked at me, and smiled. Being that I was

the only person in the waiting room, my guess was identifying me didn't take her too much effort.

"Yes, hi!" I answered enthusiastically.

"Come on with me." She spun around and headed down the hallway. I obediently followed her into a small room.

After checking my temperature, pulse and blood pressure; followed by the prick of the needle to extract three vials of blood samples, she informed me that the doctor would be with me in a minute.

The minute turned out to be more like twenty minutes, but I was here on a mission for my future so didn't mind the wait. When Dr. Horowitz finally entered the room and quietly shut the door behind him. I was as happy to see him as any human being I had ever met. At this moment, he was Santa Claus, and in his bag of toys was the one gift that was more precious and dear to me than any doll or stuffed animal I had ever wished for as a child could have ever aspired to be. This gift was the documentation that would scream to the world now and forever more that I am now a female!

While the doctor thumped my chest, listened to my heart, tapped my knees, and shoved objects into my mouth, I explained my situation and needs, all of which were responded to with clinical grunts and nods.

"So you need a DL 328, do you?" he smiled as he wrote on a clipboard.

"Yes, please" I gulped hopefully.

"I'm going to write you scripts for your Estradiol and Spironolactone. You don't need Prometrium, so you can stop taking that. You can pick your scripts up from Linda when you check out," he said flatly.

"Okay, and the DL 328?"

"Yes, she will have that too. I'll need to see you again in six months." He smiled slightly, opened the door, and disappeared into the hallway, the tails of his white smock trailing behind him.

"That will be $350 for today Ms. Anders," Linda said as

calmly, as if she was asking for $3.50.

"Wow, I wasn't expecting it to be so much." I reached into my wallet and handed her my insurance card.

"Oh, we don't accept insurance. Didn't anyone tell you that?" She laid the card on the counter.

"Um, well no. So can I pay with a check?" I put the insurance card back in my wallet.

"Visa, MasterCard, or check… or cash of course" she laughed.

"I pulled my checkbook out of my purse and agonizingly wrote a check for $350.00, tore it off the pad, and handed it to her. My savings were rapidly dwindling.

"Thank you, if you will have a seat for about fifteen minutes, I will have your paperwork, and your prescriptions, ready for you. Or, you can go down to the deli and have a cup of coffee, and come back if you want."

I grimaced as I speculated on the price of a cup of coffee in that deli. Instead, I opted to take a seat in the same chair that I had begun to sit in previously. There were two other women in the waiting room now, both intently reading magazines. I was not able to tell for certain if they were transsexual women or genetically born women, as they were both very feminine in appearance. It would not be a surprise to me for Dr. Horowitz to have a large clientele of genetically born women in addition to those from the trans community. I picked up a magazine and flipped through it mindlessly while I waited. My thoughts were coursing through a montage of images, none of which I could recall in the split second it took for my brain to move from one to the next.

It seemed like only seconds had passed when the sound of my name interrupted my hypnotic state.

"Ms. Anders, I have your papers ready…"

I tossed the magazine back onto the pile with the others, sprang to my feet, and virtually sprinted to the counter. Linda handed me the two prescriptions first, then the filled out and signed DL 328, along with the accompanying letter written on Dr.

Horowitz' letterhead.

"Could you please make a couple of copies of these for my records?" I handed the DL 328 and letter back to her.

Linda slid the two documents into the feeder of her copy machine and pressed the buttons to make the machine spit out two copies of each, then handed them back to me with the copies.

"Could you tell me please?... Where is the nearest DMV office from here?" I asked.

"There is one over in Santa Monica; it's about fifteen minutes away. Hold on, I'll give you directions." She jotted the information on a pad of paper, tore off the page, and handed it to me.

"Thank you" I looked at the clock on the wall behind her desk. It was 2:30. I would have plenty of time to get to the DMV before they closed.

My heart raced with excitement as I made the drive to Santa Monica. At every stoplight along Santa Monica Boulevard, I read and re-read Dr. Horowitz' handiwork.

"…she identifies as female and is undergoing extensive treatment to irreversibly alter her gender from male to female…"

"…she presents as female, appears female, and identifies as female…"

"… she lives full time in her target female gender…"

"…It is my medical opinion that this patient qualifies to be legally considered female within the guidelines of the state of California…"

Linda had estimated correctly, it took me exactly fifteen minutes to get to the DMV. Called up to one of the windows after a brief wait, I handed the clerk my CDL, and guardedly explained to her that I wished to change the status of my gender on my license to female. I was expecting an astonished reaction, followed by my having to recite a lengthy explanation of my life story. Instead, the response that I received was more like I had simply told her that I wanted to change my address.

"No problem, ma'am. Do you have your DL 328?" She asked with a smile.

I breathed a sigh of relief as I handed the two documents to her. My face felt as though it was about to crack in half from the huge smile that I was sure I had.

"How soon can I get my new license?" I asked.

"It usually takes about two weeks." She sounded almost apologetic.

I had hoped to get it today, but I was just pleased that everything had gone so smoothly so far. I could wait the additional two weeks to get the new license with the corrected gender.

Fifteen minutes later, I was again on the freeway back to Fontana. I had the radio turned off, and sang the simple words that thousands of mothers have sung to their children when they face setbacks in their lives.

The itsy bitsy spider climbed up the water spout.
Down came the rain and washed the spider out.
Out came the sun, and dried up all the rain.
And the itsy bitsy spider climbed up the spout again.

It was 4:30 when I arrived at the Rent a Wreck location in Fontana, to return my rental car. After checking in the car, an attendant drove me back to the OC. During the ride I gazed happily out the windows at the passing scenery along Valley Boulevard. I mentally summed up the cost of having this important change made on my CDL. Between the rental car, gas, parking fee, doctors fee… and oh yes, my tuna sandwich! I had spent $425.

This had been an unplanned, but very well spent expenditure. Despite the fact that I was much lighter in the pocketbook than I had been yesterday, or had planned to be today…I was still happy that I had spent every penny.

Yes… Even for that Beverly Hills tuna fish sandwich.

Pamela Anders; FEMALE… had arrived at the OC with a tremendous feeling of elation, and a glorious and triumphant sense of accomplishment.

234

Chapter Seventeen
Dianna

It was a typically quiet Friday night in the drivers' lounge. Most of the local drivers had gone home for the weekend and I was not expecting any company. I was busy working out some numbers with a calculator and jotting them onto a notepad when my thoughts were interrupted.

"You must be Pam?" I was startled to hear my name, as I looked up and responded.

"Yes?" I eyed the intruder of my calculations suspiciously, and laid down my pen.

The woman standing over me was very tall. Even from my sitting position, I could tell she stood well over six feet tall. She had medium length, auburn hair and one of the absolutely biggest smiles I had ever seen. She wore a tank top, Capri pants, and flip flops.

"Hi, I'm Dianna. I'm your new driving partner." I don't know how it was possible, but her smile grew even larger as she extended her right hand to me.

I reached out and shook her hand halfheartedly. "New driving partner? I wasn't aware that I had a new driving partner."

"Yup. I met with Sandra about it today." Dianna folded

herself into the chair across the table from me as she spoke. "She wanted all three of us to get together before she went home, but you were gone all day. She said we could all meet first thing Monday morning."

"No offense Dianna, but my plans are to go back to being a solo driver. In fact, I'm actually looking into leasing my own truck and becoming an owner operator."

"Really? When's that going to happen?" she asked.

"Not until the end of July. I will have been driving for six months by then, which is what they require before you can lease a truck."

"That works for me. I put in for a local driving job, but they want me to have at least a month of over the road experience first." She laughed.

She had an infectious laugh, and I could not help but smile. "Well, I really didn't want another driving partner between now and then. Besides, I don't think you want to partner with me. I attract trouble. That's how I lost my previous partner."

"What kind of trouble?" she smiled.

"A lot of people have a problem with me because of who I am." I paused for a moment before continuing. "You do know what I'm talking about, right?"

"Yeah, you're going through a sex change. So?" She shrugged her shoulders.

"Most people I work with don't have a problem with it. Obviously, you don't either, but there are a lot of people out there that do. That's where the trouble comes from."

"What kind of trouble are you talking about? What has happened?"

"Well, for starters… I'm not allowed to use the ladies room at the operating centers. A few female drivers have complained about my being in there and now I've been told that if I get caught using them I'll be fired. I have a lawyer fighting over that with Schneider right now."

"That sucks… but we can work around it. What else?"

"Oh let's see… well, I've been heckled at truck stops, called a transvestite on the CB, and have had nasty notes left on the truck."

Dianna continued smiling at me without saying a word.

I went on. "And of course there's the minor detail of the Mississippi State Troopers searching the truck because of me. Did Sandra tell you about that?"

"Aw, don't blame yourself for that. They were probably just looking for donuts," she chortled.

"Maybe I should keep a box of donuts handy… just in case." We both laughed.

"So… why do you want to be an owner operator? It's more money, but a lot more headaches from what I've heard," she asked.

"I've heard that too… about the headaches, but it makes sense for me. I'm only planning on driving for three years at the most, and I need to make as much money as I can quickly. The numbers work." I pointed to the calculations on my notepad.

Dianna studied my cryptic figures for a moment, and then looked up at me quizzically.

"Okay, let me explain. Right now, I am getting twenty-six cents per mile. I can easily average five hundred miles per day, which comes to $130.00 per day. After I have been driving for six months, Schneider will start paying me a whopping twenty-eight cents per mile, so that will go up to $140.00 per day."

"Whoopeee!" Dianna laughed.

"If I only take four days off per month, it comes out to approximately $3,600 gross per month. My take home would be less than three grand. That's not nearly enough to save the kind of money to pay for all of the surgeries I need, plus the electrolysis and other things. Not to mention child support and basic necessities."

"Like eating…" Dianna laughed.

"Yeah, that too. So, here's the same scenario if I lease a truck." I flipped the page on my pad and pointed out each calculation as I spoke.

"As an owner operator I get paid between eighty-eight and ninety-nine cents per mile, plus a fuel surcharge based on the current fuel prices. Right now the surcharge is running around twenty-four cents per mile. Using the same average miles and adjusting for four days off per month, I should gross around fifteen grand per month before expenses."

"Holy moley!" Dianna exclaimed.

"Well hold on… There are still a lot of expenses. From that gross income, I have to pay for my own fuel, and there is a four cent per mile escrow taken out for maintenance and insurance. Not to mention the lease payment of four-hundred-fifty dollars a week."

"Four-fifty a week for the lease payment? Geez!"

"Yeah, it's an open lease, so I can walk away from it anytime I want. That's why it's so high. But as long as I keep the truck moving, it will be profitable even with the high lease payment."

Dianna nodded silently. I continued.

"Okay, the lease payment works out to be nineteen-fifty per month. If I run just twelve thousand miles per month, I'll be using around fifteen-hundred gallons of fuel. At today's fuel prices, my fuel cost will run around four grand a month. My escrow will run around five-hundred dollars."

I was rapidly punching numbers into my calculator and showing them to Dianna as I swiftly moved from one computation to the next. Her eyes were beginning to glaze over as she tried to keep up.

I laughed. "Sorry Dianna, you look perplexed. Let me jump to the bottom line. If I keep the truck moving at least twenty-six days per month, and average five hundred miles per day, I can net close to six grand per month. It works out to be around forty-five cents per mile after expenses."

"So basically, you have to pay the lease payment whether the truck is moving or not. The other costs only accumulate when you are moving?"

"Yes, you are correct. The lease payment is a fixed expense. All of the others are relative to how many miles I run. Every hour that the truck is not moving costs me two dollars and sixty-seven cents." I flipped through my notes and showed Dianna the equation as I spoke.

Dianna laughed. "Geez, you don't miss a thing do you. It looks like you have this all figured out."

"I don't do anything without forethought, calculation, and careful planning, Dianna. That's something you'll learn about me." I smiled.

"Okay… so, do we have a deal? Partners?" She asked.

"It's really not up to me, but yeah sure. I guess we can work out the details on Monday when we meet with Sandra."

"Good deal! See you then!" Diana smiled, unfolded her long legs and body from the chair, and stood up. I stood as well and suddenly realized the true height of this woman, compared to me.

"I guess I'll head on home and visit my husband," she added with a laugh.

"Do you live close to here?" I asked, as we walked toward the glass doors.

"I'm about forty-five minutes from here. Do you know where Yucaipa is?" She pushed open the door and we stepped out into the cool evening air.

"Yeah, I'm vaguely familiar with it. I've seen exit signs for it on the Interstate."

"Well, that's where I live" she proclaimed proudly.

I nodded wordlessly as I stared at the sea of orange trucks and trailers in the yard. My mind was elsewhere.

"So I'll see you Monday partner." Dianna thrust out her right hand.

I shook her hand and smiled. "See you Monday."

After Dianna had left, I went back to the table to gather up my notes and calculator. I also needed to gather my thoughts. As much as I always carefully plan things out, there are often unexpected elements that require adjustments to the original strategy. I had thought I'd be a solo driver again, but now I had been presented with the prospect of remaining a team driver.

As I walked back to the truck, a myriad of thoughts tumbled through my mind. Dianna seemed like a pleasant enough woman. From our initial encounter, it felt as though we had made a friendly connection, and were both comfortable with each other.

I still could not help but wonder though, if she would be able to withstand the furies that were sure to arise as I continued to slowly progress through my transition. Nicole had assured me that she could handle anything that she might have to face, yet she had caved in and walked away.

I also wondered what kind of driver Dianna would be. I had trained with Nicole, so I knew before we even started that she was a competent driver. Dianna, however, was someone entirely foreign to me and fresh out of training. I had no idea of what her strengths and weaknesses might be. There was also the question of whether or not we would be able to co-exist in the tiny confines of the truck. Would we be able to mesh well together as a drive team?

As I nestled into my sleeper berth, a mosaic of images streamed and swirled through my mind. Today I had achieved a major accomplishment along my journey. I had obtained the legal credential of 'female' on my CDL. My plan to regain my solitude was disrupted, yet I was being gifted with the company of a pleasant driving companion.

The mathematical computations related to my becoming an owner operator paraded back and forth through my head like a marching band. The question of whether or not I could successfully partner with Dianna resounded in counterpoint in the background like a pipe organ.

As my thoughts slowly faded and I began to drift toward slumber; the marching band retreated off to a distant corner of my mind, and the blaring pipe organ magically transformed into the soothing melody of a harp. I was serene in the knowledge that it didn't really matter whether or not Dianna and I would make good truck partners. In a very short time, I would be the proprietor of my own truck and again the commander of my destiny. I would soon be the Queen of the Road.

I was jolted awake on Monday morning by the sound of banging on the door of my truck. I had gone out to Loretta's for some much needed, and long overdue, recreation on Sunday night. Having played hard, my plan had been to sleep in this morning. Obviously, this was not going to happen. I lazed in my berth with my eyes closed for a moment, hoping the intruder would simply give up and go away, but to no avail. The pounding continued. This only added to the throbbing in my head that was the result of my previous night's festivities.

I gingerly propped myself up on the berth and hoisted myself onto my half numb legs. I then wobbled to the front of the truck and pulled the curtain back enough to peer outside. It was just barely dawn, but I could clearly see Dianna standing at my door sporting her ever present grin. I pulled the curtains open completely, and then pushed the button to open the driver's side window with a soft whirring sound.

"Good morning Pam! I heard you were an early bird, so I figured you'd be up by now," she laughed.

"Normally I would be, but I went out last night. I was hoping to sleep in this morning. What time is it?" I yawned.

"It's 6:00. I have a carload of stuff to put in the truck. Can you pull it over near the employee parking lot so I can load it up?" she asked.

"I need to take a shower. Do you mind doing it while I'm in there?"

"That'd be just fine… Permission to climb aboard, Ma'am?" she laughed heartily. I couldn't help but join in with her contagious laughter, as I opened the door for her to climb in. My hangover admonished me for this outburst by a short stab of pain directly behind my eyes.

I shook two Tylenol capsules from the plastic bottle, washed them down with a few swigs from a bottle of water, and then quickly packed my shower bag. My legs were still a bit wobbly as I climbed down from the truck, but I managed to keep my balance enough to avoid a crash landing, as I headed off to the drivers' lounge. I was fairly certain that a cup of coffee and a hot shower would be able to revive me. Well, that and the soothing affects that I would soon enjoy from the two magical capsules.

After my shower, I walked back outside, and was met with a brilliant, crystal clear morning. It took me a moment to adjust my eyes to the sunlight, but I was soon able to focus, and spotted the truck parked over in one of the bobtail spots. I walked over, opened the passenger side door, and climbed in.

Dianna was busy unpacking her bags and placing her belongings on the upper berth. All around her feet and in every available inch of space inside the truck were boxes, bags, and plastic containers of food.

"Feel better? You certainly look better," she laughed. "You looked like death warmed over this morning."

"Yeah, I feel much better, thanks." I smiled while surveying the inside of the truck. It looked as if we were about to open a rolling convenience store. There was a case of Twinkies, assorted snack chips, Oreo cookies, and cans of fruit, tuna, and several plastic containers of various food items.

"Geez Dianna, you didn't have to bring all this food. We can go shopping anytime we want at any of the Super Wal-Mart stores along the Interstates." I laughed.

"I know. I just like to be stocked up. I have a Sam's club membership so I buy this stuff in bulk. Plus, I love to cook, so I whipped up some fried chicken, meat loaf, lasagna, and a few other items. I hope we have room in the fridge," she laughed.

"Well you need to hide those Twinkies, and don't you dare tell me where," I said only half jokingly. "Otherwise, that entire box will be empty by the end of this week." I laughed.

"Oh, you're a Twinkie-holic?" Dianna laughed. "They have support groups for that you know."

We both laughed raucously as we continued putting all of the food away. Once we had finished, we headed into the drivers' lounge to enjoy breakfast and wait for Sandra's arrival at the office for our meeting. By this point, I was already feeling a strong sense that Dianna and I would get along just great as driving partners.

It was 8:15 by the time Dianna and I sat down with our breakfasts. There was only a light crowd in the drivers lounge, with just a smattering of drivers and a handful of trainers in conference with students. Gennipher was seated a few tables away from us. She was engaged in an animated conversation with a stone-faced driver who was, ostensibly the unhappy recipient of a dressing down for some infraction. Gennipher and I made eye contact briefly. She gave me a quick nod before resuming her scolding of the driver.

"So what did you do before you became a truck driver?" I asked Dianna while pouring syrup on my pancakes.

She pondered for a moment before replying. "Well let's see… I have been a waitress, a convenience store clerk, a tax preparation worker, a school-bus driver, and a realtor. Then I decided to become a truck driver."

I laughed heartily. "Wow Dianna, you've had a well-rounded career haven't you?"

"Yeah, I guess I have." she laughed. "How about you? What did you do before?"

"I was in the publishing business. Magazines, actually. I've been a writer, editor, advertising salesperson, production manager, you name it. I owned my own publishing company for several years before I finally got out of it."

Dianna laughed, "That would explain your number crunching last night. You probably had to do a lot of that to run your business."

"Yes, magazine publishing is a very tough business, and you can lose your shirt if you don't plan each issue properly. It's a real balancing act trying to put out quality content, bring in sufficient advertising revenue, and keep the circulation numbers up. I used to refer to it as the "unholy trinity." I laughed.

"Why did you get out?"

"My publishing company was based in Colorado Springs.

Do you know anything about that city?" I took the last bite of my sausage and washed it down with coffee.

"I know it's in Colorado," she laughed.

"Yes, it is in Colorado." I smiled. It's also one of the most conservative cities in America, and home to Focus on the Family. Do you know who they are?"

"Aren't they that group of religious fanatics that kidnap gay kids and put them through some kind of brainwashing camp to try to turn them straight?" Dianna was frowning for the first time since I met her.

"Among other things, yes. I'm not one hundred percent sure about the kidnapping part, but there are rumors that some sort of "intervention" takes place after the parents contact Focus on the Family about their gay kids."

"Is it really possible to reprogram a gay kid and make him straight?" Dianna scooped a spoonful of her oatmeal out of the bowl and gazed at me intently.

"Nah, that's ultra right wing religious hogwash. There is no way you can program anybody's sexual orientation. If someone is gay, lesbian, or straight; that is who they are, and that's the end of it."

"So what does any of this have to do with why you quit your publishing business?"

"Sorry… I seem to have gotten off track." I smiled. "Because Colorado Springs is so ultra-conservative, and because of the influence that Focus on the Family has on the community, the idea of the publisher of a well-known business magazine having a sex change was appalling to the community!. Once word spread about my transition, it didn't take long for my freelance writers to vanish and for my advertisers to pull their ads. Remember the 'unholy trinity' of circulation, content, and advertising that I mentioned?"

Dianna nodded silently as she sipped her coffee. I went on.

"The trinity is like a tripod that holds up the magazine. Once one or more of those legs collapses, the whole thing comes crashing down. That's exactly what happened to my publishing company." I took a sip of my now lukewarm coffee.

Sandra suddenly appeared at our table holding a Styrofoam cup of steaming coffee in one hand, and a stack of papers in the other. "Hey you two, I see you've met."

"Morning Sandra." Dianna and I chimed in unison.

"Why don't you guys come back to my desk when you finish breakfast and we'll chat for a minute?" Sandra smiled as she spun around and scurried toward the office area.

"See you in a few minutes Sandra." I said, as she disappeared down the hallway.

Dianna and I both rose from our chairs simultaneously and took our trays, plates, and utensils to the bussing station. I refilled my cup with coffee and we headed to the back offices to see Sandra.

The STL area was abuzz with activity when Dianna and I entered. As we navigated through the many cubicles on our way to see Sandra, Gregg Sallavolltia appeared from behind a pillar on the way to his desk.

"Good morning Pam and… Dianna, right?"

"Yes, it's Dianna. Good morning Gregg." She smiled.

"I'm glad to see you found yourself a good driving partner, Dianna. Pam's a good driver and I think you can learn a lot from her."

"Thank you Gregg." I beamed proudly.

"You're welcome." he paused for a moment. "Pam, when you finish with Sandra, can you stop by my desk for a minute?"

"Sure thing, Gregg. See you in a few minutes." I said as Dianna and I headed over to Sandra's station.

"Hey ladies, what's happening?" Sandra asked in her usual cheery manner.

"Well I guess Dianna and I are going to be partners. We seem to have approved of each other so far," I laughed.

"Don't be so confident, Pam," Dianna quipped. Then she turned to Sandra.

"Sandra, did you know that this woman is a Twinkie-holic?

She needs professional help!" Dianna laughed.

"Twinkie-holic?" Sandra raised her eyebrows.

I laughed. "It's a joke, Sandra. Dianna packed a load of Twinkies on the truck, and I told her to hide them from me or they would be gone within days."

"Okay, I have a feeling you two are going to be trouble makers. I'll be keeping a close eye on you two." Sandra laughed. Dianna and I joined in.

Sandra switched to a more sober tone and continued. "So, what kind of commitment can I get from you guys? Sixty days?"

Dianna and I exchanged conspiratorial looks for a moment, and then I replied. "Sandra, I'm planning on leasing my own truck and becoming an owner operator as soon as I hit my six month anniversary. I had already made that decision before I found out I had a new partner. I can't commit to more than six weeks, if even that."

"Pam, have you thought this out? Being an owner operator is a big commitment. You've got to work your tail off to make a profit, and if you don't keep the truck rolling, the lease payment can eat you alive."

Dianna interjected with her infectious laugh. "Yeah, I think she has it all pretty well thought out. When I first met her the other night, it looked like she had Einstein's theory of relativity worked out in long form on her note pad."

I glanced at Dianna and smiled, then turned back to Sandra. "Yes, Sandra I have thought long and hard about it. I've been talking to people I know who are owner operators and have gotten the good, bad, and the ugly about it all. I am convinced that I can make a lot more money as an owner operator than I can as a company driver. And there is no question that I am capable of working hard enough to do it."

"Have you talked to the leasing people here at Schneider about leasing a truck?" Sandra asked.

"That's on my to-do list for today." I smiled.

Sandra changed the subject. "So... are you two ready to hit

the road today? I've got a load sitting here in the yard that needs to go to Philly and I'm going to put it on your truck, ok?"

"I'm ready!" Dianna replied enthusiastically.

"Yup, let's hit it." I added.

"Ok, I'm sending the load assignment to your Qualcomm now. You guys be safe out there." Sandra turned to her computer keyboard and began typing.

"Take care Sandra" I said as Dianna and I walked toward the hallway that led back to the drivers' lounge.

"Dianna, do you want to get the truck ready to roll and maybe hook up to our trailer while I go see what Gregg wants?" I asked.

"Sure thing Pam! By the way, I'm a night person. Do you mind if I take the noon to midnight shift?"

"Perfect!" I exclaimed. "You and I are going to get along great!"

As I made my way over to Gregg's desk, I crossed paths with Mr. Loss Prevention, Ed Paul. We locked eyes for a moment, each of us projecting our contempt for one another as we passed; neither of us acknowledging the other or exchanging even the slightest hint of a greeting. I felt no need to hide my dislike for this man, and he undoubtedly felt the same about me. I was certain that by now, a copy of the letter from Chris Daley had landed on his desk, and he was fully aware that I planned to fight him and Leary on the bathroom issue.

Gregg was talking on the phone as I arrived at his desk, and he gave me the hand signal to wait a minute. I nodded affirmatively, and stood passively while I waited. In a short time, he hung up the phone and smiled at me.

"Pam, have a seat." He pointed to the plastic chair next to his desk. I obediently sat down and smiled at him. I had a feeling this was going to be about the letter from Chris Daley. My intuition was right on point.

"Mike Leary emailed me a copy of the letter that your lawyer sent regarding this whole bathroom thing. Needless to say, it has stirred up quite a hornet's nest in Green Bay." Gregg smiled warmly.

I knew I had an ally in him, but also realized that he was caught between the proverbial 'rock and a hard place'.

"Gregg, I really didn't have much choice. My right to exercise the basic need to use the restroom has been taken from me, and I had to do something. I hope you don't think that I have anything against you or the company." I smiled slightly. "The bottom line is… I need to be able to go to the bathroom."

"Yes, I understand that. But what they're saying is that until you get your surgery… they don't want you to use the ladies rooms in any of the company facilities, despite what your lawyer says."

"I got a signed form from my doctor that says I am female, and I was able to get my CDL to say I'm a female too. Will that help?"

"Let me make a copy of your CDL, and I'll fax it to human resources." He held out his hand for me to hand him my license.

"Umm… well… It will be a couple of weeks before I actually receive it in the mail. I'll get it to you as soon as it gets here."

"That's fine, but even so… I seriously doubt that your license will be enough to change their minds on this. Until you get your surgery I believe that they will stand their ground on this."

"Even if it's a violation of the law?"

"That's what they are saying right now, Pam. I'm sorry."

"Well, okay Gregg. I guess we'll just have to see how this all plays out. In the meantime, I'll just try to avoid the operating center restrooms. If I do have to stop at one, I'll simply do my best to slink in and out unnoticed until we get this worked out."

"Thanks Pam that would be best. You are a good driver and very much liked around here. Be careful though. Leary doesn't know you the way we do, and he won't hesitate to terminate you if he gets another complaint. He sent out a memo to all the operating center managers instructing them to let him know immediately if you are seen using the women's bathroom."

"Geez, Leary really has it out for me, doesn't he?" I said in astonishment as I stood to shake hands with Gregg.

During my meeting with Gregg, Dianna had hooked up to

our trailer, performed the pre-trip inspection, and had filled the tanks with fuel. It was 10:45 am and we were ready to roll. I had the first driving shift, even though it would only be an hour long. I updated my log status to '*driving*' and pulled out of the operating center onto Valley Boulevard toward Interstate 15.

It had been an interesting weekend that had been filled with surprises, but I was on the road again at last, this time with a new driving partner.

Chapter Eighteen
You Don't Exist

I pulled the truck into the Barstow TA at 11:55, and backed into one of the many open slots. After a quick visit to the restroom, we were back on the road, now heading east on Interstate 40 with Dianna at the wheel. I sat in the jump seat and surreptitiously observed my new driving partner as she maneuvered the truck and shifted gears. Her shifting was as smooth as silk and she appeared to be every bit as competent behind the wheel of a big truck as Nicole had been. I sighed with relief, as I leaned back in the seat and peered through the windshield at the bland scenery, as we headed into the Mojave Desert.

"I saw you eyeballing me," she laughed. "Are you worried that I don't know how to drive?"

"I'm not in the least bit worried, Dianna" I smiled. "I was just making sure that I could sleep peacefully with the knowledge that there is a competent driver at the helm. Can't blame me, can you?"

"Nah, I don't blame you. So how am I doing?" she glanced over at me and laughed. "Where's your clipboard?"

"You're doing great!" I exclaimed, and then asked, "Who was your trainer?"

"Sponge Bob" she laughed. "Do you know him? His name is Greg, but everyone calls him 'Sponge Bob'. He's a good trainer and a great guy, lots of fun to be around."

"Yeah, I have met him briefly. He seems like a nice guy." 'Sponge' was one of the male trainers who had immediately accepted my transition and was always ready with a smile and 'Hello Pam' whenever I saw him.

"What about you? Who trained you?" Dianna asked.

"Gennipher. Do you know who she is?"

"Just to say hello, don't know her real well. She seems like a pretty cool lady though."

"She is" I smiled. "Way cool."

"So, what did Gregg want…. if you don't mind me asking."

"I don't mind at all. Remember me talking about the complaints about me using the women's bathroom?"

"Yeah, and you said you had a lawyer fighting with Schneider over it."

"That's right. Well the lawyer sent a letter to human resources in Green Bay, and I guess it caused a bit of a stir. Gregg was told that if I set foot in any ladies room anywhere in any of our facilities, I would be instantly terminated. The head of HR even sent a memo out to all the operating centers, instructing them to report if anyone spotted me using the ladies room," I added with a rueful chuckle.

Dianna laughed, "Geez, did they also distribute wanted posters with your mug to all the managers?"

"That wouldn't surprise me." I laughed. "Oh, that reminds me, I need to call my lawyer and give him an update."

I grabbed my cell phone from my purse, and pressed the speed dial for the Transgender Law Center. After only two rings, the familiar friendly voice answered.

"Good afternoon, Transgender Law Center."

"Hi, this is Pam Anders. Is Chris Daley available?"

"Hi Pam. No, I'm sorry, but he is in conference right now. Can I have him call you back?"

"That would be great. Tell him I have an update for him."

"Will do. You have a great day Pam." She hung up the phone and I pressed the end button on my cell phone.

"Don't forget to call the leasing people too, Pam. You said you were going to call them today," Dianna said.

"Yes, thank you for reminding me. I just need to get my notepad with their phone number on it."

I rose from the jump seat, and headed to the back to retrieve my notepad from the cubbyhole next to my sleeper berth. As I began to turn to return to the cab, something on my pillow caught my eye, causing me to take a second look. There, reposing on my pillow, wrapped in its cellophane wrapper, was a Twinkie. I grabbed it and headed back to the jump seat.

"What is this?" I laughed as I snapped the buckle on my seat belt.

"It's your daily Twinkie fix, Pam. Enjoy," she laughed.

"You are cruel Dianna!" We both laughed.

I punched in the number for Schneider Finance and was connected to a lady by the name of Rebecca. She cheerfully took my credit application over the phone.

"We are going to pull your credit report Pam. How does it look?"

"It's not the best, but it's not the worst either. I have had some financial struggles during the past few years, so there are some slow pays on the credit cards. Is that going to be a problem?"

"You don't need to have perfect credit to lease a truck through us, but it helps. If your credit is fair, but not awful, we can usually get you approved, maybe with a higher lease payment. I guess we will find out soon enough."

"How long will it be before I can find out?"

"I should have an answer by tomorrow. I'll give you a call as soon as I know."

No sooner had I disconnected with Rebecca, when my cell phone rang. The caller ID informed me that it was the Transgender Law Center.

"Hello", I answered cheerfully.

"Hi Pam, Chris Daley here. How are you?"

"I'm good Chris. Any news?"

"Nothing really. I've left three messages for Mike Leary, but haven't gotten a return call yet. I was planning to call him again today, but thought I would talk to you first. Any new developments on your end?"

"This morning I was told, by one of my bosses, that Leary sent out a memo to all the operating center managers to keep an eye out, and to report if I am seen going into any of the women's restrooms."

"Sounds like he wants to play hardball. That's okay, I can play rough too. I'm going to leave him another message, this time letting him know what we are prepared to file a complaint against Schneider, and possibly go for punitive damages if they don't allow you to use the restrooms. We'll see what happens."

"Okay, I guess this isn't going to go as smoothly as I had hoped," I said nervously.

"Hopefully it won't go to litigation, let's keep our fingers crossed. By the way, did you get in touch with Dr. Horowitz?"

"Oh, Chris I nearly forgot to tell you!" I spluttered excitedly. "Yes, I saw Dr. Horowitz last week and he signed my form 328. I went right over to the DMV and they changed the gender on my CDL to female."

"That's great. I will mention that in my message to Leary. Maybe that will get him to back off a little. Did you make a copy of your CDL and give it to your boss?"

"No, I have to wait for it to come in the mail."

"Okay, give them a copy as soon as you get it. Meanwhile let's just see what happens. I'll give you a call if I hear anything." He hung up the phone.

After replacing my cell phone in my purse, I stared at the passing desert through the windshield, while removing the cellophane wrapper from my Twinkie. After tossing the wrapper in the trash bag, I took a bite, and turned to Dianna who was intently watching the road ahead.

"The lady at Schneider Finance says she should have an answer by tomorrow as to whether or not I can lease a truck."

"I heard you tell her that your credit is not the best. What did she say about that?"

I shrugged my shoulders, "She said that if it isn't awful she could probably still get me approved. That would cause me to have a higher lease payment though."

"Define awful" Dianna laughed.

"I guess everyone's definition of good or bad credit is different, but lenders pretty much just go by the credit score now-a-days, which is a derivative of some crazy formula that nobody seems to understand."

"So how bad is yours? Do you think you'll get approved?"

"The slow death of my publishing business over a period of several months affected my credit in a very negative way. I had maxed out my credit cards trying to keep things going, and eventually fell behind on those payments. Plus I was so far behind in my car payments that I finally surrendered the car and bought a used car with cash."

Dianna stared at the road ahead without commenting. Her facial expression betrayed her thoughts.

"Yeah, Dianna", I sighed. "I have a bad feeling about this. I probably won't get approved."

"Time for a pit stop?" Dianna delicately changed the subject, as she flipped on the right turn signal for us to exit in Needles for a quick break.

Within minutes, we had both finished our visits to the bathroom, and were back in the truck, on the way toward the Arizona state line. I headed to the back to climb into my sleeper berth.

"See you in a few hours Dianna. Thanks for the Twinkie," I smiled.

Dianna laughed. "You're welcome. I hope you enjoyed it. There's more where that came from!"

I slept soundly, despite all the turmoil that was taking place in my life, and the fact that I was in the back of a truck that was hurtling across the Interstate under the control of a rookie driver whose driving skills were yet undetermined. After what seemed like eight minutes, but was in fact eight hours, the sound of Dianna's voice, on the other side of the curtain, roused me from my slumber.

"Time to wake up, Pam" she yelled.

I parted the curtains slightly, and peered out, as I sat up on the edge of my sleeper berth. Dianna was seated behind the wheel writing in her log book.

"Where are we?" I asked sleepily, while rising to my feet and opening the curtains completely.

"Gallup, New Mexico. We're at the Pilot."

"What time is it?"

"It's a little after eleven pm. I'm gonna take a shower. I thought you might want one too…"

"Is that a hint?" I laughed.

Dianna was reposing in the jump seat when I returned to the truck with my shower bag in one hand, and a steaming cup of coffee in the other. I climbed into the driver's side and tossed my shower bag into the back. I spotted a banana, apple, container of yogurt with a plastic spoon, and a boiled egg resting on the driver's seat.

"It's about time you got back from the shower," Dianna laughed. "What'd you do… get your nails done while you were in there?"

I smiled while moving the food items to the console and plopping myself into the seat. "It takes a long time to make this ugly mug of mine look halfway decent Dianna. In fact, I need a magician in there with me, not a nail tech."

"Aw don't be so hard on yourself, Pam. You look just fine." She smiled back at me.

"Thanks for the compliment, Dianna. And, oh… Thanks for breakfast. Where's my Twinkie?" I laughed while peeling the top off the yogurt container.

"No Twinkie for you until supper time missy," she replied with her familiar chortle.

"I can't wait!" I laughed as I gobbled down the yogurt, tossing the empty container into the trash bag.

After starting my log for the day, I released the brakes and put the truck in gear, slowly guiding it through the truck stop parking area toward the exit. It was just past midnight, and the lot was eerily still, the only sounds coming from the idling trucks, whose drivers were inside sleeping peacefully in preparation for another long day of driving. I turned the truck onto Refinery Road, made the left turn onto eastbound Interstate 40, gradually working the gears until I reached 10th gear.

Dianna remained seated in the jump seat, and was busy tuning the satellite radio until she found a soft rock station that we both liked. She sat back in her seat, and quietly enjoyed the music. I simply stared ahead, guiding the truck along the white lines of the Interstate.

After what seemed like an eternity of silence, Dianna turned to me.

"You mentioned that you were trying to save up money for 'all the surgeries' you need. Other than your sex change surgery, what other surgeries are there?"

"Well, it's not actually called 'sex change' surgery anymore," I glanced at her and smiled warmly. "It's referred to as 'gender reassignment surgery' or GRS for short."

"Oh, sorry for my political incorrectness," she laughed. "Now I know better."

"It's okay Dianna. Most people don't know that. Anyway, to answer your question… I need what's called facial feminization surgery. It's basically to reshape the outstandingly male characteristics of my face, and soften them up to make me look more feminine."

"Ah okay. That makes sense, I guess. What all do they do?"

"It's mainly bone and soft tissue work under the skin. The surgeon goes in and grinds things down to contour the jaw line, soften the chin, brows, and forehead, and whatever else is needed."

"Ouch!" Dianna exclaimed. "That sounds painful."

"Fortunately, I'll be under anesthesia, so I won't feel anything. I'm sure I will be sore for a few days afterwards though."

"How much does all that cost?"

"I'm not sure. I have an appointment with a plastic surgeon in Dallas next month, so I guess I'll find out then."

As we passed through Albuquerque, I tore the skin off my banana, and munched on it, as I skillfully held it in one hand and steered the truck in a straight line with the other. It was now 2:00 am and it seemed as if we were the only vehicle on the Interstate. Dianna appeared to be in a talkative mood, so I continued the dialog.

"So, do you have kids?" I asked.

"Yeah I have two grownup kids, a son, and a daughter" she said. My daughter is pregnant, so I am soon to become a grandma." Dianna beamed with pride.

"Congratulations! What about your son?"

Dianna looked out the side window for a moment, and then turned back to me. "Well, he's not doing so well. The last we heard, he was living in his car somewhere. We don't talk to him."

"Oh, I'm so sorry" I said quietly.

"Yeah, well sometimes things don't work out the way parents plan for their kids. It's just the way it is," she replied ruefully. Again, she turned to stare through the side window. I could sense that she was deep in thought, reflecting on the pain and regret that she surely must have been enduring.

We had now passed through Albuquerque with its well-lit, urban slice of the Interstate, and were once again driving through the moonlit, rural portion of New Mexico. Beyond the reach of our headlights, a dark ribbon of asphalt lay in wait before us, as the truck careered eastbound at 65 miles an hour. Dianna and I remained silent, with the only sounds being the throaty purr of the truck's engine, and 'The Carpenters' softly singing, *Hurting Each*

Other", on the satellite radio. A lighted road sign informed me that it was 100 miles to Santa Rosa, 156 miles to Tucumcari, and 280 miles to Amarillo; where I would stop to top off the fuel tanks and take a break. We would most likely switch drivers in Oklahoma City.

Dianna broke the silence, interrupting my thoughts.

"What about you? Do you have kids?" she asked.

"Yes, I have three… a daughter, and two sons. My daughter, Cheryl, lives in Daytona with her two sons. My boys, Gregory and Steven, live in Texas with my second ex-wife."

"Oh, so you're a grandma!" she laughed. Are you close to your kids?"

"I'm pretty close to my boys. They're just barely teenagers. My daughter is another story though."

Dianna nodded silently, apparently not wanting to pry, but nonetheless curious about my relationship with my daughter.

I continued. "Cheryl and I have been in and out of each other's lives for several years, ever since her mom and I got divorced. I disappeared from her life for several years while she was a child, and then reappeared when she was a teenager. We briefly restored our relationship, and she lived with me until she graduated from high school. After that, she made some choices in her life that made me angry, and I reacted poorly. In essence, we both made some bad choices which resulted in a very strained relationship."

"Are you on good terms with her now?"

"I haven't talked to her in a long time, so I'm not exactly sure where I stand with her. I know I need to call her and try to mend fences, but I haven't been able to muster up the courage to call her."

"Well Pam, I don't want to tell you what to do, but I think you should call her before it's too late."

"Yeah, you're right Dianna. I need to call her," I said plaintively.

"Holy cow! It's almost 3:00 am!" Dianna exclaimed as she looked at the clock on the dashboard. I guess I'd better get some sleep." She rose from the jump seat and headed to the back.

"Okay, sleep well. I'll see you at noon." I smiled.

It was 5:45 am when I pulled up to the fuel pump at the Pilot in Amarillo, As I began filling the tanks, Dianna emerged from the truck, and headed into the building for a potty break. Only a few minutes later she padded sleepily back to the truck. By the time I had finished re-fueling, she was already back in the sleeper berth with the curtain closed.

I headed into the travel center to take a bathroom break, and to get a fresh cup of coffee. I had become somewhat accustomed to the stares that I received from people, who were essentially trying to figure out if I was male or female. It was becoming progressively easier simply to ignore their stares. Occasionally, I would overhear whispered comments as I walked past a group of people, but I had learned to ignore those as well. I had even learned to contain my anger when a clerk referred to me as a male by calling me 'sir'. I experienced all of these things on this particular visit to the Pilot travel center, but I was able simply to take it in stride. There was nothing to gain by responding to the stares, comments, or misgendered greetings, so I held my emotions in check. It would be delusional thinking to believe that with my present facial configuration I could successfully present myself as a female without question, so I simply ignored it all. Instead, I mentally focused on the solutions that awaited me just over the horizon.

I returned to the truck, started the engine, updated my log, and buckled my seatbelt, before putting the truck in gear and pulling out of the truck stop and heading back out onto Interstate 40. It was another 260 miles to Oklahoma City, and I would arrive just as my driving shift ended. So far… I was pleased with my new driving partner in terms of her driving ability and her personality. This made me smile as I headed east across the Texas Panhandle.

It was nearly five hours later when Dianna popped her head through the part in the curtain, as I backed the truck into a parking spot at the TA in Oklahoma City. "What time is it?" she asked.

"It's a little after eleven," I answered while setting the air brakes. "I'm hungry!"

"Me too!" Dianna responded enthusiastically, as the sleeper berth curtains flew open, and she emerged. "How about some of my homemade meatloaf?" she asked.

"Sounds good to me" I replied.

As Nicole and I had done on many occasions, we took our food inside, where the truck stop provided a microwave oven, and heated it up. We purchased a few side items and drinks to go along with our meatloaf, and sat down at one of the tables to eat.

"This is good meatloaf," I commented, after popping the first forkful into my mouth and savoring the flavor.

"Thanks, it's my mom's meatloaf recipe. I think she got it from her mom." Dianna laughed.

"My compliments to your mom and your grandma!" I said. And also to you, of course."

"Thank you," Dianna said and then changed the subject. "I don't suppose you've heard back from that lady about your truck lease have you?"

"Nope, nothing yet." I felt my stomach knot up as I responded. I was not feeling optimistic about what the answer might be.

"I figured that you would certainly have said something to me if she had, but I was curious. Well, at least she said she would have an answer for you today. Hopefully it will be good news," she responded. "Just try and think happy thoughts."

"Well, that's what I've been trying to do, but I can't help worrying that they're going to turn me down," I said.

She finished her soda and laughed, "Well, I'm sure that it'll all work out just fine for you. I mean, even if for some reason they deny you, or even just delay it for you… you still have me!"

I smiled, "That's one good thing that I have to be thankful for! I'm glad I ended up with you as my partner. I feel like we really get along on both the friendship and the professional levels. You're a good driver. And a good friend."

"Thanks!" she said. "I feel the same way too. Besides… you wouldn't be eating my grandma's fantastic meatloaf if we hadn't been put in each others paths!"

After we had finished eating, we tossed our paper plates and plastic forks into the trash can, and headed back across the parking lot to our truck. The air was cooler in Oklahoma City than we were used to, but the sky was a heavenly blue, with just a few puffs of white clouds slowly drifting about. Most importantly, the sun was shining; which made it a perfect day.

I sat in the jump seat completing my log for the day, while Dianna performed her pre-trip inspection. When she had finished, she climbed into the driver's seat and began her log. When she was done, she started the truck as we both buckled our seat belts. Within minutes, we were back on Interstate 40 heading east to Interstate 35. We would take this as far as the turnpike, northeast toward Tulsa, and then on into Joplin, Missouri.

We had just entered the turnpike when the ringing of my cell phone emitted from my purse. After exchanging ominous looks with Dianna, I reached into my purse and grabbed the phone. A quick glance at the caller ID told me it was not the call I was expecting from Schneider Finance, but was instead from the Transgender Law Center. I answered the phone anxiously.

"Hi Pam, its Chris Daley. I just wanted to let you know that I had a conference call with Mike Leary and Schneider's corporate counsel this morning. I pretty much laid down the law with them about the bathroom situation."

"Okay, and what did they say?" I was eager to get the details.

"Leary was still adamant about preventing you from using the women's restroom, but the attorney was a lot more level headed. He told me they would confer on the matter and make a decision as to how they want to proceed."

"How they want to proceed? What does that mean?"

"It means I gave them a choice to either back off of this bathroom restriction they have on you, or get served with a formal summons and complaint."

"Did they say how long it would be before they would decide?"

"I gave them twenty-four hours to give me a decision one way or the other. I also told them that if I didn't hear from them in that time frame, I would be forced to assume that they had chosen litigation to resolve the matter."

"Okay Chris, thanks for the update." We said our goodbyes and disconnected.

As I dropped my cell phone back into my purse, the very small knot that had been in my stomach earlier seemed to have now grown to the proportions of a much, much larger one. Dianna took her eyes off the road just long enough to spare me a quick glance, before returning them back to the road.

"Bad news?" she asked.

"I'm not sure… the lawyer gave Schneider until the end of the day tomorrow, to either allow me use of the women's restrooms, or go to court. It's making me nervous."

"Shit or get off the pot, huh?" Dianna laughed aloud at her unintentional, yet ever so accurate, metaphor.

Despite the earthquake that was currently taking place in the pit of my stomach, I could not help but laugh along with her. "Yeah, I guess that's pretty much it."

The sound of my cell phone ringing, once again, trumpeted from inside my purse. I reached into my purse, extracted the device, and peered at the caller ID, only to find that the number was 'unavailable'.

"Hello?" I answered nervously.

"Hello, Pam? It's Rebecca from Schneider Finance. How are you today?"

"I'm good, how are you?" I tried my best to conceal my anxiety. I was certain she could sense it, even over the phone.

"Well, I have some good news and some not so good news." she said with a cheery tone. "Can I give you the bad news first?"

"Sure." The earthquake in my stomach had reached a 9.5 on

the Richter scale, and was now joined by a tsunami of stomach acid. I gulped, while awaiting the bad news.

"Actually, it's not really bad news… it's more like weird news." She paused for a moment before continuing. "You don't exist," she said pointedly.

"I don't exist?" I exchanged looks with Dianna who looked as puzzled as I felt.

"You told me that you had a bad credit report, something about slow pays on credit cards and so forth?" Rebecca went on.

"Yeah?"

"There are no credit cards on your credit report, no car loans. There is absolutely nothing on your credit report, neither good nor bad. You don't even have a credit score. It is almost as if you don't exist."

"Wow, Rebecca. You're right, this is really weird. What does this do for my chances for leasing my own truck?"

Rebecca laughed. "Well… now for the good news. Since you don't have bad credit, and since we will be in control of your revenue and your truck, we approved you for a lease with a five hundred dollar per week payment. I know the payment is high, but it was the best we could get for you."

"Wow Rebecca, that is awesome!" I exclaimed. I looked over at Dianna, who was now beaming with an ear to ear grin. She held up her hand and I slapped it with a celebratory high-five.

"So what happens now?" I asked.

"From here we submit the paperwork to corporate. As long as you have a clean driving record and no driver complaints, they will approve your transfer into a lease operator contract. Once that is done, you just need to come to Charlotte and meet with me to go over the lease, sign the documents, and get your truck."

"Charlotte? As in North Carolina? I thought you were in Green Bay."

"Nope. All owner operators are dispatched out of the Charlotte operating center."

"So do I just wait to hear back from you then?"

"Yup, that's the plan." she said cheerfully. "Congratulations!"

I got off the phone and turned to my partner, "Wow Dianna, this is really crazy! She said there is no credit file for me. How can that be?"

"It must just be some sort of computer glitch. Maybe because of your name change, everything is on your old name, and didn't get put on our new name." Dianna speculated.

"Who knows?... But the important thing is… I got approved for a lease! That means in a few weeks I will be an owner operator!" I could hardly contain my enthusiasm. A flock of butterflies had now replaced the natural disasters that had been occurring in my stomach only minutes before.

"Congratulations Pam!" Dianna beamed with genuine happiness for me.

"Thank you! I am so happy now! I'm going to sleep like a baby tonight!"

Chapter Nineteen
Independence Day

Dianna and I switched seats in Vandalia, Illinois. After only a brief chat, she was asleep in her berth by 1:00 am. I had the satellite radio tuned to my favorite classic rock station. I turned the volume up just enough so that I could enjoy the music without disturbing my partner, who was snoozing in the berth behind me. It was a beautiful early morning, featuring a clear moonlit sky peppered with shining stars. I set the cruise control to the maximum truck speed in Illinois of 55 mph, and simply let the truck cruise eastbound along Interstate 70. The moment I crossed the state line into Indiana, I would increase my speed to 60 mph, which is the speed limit for trucks in that state.

My telephone conversation with Rebecca the previous day had left me in a very euphoric state of mind. I was now content in the knowledge that my goal to become an owner operator would soon be coming to fruition. Adding to my bliss, was the fact that in a very short time, I would be visiting Dr. Raphael for a consultation regarding my facial feminization surgery, and I then would have my session at E2000 to have my facial hair removed. Things were slowly coming together for me.

The only dark cloud casting a shadow on my sunny state of

being, was the uncertainty of how Schneider would respond to the demand put on them by Chris Daley. Would they concede to the fact that the law protects my use of the women's restroom, or would they choose to take their chances in court? I would prefer that we avoid a legal battle, but was also willing to stand and fight if the need arose.

The answer to my question came to me in a much-unexpected fashion… on the Qualcomm.

At 8:45, I pulled into the Pilot truck stop in Zanesville, Ohio to top off the fuel tanks, refill my coffee, and take a stretch break. After refueling, I backed the truck into an empty slot, and set the brake. Dianna was now awake, and joined me for a bathroom break.

Upon our return to the truck, Dianna climbed back into the sleeper berth and closed the curtain. I sipped on my coffee while updating my log. From the corner of my eye, I noticed the light flashing on the Qualcomm console, an indication that there was an unread incoming message. I set my coffee into the cup holder, and reached for the console. I then pressed the button to read the message.

After reading the text on the display, I blinked, and then read it again. I could not believe my eyes, so I read it one more time. After reading the message three times, I let out a loud and audible exclamation.

"Holy shit!" I yelled.

"What's wrong?" Dianna exclaimed as the curtain flew open.

"Oh, sorry Dianna, I didn't mean to wake you. You are not going to believe this message on the Qualcomm. I don't know whether to cry with joy, or just laugh."

"What does it say?" she asked sleepily.

"Here, you read it." I reached back and handed the console to her, as she sat up on the edge of the berth, and reached with her long arms to take it from me.

"Holy shit is right," she laughed as she handed it back to me.

"This is good news for you, but it's also pretty hilarious the way they worded it."

"Yeah, well I don't think they meant it to be funny, but it is," I laughed.

I gazed at the display on the Qualcomm, and grinned, as I once again read the message that Sandra had sent me:

"Pam, the following message was sent by human resources to all the operating centers. I thought you would like to know"

'To: All Operating Center Managers:
Please be advised that Pamela Anders is now qualified to use the women's restroom.'

Dianna laughed, "Congratulations. So... how did you qualify to use the women's restroom? Did you have to pass a test?"

I chuckled, "Yeah, it was a tough test. I nearly failed the part where I had to pass a wad of toilet paper to the lady in the next stall, but I made up for it in the toilet seat doily competition."

"So I suppose they will be sending you a qualification card to keep in your wallet, for the next time Junior and Bubba in Mississippi question you, huh?"

We both laughed heartily.

Dianna continued the banter, "I think you should celebrate at the next OC we come across by running around naked in the ladies room." By now we were both laughing hysterically, as she closed the curtain and lay down to enjoy a few more hours of sleep.

I started the engine, released the brakes, and put the truck in gear. While maneuvering toward the exit, on my way back onto Interstate 70, I felt all aglow, as the song from my childhood once again streamed through my mind.

'....the itsy bitsy spider climbed up the spout again.'

Over the next few weeks, Dianna and I proved to be perfectly compatible driving partners. We shared similar taste in music, food, and movies, and we each possessed an identical sense of humor. Unlike Nicole, Dianna loved to shop for clothing, shoes, and jewelry. We stopped frequently at the outlet malls that we discovered strewn along the Interstates, where we parked our big rig in the enormous parking lots designed specifically for our purpose, as well as for the convenience of the thousands of motor homes that zigzagged across the country.

In a short time, I had compiled a decent wardrobe of clothing and jewelry, thanks in part to Dianna's guidance. We also stopped periodically to get our nails done, and I now sported a full set of beautiful acrylic nails.

I now possessed my new CDL with the female marker, and was pleased to present it on demand at the guard shacks as we entered distribution centers.

During our travels from coast to coast, and border to border, we had stopped a few times in Fontana. During these stops, Dianna took time off to spend with her husband, and I hung around the operating center, where I checked my mail, and caught up on the many friendships I had developed. I had become a regular at Loretta's, where I spent much of my days off partying with Alice, Mikey, and some of the other patrons who had befriended me.

At 11:30 am on June 30th, I backed the truck into one of the many docks at the enormous Anheuser-Busch facility in Fort Collins, Colorado. Within minutes, the dockworkers began to load our trailer with 30,000 pounds of Budweiser; destined for a beer distributor in Terre Haute, Indiana. Dianna awakened from her slumber by the bouncing of the truck, as the forklift roared in and out of our trailer, dropping pallet after pallet of product. Within 40 minutes, our trailer was laden with beer, and we headed south on Interstate 25 with Dianna now behind the wheel.

"Happy birthday, Pam!" Dianna exclaimed. She looked over at me with her familiar ear-to-ear grin.

"Oh, um… thank you Dianna." I smiled. "How did you know?"

She laughed, "A little birdie told me."

"A little birdie, huh?" I laughed. And who might this little birdie be?"

"The Qualcomm, silly!" She handed me the console, "You didn't see the message on there?"

I scrolled through the most recent messages and found one that had escaped my notice from earlier in the morning. It was from Sandra.

'Happy birthday Pam! Have a great day'

"Wow, I didn't even notice that message," I said, as I typed, *'Thank you'* on the keyboard and hit the send button.

"Since it's your special day, you get two Twinkies today," Dianna chortled.

"Oh, I'm so excited" I laughed. After a brief pause, I continued, "It's rather a cruel irony though, don't you think?"

Dianna glanced at me, "What is?"

"Here it is my birthday and I've got a fifty-three foot trailer loaded with 30,000 pounds of beer… but I can't drink," I sighed.

Dianna laughed, "You're right, that is pretty cruel!"

"So, did you get birthday greetings from your kids?"

"Yeah, the boys called me this morning to say happy birthday. I also got a text message from my sister."

Dianna looked at me with a concerned expression, "… and your daughter?"

Pangs of guilt stabbed me like a knife at the thought of my daughter. I stared silently through the windshield for a moment, and then turned to Dianna.

"I haven't heard from her." It was all I could think of to say.

"Pam, why don't you just call her?"

"I will. Her birthday is in four days, I will call her then."

"Fourth of July baby huh?" she laughed.

"Yeah" I smiled. "I remember it like it was just yesterday. When I walked out of the hospital after she was born, there were fireworks everywhere. It felt as if the whole world was celebrating her birth."

"How old is she now?"

"Thirty-five," I replied morosely.

After our beer delivery in Terre Haute, Sandra gave us a load to Saint Paul, Minnesota, and then another one back to Fontana.

Bren at E2000 had instructed me to prepare for my treatment with at least a four-day growth of beard, so I had stopped shaving on July 2. The stubble on my face made it impossible to present as a female, so for the first time in nearly two months, I reluctantly returned to life as a male.

Although Dianna was able to find humor in just about any situation, including this one. I was having a difficult time coping with it. My appearance forced me to return to the men's restrooms at the truck stops, which I found horribly appalling. Each time I entered, the all too familiar site of urinals lining the walls, and obscene graffiti displayed inside the stalls greeted me.

On Sunday, while en-route from St. Paul to Fontana; we stopped at the Pilot in Big Springs, Nebraska for showers. As Dianna and I stepped up to the counter to request showers, I rubbed my face and grimaced at the rough feeling of the stubble.

The clerk addressed me as 'sir' no less than four times during the transaction; as if he was trying to drive home a point:

'Sir, you are male and will never pass as a female'

With the sound of each 'sir', a dagger seemed to pierce my heart, deeper and deeper. I headed to the shower, my thoughts heavy with the reminder that without makeup and female clothing, I have the distinct appearance of a male, whether I want to admit it or not.

Once inside the sanctuary of my shower, I let the hot water pound against my skin as I again drifted into the deep, relaxing meditation that I was always able to find under the soothing fingers of a shower nozzle. I found myself once again a member of the male populace while temporarily under suspension from the girls club.

The stubble on my face reminded me once again, that my body was coursing with testosterone, despite nearly a year of hormone replacement therapy and testosterone blockers. The fact remained that my body was producing the male hormone faster than I could block it. My face remained ingrained with thousands of hair follicles, and chiseled with male contours. The only solution now, was to kill the follicles, and reconstruct the shape of my face. I was but days away from those solutions.

As I walked back to the truck to meet Dianna, I stopped for a moment in front of the entrance to the women's restroom. It was just weeks ago that a woman had served up the chilling wake-up call on the CB when she referred to me as a transvestite. Perhaps she had inadvertently done me a favor by calling to my attention the fact that I very much presented myself as a man, dressed as a woman. I had been delusional up to that point, thinking that the hair, nails, makeup, jewelry, and clothing were all it took to be a female.

At this point, I was eager to get through this phase of my transition as quickly as possible, so that I could return to my more comfortable female presentation.

We arrived at the Fontana operating center on the morning of July 4. Dianna went home to spend the holiday with her husband, and would return early the following morning. We had a load for Dallas that I had requested, so that I could be there on July 6 for my consultation with Dr. Raphael, and my facial hair removal session with E-2000. In order to pull this off, we needed to leave by 6:00 am, and Dianna promised to be back to the truck by then.

While parked in the Fontana yard, I kept a low profile in order to avoid anyone I knew, with what was now two days of stubble on my face. After Dianna had departed, I ate a cold can of soup directly from the can while contemplating the phone call that

I needed to make.

Making a phone call to a loved one with whom you have a strained relationship is one of the hardest things a person can do. I knew I had to make this call, and it took every ounce of courage I could muster to punch Cheryl's phone number into the keypad of my cell phone. After staring blankly at the phone for several minutes, with my stomach churning, I finally found the strength to push the send button. After two rings, she answered.

"Hello?"

"Hi Cheryl, it's me. Happy birthday," I said cheerily.

"Thanks," She responded flatly.

"So how are you?"

"I'm fine, how are you?" Her tone remained terse.

"I'm okay. Lots of things have changed in my life. I'm an over the road truck driver now."

"Yeah I know, Laura told me." Her responses remained clipped, and I could sense the awkwardness of this conversation.

"Did she tell you anything else about me?" I wondered if Laura had told my daughter about my transition.

"She said something about you guys splitting up. She didn't really get into the details and I didn't ask."

"Yeah, well relationships don't always work out as you expect them to," I sighed.

"Yeah, tell me about it," she replied curtly. The bitterness in her voice felt like a dagger.

"What do you mean?" I asked sheepishly, knowing exactly what her response would be.

"What do I mean? What do I mean?" She said it twice as if to drive home the folly of my question.

I stared at the steering wheel silently, unable to respond. After a few seconds of awkward silence that seemed more like hours, Cheryl continued the diatribe.

"All my life all I ever wanted was to be loved by you. All I wanted was for you to be there with me. Instead, all I have ever gotten were pieces of you as you drifted in and out of my life. And the times that you were in my life, it seemed like you were always either criticizing me about something, or completely ignoring me."

"Cheryl, I realize that I have not been the best parent in the world, but you have to understand that I have always loved you, and always wanted the best for you, even when we were apart.

"You love me? And you show your love by staying away for years at a time?"

"I regret that now. I regret many of the choices I have made and the things I have done in the past. But that's in the past, and now is the present. I am in the process of making some changes that will correct the problems I had back then, and I am on the path to becoming a different person."

"What can you possibly do to erase the past? Can you turn back the clock and come to my eighth grade graduation that you missed? Can you erase my memories as a little girl wondering why you hated me so much that you abandoned me?"

"No Cheryl, I can't change any of that. All I can do is explain, apologize, and do my best to make up for it. I'm going through something right now that is going to solve many of the personality problems I have had, and make me a better person. It's impossible for me to explain on the phone, but I would like the chance to sit down with you and tell you in person. Are you open to that?"

"Yeah sure." She sounded unconvinced.

"Okay, I'm going to see what I can do to get a load into Daytona, and meet you for dinner. Fair enough?"

"I'll believe it when I see it," she said skeptically.

"OK, can I talk to Jacob and Lucas for a minute?"

After my conversation with Cheryl and my two grandsons, I wearily tossed my cell phone into my purse and gazed blankly through the windshield, oblivious to the activity in the yard around me.

How could I have allowed myself to be such an awful parent? By running away from myself so many years ago, I had also run away from my daughter, who I loved dearly. My own selfish behavior had planted seeds of self-doubt in the mind of a nine-year-old little girl, whom I had left behind to wonder who and where I was, and why I did not love her.

Even during her teenage years when we were reunited and she lived with me in Dallas, I was inattentive and distracted by the preoccupation of my own inner demons. I had somehow become the incarnation of my own mother, and had been unintentionally neglecting my own daughter in the same manner as my mother had neglected me.

Cheryl had every right to be hurt and angry, just as I had been hurt and angered during my childhood. The demons, however, are now gone… I am a different person. With a lot of work, there is hope that the two of us can somehow restore this crumbled relationship. I vowed to do whatever I needed to do. I hoped that Cheryl would do the same.

There are not enough nooks and crannies in the cab of a truck to conceal a box of Twinkies, and I had long ago discovered Dianna's hiding place. After extracting one of the cellophane wrapped treats from the box, I sat on the edge of my berth while removing the wrapper. Thoughts of my daughter as a little girl streamed through my mind like an eight millimeter film, as I rapidly devoured the Twinkie and quickly unwrapped a second one, and then another.

Visions of a sad little girl appeared on the movie screen behind my eyes; she is alone in her room and writing in her diary. Tears welled in my eyes, as I felt the tears of my daughter tumbling onto the pages of her diary, as she wrote the words that nobody would ever see. Her heart cried out in bewilderment to her father who had left her. '*Why did you leave me? What did I do? Why don't you love me?*'

I knew there were no answers to her questions, other than more questions. I had been a coward. Unable to face my own inner turmoil, I had chosen to run away with no regard for the pain and destruction that I would leave behind. Through my own act of selfishness, I had hurt my little girl, and now it was time to repair the damage. I hoped that it is not too late.

I reached into the box for another Twinkie and discovered that it was now empty. Cellophane and cardboard collected about my feet; glaring evidence that I had been on a stress induced binge while reflecting on my parental transgressions. After gathering up the wrappers and stuffing them into the now empty box, I opened the door and climbed down to take it to the nearby trashcan.

After returning to the truck, I closed the curtains, brushed my teeth, changed into pajamas and slid into my berth. Thoughts of my baby girl continued to stream through my mind, as I slowly drifted off to sleep.

I woke up at 5:00 am to the sound of Dianna returning to the truck. Although I was unhappy to have my slumber disturbed, I was pleased that she had returned on time so we could get on our way to Dallas. I was eager to get our load delivered and get to my appointment with Dr. Raphael on Tuesday, and then to my E2000 session.

After a quick shower, I updated my log, performed a pre-trip inspection, and pulled out of the operating center at 5:45.

"How did it go?" Dianna asked as I merged with the eastbound traffic on Interstate 10.

"How did what go?" I glanced over my shoulder at her with a curious look. I had a suspicion what she was referring to, which turned out to be correct.

"Did you call her? Did you call your daughter for her birthday?" Dianna was in the back busily arranging her bed and putting fresh clothing into her cubbyhole.

I shifted into tenth gear and simultaneously changed into the middle lane. I then looked over at my driving partner, now seated in the jump seat. Her face was just barely visible in the early morning light, but I could see enough of her expression to know that she was not wearing her usual grin. This time her face held an expression of genuine concern; conveying the message that she truly wanted me to mend my relationship with Cheryl.

"It went pretty much as I expected it would" I responded

feebly, fully knowing that this would not satisfy my friendly inquisitor.

"Ok, so how did it go? Did you patch things up?"

"Dianna, I'm not sure if I have an answer for that question. I could tell there was a lot of bitterness on her part, for which I can't say I blame her... I just don't know what to say to her at this point."

"How about just telling her that you love her? How about telling her that you have always loved her despite any perceived wrongdoing, and that parents aren't always perfect and are allowed to make mistakes?"

"Yeah Dianna... I guess that will be in my next conversation with her."

Dianna nodded her approval as she opened up the road atlas and began to flip through the pages tracking our route. She then asked without looking up, "So are we on track to get to your appointments in Dallas on time?"

"Unless something unforeseen happens along the way, we should make it to the Dallas OC with plenty of time to spare. It's a little over 1,400 miles and we should get there by 6:00 am tomorrow. I figure we can switch drivers in Tucson, and then again in Abilene."

"Well, we're going to have to stop at a Wal-Mart somewhere along the way." Dianna looked up from the atlas and gazed at me, the familiar grin had returned to her face.

I glanced sideways at her while trying to keep my eyes on the road ahead. "Why do we need to go to Wal-Mart?"

"Someone ate all the Twinkies."

Chapter Twenty
Nouveau Visage

We arrived at the Dallas operating center at 5:00 am, and quickly dropped our loaded trailer into an empty slot. Our truck was due for mandatory preventive maintenance and we had strategically arranged to have it performed at the Dallas operating center. Because of the overnight maintenance, the company pre-authorized a paid night's stay in a nearby hotel.

After we checked the truck in at the shop, Dianna went into the driver's lounge to purchase a new pair of driving gloves at the driver's concession. I stood outside and watched for the hotel shuttle to arrive. There were several male drivers milling around me, and I was pleased that I didn't recognize any of them, and none of them seemed to know me. With my four day growth of facial hair, I simply blended in as 'one of the guys'. My serenity was short lived, however.

"Pam?"

I instinctively spun around at the sound of my name to come face to face with one of the drivers from the Fontana OC.

"Pam, is that you?" He stared at me in disbelief.

It was Andy Helmke, a driver and part time trainer in Fontana. I had met him at one of the annual 'Spring Training' sessions, in which he was one of the instructors. Andy is an extremely likeably man, who had immediately taken me in as a friend.

"Hi Andy" I said sheepishly. As much as I adored this man, he was one of the last people on earth that I wanted to see at this moment.

"Wow, what's going on with your face, Pam? You look like the bearded lady at the circus," he laughed.

"Andy, I am so embarrassed. I'm getting electrolysis today and I had to grow this out. I know I look hideous. I'm sorry."

"Don't be sorry, Pam. I understand. I think you are an awesome person for doing what you are doing."

"Thanks, Andy" I said as I stared at the ground. I really wanted to crawl into a hole at this moment.

"Well, I gotta run, Pam. I'm running behind schedule. I hope to see you soon," he smiled.

"See you later Andy," I sighed as he walked toward the sea of orange trucks. He was one of my favorite male drivers in the company, one who I had fleetingly imagined I could one day be with. All hope was now dashed, as he would forever remember me as the bearded lady.

Dianna and I boarded the shuttle to the hotel. After checking in, I took a quick shower, and grabbed a cab for my consultation with Dr. Raphael. Dianna was dozing, with the television remote control in her hand when I left.

Dr. Peter Raphael is one of the partners at the American Institute for Plastic surgery, located north of Dallas, in the suburb of Plano. I arrived at 7:55 am, five minutes early for my 8:00 appointment. Upon my entry, I found myself in a superbly appointed lobby, with hardwood floors, plush sofas and chairs, and walls covered with exquisite artwork accentuated by soft track lighting. Had I not known better, I could have been in an art gallery. As I walked from the entrance to the receptionist window, I gazed about in awe at the magnificence of this office.

Behind the window, a stunningly beautiful woman greeted

me with a dazzling smile. As I stepped up to the window, I observed two equally stunning women behind her, each performing various office tasks. Clearly, these three women were the product of the skills performed by the surgeons at this clinic.

"You must be Pamela," she said cheerily. "I'm Kaylee."

"Hello Kaylee, nice to meet you," I smiled meekly. I was dressed in blue jeans and an androgynous polo shirt; and sported dangling earrings that were neither masculine nor feminine. The four-day growth of stubble on my face eliminated even the slightest possibility that she would view me as a female. However, as distraught about my appearance as I felt, there was no point in worrying about her impression of me. I just needed to get through this.

The beautiful smiling young woman handed me a clipboard and asked that I fill out the attached sheaf of papers. I accepted the clipboard from her, and took a seat on one of the plush sectionals, where I began to fill out the all so familiar paperwork. Having become so proficient at this task, I was finished in just a few minutes, and strode back to the window to hand them back to Kaylee.

"Go ahead and have a seat. Katherine will be with you in a few minutes." She smiled, while removing my completed paperwork from the clipboard. As unlikely as it was, I inwardly hoped that Dr. Raphael was skilled enough to make me as beautiful as Kaylee.

I returned to the same sectional on which I had filled out my paperwork, and gazed around the office. There were several women seated in the waiting area; some of which sported bandages on various parts of their faces. Curious eyes peered at me over the tops of magazines, undoubtedly in wonderment of this strange looking person with the long hair and fingernails, dangling earrings, and facial stubble. At this point, I was no longer concerned about the stares. I simply wanted to get on with it, so I could move forward with my life.

Within a few minutes, yet another incredibly beautiful woman appeared in the lobby, and approached me with a brilliant smile on her face.

"Pamela?"

"Yes." I sprung to my feet and tried my best to smile.

"Hi Pamela, I'm Katherine. I spoke with you on the phone." She extended her right hand in an offer of a handshake, which I eagerly accepted. "Come on back with me."

Katherine spun around and headed to the back offices. I followed her into a room, which contained a small desk, a few chairs, a stool, and a photographic backdrop. Katherine retrieved a camera from the desk.

"The first thing I'm going to do is take some pictures of your face, Pamela. Just stand in front of the backdrop."

"Oh geez, I look like crap," I said while rubbing my scruffy face. "You don't really want to take pictures of me looking like this."

Katherine laughed, "Don't be silly. With the magic of Photoshop, we'll have you clean-shaven faster than even the most expensive shaver can! The doctor will then use these photos to determine what procedures would be best to feminize your face."

I smiled weakly as I stood in front of the light blue paper. She proceeded to take pictures from the front, each side, and various angles. When she finished, she asked me to take a seat and wait for the doctor. She then slipped through the doorway, gently closing the door behind her.

I discovered a stack of magazines on the small table next to my chair, and sifted through them in search of something interesting to read. There were a couple of editions of Cosmopolitan, Glamour, and People. I selected one of the copies of People Magazine, and began to leaf through it mindlessly. My thoughts were elsewhere.

After forty-five minutes and three magazines, the door flew open. Katherine appeared, holding several sheets of paper in her hand. Following closely behind her was a man in a white smock, who stood at least three inches shorter than she did. He appeared to be in his mid to late forties, with dark brown hair.

"Hello Pamela, I'm Dr. Raphael. I understand you want some feminization work done on your face." He smiled, as he extended his hand.

"Hello Dr. Raphael, nice to meet you." I returned the smile, while gently shaking his hand.

Katherine handed the papers to Dr. Raphael, taking a seat at the desk. The doctor sat on the small rolling stool, wheeling himself close to my chair. He leaned toward me, holding the papers so that I could see what appeared to be several rows of before and after photos. On the left of each row were color printouts of the various photos that Katherine had taken of me, with the stubble magically erased. To the right of each of these photos was a picture of a female in an identical pose. She bore only a faint resemblance to me.

After methodically going through each of the before and after photos, and the main differences in each, the doctor recommended a variety of surgical procedures that would accomplish that change in appearance. As he meticulously explained each procedure, and what it would accomplish, Katherine began writing. When he was finished, Katherine handed me a form on which was listed each of the procedures that the doctor recommended for me. I took the proposal from Katherine, and my eyes quickly darted to the bottom line.

"Eighteen thousand dollars?" I exclaimed while looking up from the paper at Katherine and then at Dr. Raphael.

"The cost covers not only the surgical procedures, but also the surgical room and anesthesia," Katherine replied pithily, as if the fact that I did not have to pay extra to be unconscious during the surgery would make the cost more palatable.

"It's going to take me forever to save that kind of money. I don't suppose you have an installment plan, do you?" I asked desperately.

"No Pam, I'm afraid we don't," Katherine replied compassionately. I was sure that I was not the first patient to ask this question, and her response came as no surprise.

"I didn't think so, but I had to ask," I smiled. "Is there any way I could break this down into multiple surgeries so I can at least get some of it done now?"

Dr. Raphael pulled a gold pen from the pocket of his white smock and took the proposal from me. After circling several items, he handed it to Katherine, who then looked it over, began punching into her calculator, made some notations on the paper, and then handed it back to the doctor.

After examining the proposal for a moment, Dr. Raphael handed it back to me and then used his pen as a pointer as he went over the details.

Dr. Raphael smiled, "Pam, I highly recommend we do the rhinoplasty… or nose job as most people know it, plus the lip lift, chin contour and lip augmentation. This will give you an immediate feminine appearance. We can do the work on your forehead, brows and jaw line on the next phase."

I studied the notations that Katherine had made on the proposal for a moment, and then looked at Dr. Raphael.

"Okay, $9,100.00 for starters. I think I can pull that off, even if I have to borrow some of the money. Can we schedule something for September?"

"Sure you can Pam. Katherine will take it from here." Dr. Raphael stood, extending his hand while he spoke.

After shaking hands with Dr. Raphael, the three of us exited the room. Dr. Raphael headed back to his office. Katherine and I went to the appointment desk to schedule my surgery date. After a few minutes of shuffling our calendars, we settled on a date. I would have my first facial surgery on September 15.

From Dr. Raphael's office, I caught a cab to the E2000 facility in North Dallas. I arrived there at 10:30 and after only a brief wait, the receptionist ushered me into one of the treatment rooms. Three women greeted me as I entered the room.

"Hello Pam, I'm Bren. I spoke with you on the phone." The older of the three smiled. "This is Andrea and Carly, they will be your technicians today. I will be in and out and will be periodically administering the local anesthesia, as needed."

"Nice to meet all of you," I smiled. I'm eager to get this mess off my face," I said as I rubbed the stubble for what I hoped to be the last time.

I gazed around at the starkly decorated treatment room. Aside from a few posters on the walls, there was very little decor. In the center of the room was the treatment table. On either side of the table were the electrolysis machines, and stools on which the technicians would sit.

Bren patted the treatment table invitingly. "Go ahead and lay back on the table, Pam. As soon as you get settled, I will give you a couple of injections, and the girls can get started."

I obediently lay back on the table and watched as Bren prepared the syringe. My eyes felt as though they were going to pop out of my head, as she moved the needle toward my face, pushing it into my skin. After briefly pressing the plunger, she removed the needle, only to pierce another part of my face and press the plunger again.

I nearly screamed in pain when she moved the needle to my upper lip and penetrated that area. Relief, however, came within seconds, as the skin on my face slowly transformed into numb plastic.

Andrea and Carly sat on each side of me, as I stretched out on the treatment table. Once they were confident that my face was completely numb, they began the treatment. Bren stood by and watched.

"Are we going to be able to get all this crap off of my face today?" I mumbled through my plastic lips.

"Pam, the average male face has around 10,000 hairs. Some males have as many as 40,000 individual hairs on their face. A tech can usually kill 100-150 hairs an hour…but then there is always re-growth, which means we have to treat the same follicle many times. Looking at you, I would say you're probably on the low end. I can't say for sure, but I would guess that you will need over 100 hours of work."

I had learned from my previous electrolysis sessions that the process is slow, tedious, and mostly painful, with every individual hair treated one at a time. Each insertion of the tiny metal probe into the hair follicle applies electric current to destroy the hair root. It feels like a bee sting. Nerve centers are scattered about the face, so the pain levels vary from spot to spot. In some parts of the face, it feels like the technician is simply tweezing the hairs. However, in most parts of the face, particularly around the lips and nostrils, it feels more like the sting of a wasp. A one-hour session of electrolysis can often leave the patient with the feeling that she just stuck her face into a beehive.

Bren continuously reappeared in the treatment room to give me additional shots to keep my face numb. The shots were painful, especially around the lips; but the pain was short lived as the anesthesia continued to work its magic.

We finished at 4:30. Bren once again explained to me that the six-hour session was not enough to clear my entire face, and that I would need more treatments.

"Many of the hairs we killed today will grow back, so expect a great deal of re-growth," she said while preparing my bill. "Although the girls were able to remove a large amount of the facial hair today, and there will be a definite improvement in your appearance, there is still a lot of work needed."

My lips were still numb, so I simply nodded silently.

She went on with her post treatment consultation. "Your face is continuing to swell up due to the cauterization of the follicles and the injections. The swelling will go down gradually over the next 3-4 days."

I paid Bren, and then stepped into the restroom to inspect the work they had done. When I looked into the mirror, I was horrified at what I saw. I barely looked human, my face badly swollen. Katherine had been right when she said my face would be swollen like a pumpkin. I looked like the Elephant Man!

I then called Candy. She had offered to treat me to a haircut and style as a gift for my birthday, after which we had planned to go out to dinner. I felt so appalled by my appearance that I tried to beg off, but she just shrugged it off and told me not to be concerned about it.

My sister arrived to pick me up 30 minutes later, and we headed directly to her favorite hair salon. There, she treated me to a nice, new hairstyle. Afterward, we had dinner at one of her favorite Cajun restaurants. Our waiter was a charming young man who spoke with a French accent.

"I'm getting a new face," I said jokingly to him, as a way of explaining my distorted face.

"Oui, nouveau visage," he smiled.

Candy and I laughed.

While enjoying our meals, I told Candy about my plans to become an owner operator, explaining the financial benefits.

"Have you thought about the potential risks?" she asked with a concerned look on her face.

"Of course," I smiled. The biggest risk is if I do not keep the truck moving. As long as I stay focused and work hard, I will earn enough money to cover the expenses, and make a decent profit."

After we had finished dinner, Candy drove me back to the hotel. I called Dianna to tell her that I was on my way.

"How did it go?" she asked.

"My face is swollen. Promise you won't laugh when you see me"

"How bad is it swollen?"

"Pretty bad. I look like the Elephant Man."

"Well, I got some good news today" Dianna said cheerfully.

"Really? What?"

"I've been accepted to the Sears dedicated fleet. I will be a local driver, and will be home every night. No more over the road for me."

"That's great! When do you start?"

"In three weeks. August 1ˢᵗ"

"That's perfect" I exclaimed. "That's right around the time that I will become an owner operator."

By the time I finished my conversation with Dianna, Candy had pulled in front of the hotel, and we both got out of the car.

"Thank you for treating me to a haircut and dinner. You really are a good big sister," I said as I gave her a hug.

"You are very welcome… and good luck with your new venture as an owner operator. Knowing you, you will do great" she smiled, walking back toward the driver door of her car. "And if you need me to help you out with a loan for your facial surgery, let me know. We've got to get your face fixed, don't we?"

I stood outside the hotel entrance for a moment while watching her pull away. I felt very fortunate to have a sister who was so supportive of me, despite the fact that she has always been my worst critic.

Dianna was seated at the small round table watching a movie on the television when I walked into the room. She looked up at me, immediately breaking into hysterical laughter.

"Oh my god, Pam. You DO look like the Elephant Man" she chortled.

"Dianna, you promised you wouldn't laugh!"

"No I didn't!" she continued laughing, now even heartier.

"You did"

"No I didn't. You asked me to, but I never did."

Now we were both laughing.

"Dianna, quit making me laugh. My face hurts."

"Your face hurts? Hah, it's killing me!"

We were both now roaring with laughter.

The next morning Dianna and I took turns taking showers in the hotel room, and rode the shuttle back to the operating center to get our truck.

Once we were in the truck, we checked the Qualcomm, and discovered that we had a load assignment. We were to pick up a load of plastic pellets in the Dallas suburb of Arlington, and take it to Hartford, Connecticut. With my stubble free, yet peculiarly swollen face, I guided the truck toward Arlington, to pick up our load to get us back on the road.

Chapter Twenty-One
Exodus

The last three weeks of July seemed to have flown by, as Dianna and I counted down the days until both of our careers would take a turn for the better.

We were jubilant as we crawled along Interstate 80, amid the bumper-to-bumper evening traffic through a congested Chicago. Headed to Des Moines, we were to pick up a loaded trailer and take it to the Fontana yard. Our partnership would end after this run.

Dianna would take a few days off before starting her new assignment with Sears dedicated, and I would get a load to Charlotte where I would turn in my company truck, and pick up my leased truck. It was a major milestone for each of us, as Dianna would finally get her wish to be home every evening with her husband, and I would become an owner operator and once again regain control of my life.

The feeling of exhilaration for the two of us was evident as we danced in our seats and sang along to David Lee Roth and Van Halen's 'Jump', which was playing at full volume on the satellite radio. Our jubilance did not escape the attention of the drivers in the lanes on either side of us, as our CB crackled with comments such as '*Show us your tits girls*' and '*Pull over and I'll show you how to party*'. Despite the lewdness, we found humor in the comments from the male drivers, which only added to our jubilance. Nothing could dampen our euphoria; not even the rush hour stop and go traffic of Chicago.

We finally broke through the congestion, and at 5:45 pm, Dianna pulled the truck into the Pilot in Minooka, just west of the city. After a quick bite to eat and a restroom break, she pulled the truck back onto Interstate 80, and I went into the sleeper berth for some much needed rest.

As I tossed and turned in the berth trying to shake the excitement from my mind so that I could go to sleep, I ran my fingers gently across my face. I had done this many times since my session with E2000 and was still in awe of the smoothness that I felt, contrary to the rough sandpaper-like texture to which I had become so accustomed. I rolled over onto my back, nestled my head into the pillow, then closed my eyes. As I reposed silently, the only sound I heard was the soft drone of the Cummins diesel that propelled the truck westward toward California, and the advent of my new business.

The events of the past six months seem to have occurred over six years, yet had gone by in a blur before my eyes. I had overcome fear, had bounded over hurdles, and had prevailed against unexpected obstacles.

The future looked bright as well. In the short term, I was just days away from realizing my goal of acquiring my own truck. Over the next few months, I would have the surgery that would correct my appearance; I would reunite with my daughter; and I would begin planning for my triumphant return to the publishing business.

My vivid thoughts slowly transformed into opaque images as I drifted away toward a peaceful slumber.

Thirty-six hours later, after picking up our load in Des Moines, and a stop in Denver for one last shopping foray and manicures, we arrived at the Fontana OC.

After I backed the trailer into an empty slot and set the brakes, Dianna came to life and emerged from the sleeper berth.

"Well Dianna, this is it. The end of our partnership," I said halfheartedly.

"Yeah, at least it is ending on a good note…unlike the way your last partnership ended." She laughed, while gathering up her clothing and stuffing them into her travel bag.

"It's been a good time. I am going to miss you… and of course your delicious meatloaf," I laughed.

"Here's a going away present for you," she chuckled.

I looked up just in time to see a box of Twinkies sailing through the air toward me. Miraculously, the box landed on my lap. I peered inside to find it more than halfway full of the delicious, cream filled treats.

"Thank you Dianna, I will savor every delicious bite," I snickered.

After Dianna had gathered all of her personal belongings, we both climbed down from the truck and headed toward the drivers lounge. It was 7:00 am, and the yard was bustling with activity. As we approached the double glass doors that led into the lounge, the familiar vans pulled up into the drive; the passenger compartments filled with students, eager to learn how to drive a truck. It was difficult for me to comprehend that a mere six months ago, I was among them.

Many of the familiar faces were in the lounge as we entered. The trainers were at their usual table in the corner. At another table, Alice and Mikey were engaged in an animated conversation. Russ and his staff were busy behind the food counter, serving hungry drivers. CNN blared on one television, and the Weather Channel on the other. Sly and Stella were busy behind the fuel desk tending to the needs of drivers, and office personnel bustled into the back offices with arm-loads of papers, and steaming cups of coffee in hand. It was just another day in the drivers lounge.

After a quick visit to the restroom, Dianna and I ordered

breakfast, and joined Alice and Mikey at their table.

"Good morning kids," I said cheerily as Dianna and I set our trays on the table and sat down. "This is my driving partner, Dianna. Dianna, this is Alice and Mikey."

"Nice to meet both of you" Dianna smiled. After the perfunctory handshakes were completed, Alice wasted no time in getting her usual banter underway.

"Damn, you are a tall one Dianna. How tall are you?"

"I'm six foot two." Dianna beamed proudly while shoveling a spoonful of oatmeal into her mouth.

"Well, you must be quite a woman to put up with this one as a partner." Alice jabbed at me playfully.

"Well, aside from her Twinkie addiction, she's a fairly decent person," Dianna answered with her contagious laugh.

"Yeah, but she sucks at karaoke. Every time she picks up that karaoke microphone at Loretta's the place clears out." Alice laughed.

Mikey added to the teasing, "She's a halfway decent pool player though… when she manages to keep the balls on the table."

"Wow, I had no idea there was a 'Pam roast' scheduled for today." I chuckled, as I pushed my empty plate to the side.

Alice changed the subject and asked, "So, are you still planning on becoming an owner operator, Pam?"

"Yes, Alice…this is the last day that Dianna and I will be driving partners. She is transferring over to Sears dedicated, and I am heading to Charlotte to get my lease truck."

"Be prepared to work your ass off, woman. Like I told you, if you want to make money as a lease operator, you've got to keep the truck moving," she said while glancing up at the clock on the wall. "Speaking of which, I need to get rolling. Nice meeting you Dianna."

"I need to get to work myself," Mikey added as he stood up. "Nice to meet you, Dianna… and good luck to you Pam."

"Nice meeting you guys too," Dianna said, while unfolding herself from the chair. "I'm going to head over to the trainer's table and say hello to Sponge Bob."

After the trio had departed, I rose from my chair and walked over to the concession stand to refill my coffee cup. Ed Paul, the Loss Prevention Manager was filling his cup, and I stood by waiting for him to finish. As I locked eyes with him, I detected an evil grin on his face, which gave me the feeling that he was up to something. I walked back to the table with my steaming cup of coffee in hand, and the ominous feeling that he knew something that I did not.

As I sipped my coffee, the sight of Nicole walking into the lounge caught my attention. Although apprehensive, I was happy to see her. We exchanged waves as she headed over to get a cup of coffee. In a few minutes, she joined me at my table.

"Hello stranger, how have you been?" I asked. I held no animosity toward her, in spite of the uncouth manner in which she had terminated our partnership.

"I'm good. I am on truck-rail now. I spend all my days running around picking up trailers from the rail yards, and I'm home every night," she smiled. "You look great! How have you been?"

"Thank you. I'm doing pretty good… going to become an owner operator. I'm heading to Charlotte to pick up my lease truck."

"Wow, that's awesome dude!" she replied enthusiastically. "You will do great, I'm sure."

"How are things with you and Rachael?" I asked.

Nicole frowned for a moment, and then answered. "Oh, well… we sort of broke up a few months ago," she said morosely.

"Oh, I'm sorry to hear that." I couldn't think of anything else to say.

"It's ok. I'm over her now," she smiled.

"That's good." I returned the smile and took a sip of my coffee.

"Did you hear about Terry?" Nicole asked.

"Terry? Terry who?" I looked at her quizzically.

"Terry… Terry my almost driving partner. Don't you

remember him?"

"Oh, yeah. The guy with the drugs in your truck. What about him?"

"Apparently he got a job with another trucking company. A few months ago, he rear ended a church van on the freeway. The van caught on fire and killed nine people. The cops did a drug test on him and discovered that he was high on meth at the time."

"Jesus Christ" I muttered softly.

Nicole put her hand on mine and sighed. "Pam, I'm really sorry about how things ended with us. Rachel really had me messed up in the head, and then all that crap was happening with you, and well… I just lost it. I really did enjoy being your partner."

"It's ok Nicole… I understand," I said, as I patted her hand tenderly with my free hand.

Gennipher suddenly appeared next to our table on her way to the offices.

"Hail, hail, the gang's all here" she said in a singsong manner. "It's good to see you two kids sitting together playing nicely."

"Good morning Gennipher." Nicole smiled.

"Hey Gennipher," I added.

"I wish I could chat, but I've got to run…good luck on your new venture as an owner operator, Pam. I know you will do great!" she said as she scurried toward the door to the office area.

Nicole took the last sip of her coffee. "I've got to get going too. Pam, it was nice seeing you, and good luck."

We both stood and exchanged warm hugs, just as we had always done during our days of driving together. After Nicole had departed, I sat back down to enjoy the remainder of my coffee. I glanced at the clock on the wall. It was now 8:00 am in California, which meant it was 11:00 in Charlotte. I dialed Rebecca's number on my cell phone. I reached her voice mail greeting, and left her a message.

"Hi Rebecca, it's Pam Anders. I'm in Fontana and I'm going to be getting a load to Charlotte so I can do the paperwork and get my lease truck. I should be there in a couple of days."

A moment after I had laid my phone on the table, it rang. A glance at the caller ID informed me that it was Rebecca.

"Oh Pam, I was just about to call you when you called and left your message. Have you talked to your manager?"

"No, not yet. Why?"

"Pam I am so sorry, but they turned you down." She said sympathetically.

"They turned me down? Who turned me down? You told me I was approved!" I asked incredulously.

"Yes Pam, I told you that you had been approved for a lease. But remember, I also told you that we had to submit your owner operator application to corporate for their approval?"

"Yes, I remember you saying that, but you told me it would be based on my driving record. I have a perfect record."

"Yes Pam, I see that you have a good driving record. But apparently they made this decision based on other factors, and there is nothing I can do to change it."

"Other factors? What other factors?" I was practically screaming into the phone.

"I don't know the details. All I know is that one of the higher ups at the Fontana operating center filed a report stating that there have been some disciplinary problems with you. Whoever it was said that they would not recommend that you become an owner operator."

"Geez, I have disciplinary problems? Who was it that said that?" I was so angry that I was tempted to throw my cell phone across the room.

"I don't know who it was Pam. You might want to call corporate and talk to them. Maybe you can get them to change their decision."

"Ok, who do I need to talk to at corporate?"

"His name is Mike Leary. He is the one who made the final decision."

The sound of Mike Leary's name made me want to vomit. Of all people in the company to have to call and beseech to reconsider this decision, he was the last one.

"Thank you Rebecca" I said meekly.

"I'm so sorry Pam. Good luck." Rebecca said as she hung up the phone.

I headed back to the offices and straight to Gregg's cubicle. He was just finishing a phone call as I approached, and frowned at me while hanging up the phone.

"Hello Pam. I'm guessing you got the bad news?" he said deadpanned.

"Yeah, I got the bad news" I fumed. What the hell is this about me being a 'disciplinary problem'?"

"Pam, it has to do with that dispute about your use of the women's bathroom I guess. A lot of feathers got ruffled when you hired a lawyer."

"What was I supposed to do, just roll over and let them deny my rights to use the restroom? They're calling that a disciplinary problem? Now I'm being denied the opportunity to become an owner operator because of it?"

Gregg nodded solemnly, "Actually, it's even worse than that, Pam."

"Worse? Worse in what way?"

"Pam, they're putting you back on Western Regional. You will only be running up and down the west coast."

"Gregg, I can't make a living on Western Regional. I have based my entire budget on being an owner operator. I will starve to death!"

"Pam, I wish there was something I could…"

Gregg looked over my shoulder, and I spun around. Ed Paul had walked up to Gregg's cubical and was now standing behind me. He had a smirk of satisfaction on his face.

"Ed, is there anything we can do to help Pam out here?" Gregg asked.

Ed replied smugly, "It's not my decision to make. I just filed my report on Mr. Anders. My feeling is that he is not a team player and is very unstable. Corporate made the final decision, not me."

"Every instinct in my body commanded me to punch this putrid little man in the face, and it took every ounce of prudence I could muster to restrain myself. Instead, I chose diplomacy, as I stared angrily into the evil eyes of Ed Paul.

"Simply because I fought for my legal right to use the restroom that corresponds to my gender, you have labeled me 'unstable'? 'Not a team player'?" I fumed.

Ed looked at me with the smirk still painted on his face as he replied arrogantly, "Sir, you can hate me if you want, but the fact remains; you will never be an owner operator with this company, period!"

I took a deep breath before replying. I fought to keep my clenched fists at my sides.

"Ed, I don't hate you… I don't hate anyone. I just dislike people in varying degrees, and on a scale of one to ten, you are an eleven."

I resisted the temptation to push this little man out of my way, but instead walked around him, as I left Gregg's cubicle and stormed back into the drivers lounge and through the double glass doors out into the yard.

As I walked to my truck, an assortment of emotions was boiling like a stew inside my brain. I was angry with Ed Paul for his insensitivity, as he repeatedly referred to me as a male. I was frustrated with the seemingly endless barrage of bigotry with which management confronted me. I was hurting emotionally. Moreover, the revelation that Schneider would not allow me to become an owner operator was a tremendous blow to my spirits and my financial plans. However, despite it all, I refused to concede to defeat.

Dianna and I had accumulated a sizable collection of trucker magazines that we had picked up at magazine racks at truck stops along the way. The shortage of truck drivers remained rampant, which meant that each of the magazines was replete with advertisements recruiting drivers. I spent the next several hours in the truck going through the ads for lease opportunities, selecting the ones that sounded the most appealing, and making phone calls. After lengthy conversations with the recruiters at five different companies, I settled on one that had made the most appealing offer.

Stugel Trucking, based in Fontana, is just a few blocks down the street from Schneider's Fontana operating center. They are a small trucking company, in comparison to the behemoth Schneider, but sizable enough to have plenty of opportunity for an eager driver such as myself. An additional factor in my choice was the fact that they have a terminal in Dallas, which would ensure plenty of opportunity to visit my boys. Linda, the recruiter, had also ensured me that there would be occasional loads to Florida, which would allow me to visit Cheryl and her two boys.

After giving Linda the information she needed in order to perform the perfunctory background check, we arranged an interview for 1:00 pm. I headed back into the driver's lounge with newfound enthusiasm, and took a shower. Dressed and made up to look my professional best, I walked the quarter of a mile to the Stugel facility.

After a brief and informal interview with Linda, I took the mandatory drug-screening test. Linda had already pulled my driving record from the DMV, which she assured me was perfect. It would take a couple of hours more to receive the results of my background check, which I was confident would also be clean.

It was time for me to disclose the truth. There was no sense in fooling myself, knowing that the background check would reveal my past.

"Linda, my background report will reveal that I have had no misdemeanor or felony convictions, nor are there any warrants out for me. However, there is one thing that you will probably discover about me that I should tell you now so you don't think I was withholding it."

Linda looked at me curiously, "What is that?"

I gulped nervously before replying, "I am a transsexual woman. My background report will most likely reveal that up until six months ago I had a male name. I hope this doesn't affect my chances to become a driver here."

Linda laughed, "Actually, I already guessed that. Pam, as long as you are a safe, reliable driver and get along with your dispatcher and the other drivers… and of course the customers, that doesn't matter one bit."

I sighed with relief, "Linda, you have my word that I will be one of the best drivers in the fleet. So, when do I start?" I asked enthusiastically.

"Ok let's work on the presumption that your drug test and your background check come back ok. Can you be here for a half day of orientation tomorrow?"

"Absolutely!" I exclaimed eagerly. What time?"

"Be here at 7:00 am. We require that you take a quick road test with one of the other drivers. After that, you will spend a couple of hours on paperwork and procedures. Then, you get to pick out your truck and meet your dispatcher," she smiled.

We both stood simultaneously and shook hands. "It's a deal. See you then!"

I was practically walking on air as I left the Stugel facility and walked back to the Schneider operating center. After a brief meeting with Sandra and Gregg, I tendered my resignation, with the promise to have my truck emptied out in two days.

The following morning, after one final shower and breakfast in the drivers lounge, I headed over to my new trucking company. The day started out with a road test with one of the Stugel drivers in one of the thirteen-speed International trucks. It took me some getting used to the thirteen speed after having driven the ten-speed Freightliner for the past six months, but before long I mastered it. I then spent two hours in a meeting room with the various department staffers, who went over everything from logging procedures to payroll. Later in the day, I met my dispatcher, Charlotte. I found everyone in the company to be friendly and cordial, and they all made an effort to make me feel welcome.

After the orientation was completed, Linda walked with me out to the yard to select my truck. A dozen brand new 2006 International trucks reposed in a row: Three blue, six white, two green, and one cherry red. My eyes immediately locked on the red truck. I knew immediately that this was going to be 'my truck' as I walked up to her, and opened the door. I climbed aboard and gazed at the interior. This was my new home. I climbed back down and smiled at Linda.

"I want this one."

"You got it Pam. We just need to go back inside and type up the paperwork and it's all yours."

I stepped back and admired my new truck. She was a beautiful sight, and I was eager to start driving her. My dream to be an owner operator was about to come true, with a beautiful cherry red truck, and with a new company to boot.

I stared for a moment at the number imprinted the sides of my truck, and then turned to Linda who was busy writing on her clipboard.

"I am going to name her 'BJ'," I exclaimed proudly.

"BJ? That's an interesting name for a truck," she laughed. Why do you want to name your truck BJ?"

"It's her number… Three Seven Three Eight" I smiled.

Linda gazed at the number and read it aloud several times, "Three-seven-three-eight… three-seven-three-eight… thirty seven thirty eight… How do you get 'BJ' out of the number Three-seven-three-eight?"

"I know it sounds complicated Linda, but it's really fairly simple," I smiled. "Give it some thought and I'm sure you'll get it. If you don't figure it out, I will tell you someday."

Chapter Twenty-Two
Jaxon

I guided BJ into the Petro Truck Stop at exit 21 on Interstate 80, in Sparks, Nevada. After refueling, I backed into a parking slot and set the brakes. I had left Sacramento at 1:45 pm with a load of lawnmowers destined for Baltimore, and had made it to the Sparks Petro at 4:00. Luckily, there were plenty of empty slots from which to choose.

I changed the status on my log to "*Off Duty*," and completed my post trip inspection. After climbing back into the cab and entering the inspection on my log, I mused on the date; January 27, 2006. On this very date, exactly one year ago, I had pulled a big orange truck out of the Schneider yard in Fontana for my first run as a professional truck driver.

BJ's long red hood sparkled under the lights of the parking lot, as I stared blankly through the glass at the activity around me. I reflected on the events of the past twelve months. During that period, I had made my successful debut as a female; had my name legally changed; had overcome a legal question as to my use of the women's restroom; encountered bigoted law enforcement personnel; and forged new friendships. During the first six months, I had driven with two different partners, and still maintained a friendship with one of them. I had also maintained close friendships with Alice, Gennipher, and Marla, all of whom I kept in contact by telephone and occasional visits. I was now a familiar face at Loretta's, and had developed friendships with most of its staff, and many of its patrons.

During the past six months, BJ and I had travelled across the country dozens of times, and hauled thousands of tons of freight. Absent now was the restriction of the governed Schneider trucks, which were limited to 65 miles per hour. I was now capable of keeping pace with the 75 mph speed limits in Arizona, New Mexico, and other states. I push the hours of service to the maximum, and maintain an average of 600 miles per day. On many days, I exceed 700 miles. The money is now rolling in at a steady pace, and I am able to afford the electrolysis and facial surgeries that I need, and save money for my GRS.

Hurricane Katrina had managed to thwart my original plan to have the initial stage of surgery performed on September 15th. After the storm devastated New Orleans, a call had gone out to any truck drivers who were willing to help FEMA with the efforts to get supplies to the victims. I put off the surgery so that I could help the cause, by hauling trailer loads of bottled water into the city from various distribution points across the country.

On October 7th Dr. Raphael performed the rhinoplasty, lip lift, chin contour and lip augmentation that we had originally scheduled for September.

Although I was very satisfied with his work, I chose a different surgeon in Guadalajara, Mexico for the remainder of the bone work that needed to be done, and had traveled to Mexico in late November to have that work performed.

My female presentation was now nearly complete, with the exception of the persistent facial hairs that were still scattered about my face.

I had discovered a mother-daughter electrolysis team in West Los Angeles, near Santa Monica, and had made frequent visits to Layla and her daughter for two-hour sessions, at which they both worked on me simultaneously. I had managed to build up a strong resistance to the pain, and somehow endured marathon treatments. I often stopped on my way out of Los Angeles with a load, parking my 70-foot truck on Santa Monica or Wilshire Boulevard. BJ frequently received not one, but three parking tickets at a time from the City of Los Angeles. Most of them remain unpaid.

The week before Christmas of 2005, I had taken my two sons to the Aerosmith and Motley Crue concert in Dallas. They finally saw me for the first time as Pamela when I picked them up in the school parking lot. Neither of them displayed even the slightest hint of shock when they saw me. Prior to the concert, while enjoying dinner at a Mexican restaurant, I could not resist asking,

"So what do you think? Neither of you has made a comment."

"About what?" Greg and Steven asked in unison.

"About the way I look?" I replied while making a sweeping motion along my face.

"Oh, that? No biggie. You're still the same person inside, right?" Greg said while taking a bite of a taco.

"Is this what you meant about turning into a frog?" Steven asked.

"Yes, Steven. This is exactly what I meant. And yes, I am still the same person inside."

"Awesome! I'm glad you're not a frog," said Steven.

"Cool!" added Greg.

My daughter Cheryl had been a different story. I had not been able to conjure up the courage to tell her about my transition, and had presented as androgynously as possible when I stopped in Daytona to have dinner with her and her boys. Their curious stares made it apparent that my feminine facial features, acrylic nails, soft voice, and long hair had not escaped their attention; yet none of them asked questions.

The chill between Cheryl and I had begun to melt away as we talked more and more on the phone, and over dinner. I knew, however, that there was much effort still needed to restore our relationship, and many amends needed by both parties. I was in constant turmoil over how she would take the revelation of my gender change, and how it would affect the chances of our reconciliation.

The ringing of my cell phone interrupted my reverie. A quick glance at the display revealed that the caller was Alice.

"Hello Alice" I answered cheerfully.

"Hey slut, what are you up to?" Alice was in her usual jovial form.

"Nothing much, I just parked at the Petro in Sparks. I'm going to shut down here."

"You bitch! I wish I were there. You're going to go in and play in the casino, right?"

"Well, I hadn't really thought about it. I have a load going to…"

"Pam, watch out for the poker dealer with the long blond hair… Her name is Sherilynn or Carrielynn or something like that. I think she's in cahoots with some of the regulars."

"Well actually I was going to just grab a bite to…"

"Yeah, go to the restaurant inside the casino and get the $6.99 prime rib. It's really good."

"Okay Alice, I'll check it out."

"Call me tomorrow and tell me how you did in the casino. I am so jealous!" Alice disconnected before I could reply.

The Alamo Casino is adjacent and connected to the Petro truck stop. On my way to the restaurant to have dinner before retiring for the night, I walked through the casino, past the sea of slot machines, the rows of blackjack tables, the roulette wheels, and the poker pit. Gambling is a passion of mine, and I was having a difficult time staying focused on my normal routine of getting to bed early and getting on the road early. My load was not due in Baltimore for two days, and I had plenty of time. My desire to gamble prevailed.

After extracting $200 from the ATM, I headed over to the

blackjack area and found a table at which only one other person was playing. Blackjack is one of the many casino games in which the gambler is playing against the house rather than against the other players. It is also a game of probabilities, and if one knows what the odds are in various situations, and follows a few simple rules, they can master the game. I had mastered the game of blackjack many years ago, and although it has been awhile since I played, it would not take me long to regain my rhythm.

For the next several hours, I migrated from one blackjack table to another, as the cards went from hot to cold, and I endured the ebbs and tides of fortune. When the cards got cold and my simple rules of play were not working, I simply picked up my chips and moved to another table and another dealer, where I would play as long as the cards worked in my favor. I kept a watchful eye on the other players, and if I found myself at a table with a horrible player who was disrupting the flow of cards with his poor choices, I simply drifted to another table. Thus has always been my method of winning at blackjack.

As I trekked from one table to the next, I could not help but notice the man who had been observing me for the past hour while playing the slots. He moved from machine to machine, pumping money into the device and pulling the handle; often times pouring winnings into the plastic cup the casino provided. His eyes were on me whenever I looked in his direction, and he made no effort to conceal his interest in me. As I changed tables, I began surreptitiously watching for him, and before long, I would spot him walking by with his cup in hand, gazing at me with no particular expression on his face.

After three hours of blackjack, I found myself $600 ahead. It was time for me to move over to the poker tables. Poker is also one of my favorite games, and I have been playing it regularly since I was a teenager. One of the major differences between poker and blackjack is; rather than playing against the house such as in blackjack, in poker, the players are competing against each other. The house takes a percentage of each pot (known as the rake) from each hand, which is how they make their money. The dealer and the house do not care who wins each hand, only that they build up a substantial pot, which results in a healthier rake.

I sat down at one of the Texas hold 'em tables and joined five men and a woman who were already seated and playing. Texas hold 'em is a game which requires a combination of skill, luck, guts, and the ability to know when to quit. As Kenny Rogers implores in his song, 'The Gambler': 'You have to know when to hold 'em and when to fold 'em'.

My skill as a poker player was a bit rusty, but still intact; and Lady Luck was with me on this night. Hand after hand I either successfully bluffed the other players into folding their hands, or the cards that I needed fell upon me like manna from heaven. If I didn't get the cards that gave me the confidence to bet, I simply folded the hand and waited for the next one. As I played each hand, I looked up to see my admirer watching me from the corner. He was tall and very muscular, neither attractive nor ugly. He had olive skin, short brown hair, and dark eyes. His gaze was neither menacing nor inviting, and I was not sure how to react to his apparent interest in me.

I played poker for what seemed like an hour, but turned out to be three hours. Although I had been winning all night, I had lost the last three hands. It was time to quit. I was tired, but happily $1,600 ahead… I was also hungry.

After cashing in my chips at the cashier window, I headed over to the restaurant to get something to eat before heading back to the truck for the night. It was an austere restaurant, with plain tables and cheap metal chairs with red plastic seats and backs. The blackboard at the entranceway boasted the $6.99 prime rib that Alice had trumpeted.

After the hostess seated me, I sat at the table with a smile on my face, while quietly basking in my triumph over the casino games.

"Do you know how to convert kilograms into pounds?"

I looked up at the voice that had seemingly come from

nowhere, to find the man that had been watching me all night standing next to my table.

"Excuse me?" I replied while gazing curiously at him..

"Sorry to bother you miss, but I've got this load, and the bill of lading is in kilograms. I just need to know what the formula is to convert it to pounds."

"You divide kilos by .45 to convert them to pounds," I answered suspiciously.

"Ah, Okay. Thanks" he smiled. He remained standing next to my table.

"Okay, so you have been watching me all night, and then you followed me into the restaurant. All this just so you could ask me how to convert kilograms to pounds?" I laughed.

He laughed, "Well actually I have wanted to meet you all night, and that's the only pickup line I could think of."

"Well, it's a unique pickup line. I've got to give you credit for that," I chuckled.

"My name is Jaxon. Can I join you for dinner?"

"Sure Jackson. My name is Pam." I extended my right hand, which he clasped gently with his large hand. He then settled into the chair next to me.

"Just so you know, Pam. My name is spelled J-A-X-O-N. Most people spell it like the city in Mississippi."

"Yeah, that's what I would have thought. Okay Jaxon, nice to meet you" I smiled.

The server came by, and we each ordered the prime rib and a bottle of Heineken. After she had departed, I gazed at Jaxon for a moment. He had a nondescript face that one would not notice in a crowd, yet shouted loudly with warmth and sincerity. He had a pleasant smile, and eyes that invoked trust. I found myself quickly becoming very comfortable with this man.

"It looked like you were doing pretty well out there at the tables. Why did you quit?"

"I guess it was just time," I smiled.

"But you were winning. You could have won a lot more."

"Jaxon, in order to be a winner you have to know when it's time to quit. You can never win if you quit too soon, or quit so late that you give all your winnings back to the casino… which is what most people do."

"That makes sense… so, how long have you been driving?" he asked after the server had dropped off our beers and scampered off to another table.

"Exactly one year today" I exclaimed proudly while taking a sip of my beer.

"Congratulations." He smiled, while lifting his bottle in a toast. I tapped his bottle with mine and took another swig.

"How about you? How long have you been driving?" I asked.

"Too long," he laughed. "Actually I'm going on ten years over the road."

The server breezed by our table and placed our platters in front of each of us. I quickly cut off a piece of prime rib and slid it into my mouth.

"Where do you live?" I asked, while chewing.

"St. Cloud, Minnesota. I'm sure you know where that is." He took a bite of his prime rib and washed it down with the beer.

"Yup, sure do. I've been through there many times on my way in and out of Minneapolis. I've even shut down a few times at the Pilot there."

"And you? Where do you live?" he asked.

"I'm based out of Fontana, California. My CDL says I live there, but I really just live out of my truck. Actually, I'm not sure where I live." I said with a rueful chuckle.

"Where do you want to live?"

I turned my head and stared blankly at the huge keno board on the back wall of the restaurant, as the red LED numbers appeared one by one. Around the restaurant, customers scratched eagerly onto their keno cards in the hopes of catching the right numbers and winning big. I then turned back to Jaxon.

"I'm not sure. Maybe I'll stay in California. Maybe go back

to Texas or Colorado. Maybe even back to Chicago. I don't know right now."

"How about Minnesota?" Jaxon smiled.

"No way! The winters are way too cold!" I exclaimed with a laugh.

Jaxon chuckled, "Yeah, that's what everyone says. But actually, Minnesota has some redeeming qualities."

"Such as?" I smiled.

"Well, we have a lot of nice lakes. The summers are pleasant. And of course, we have the Vikings," he smiled.

"The Vikings?" I laughed. I'm from Chicago. Why would I consider the Vikings to be a 'redeeming quality'?" I picked up a stalk of broccoli from my plate and playfully tossed it at him.

He caught the broccoli in mid-air and laid it on the table. "Ah, so you are a Bears fan?" he laughed.

"Well, I grew up a Bears fan and was taught to hate the Vikings. But I'm actually more of a Cowboys fan now" I grinned.

Jaxon picked up the broccoli that I had thrown at him and tossed it back at me. I quickly dodged, and it sailed over my shoulder and fluttered onto the floor behind me.

"Of all the women in Sparks, Nevada… I flirt with a Dallas friggin' Cowboys fan!" he chortled.

"Of all the men in Sparks, I invite a Vikings fan to have dinner with me!" I laughed.

"You didn't invite me. I invited myself."

"Yeah, but I taught you how to convert kilograms to pounds. What would you have ever done without me?" I laughed.

"Hah! I already knew how to do that. I was just using that as a pickup line," he chortled.

"Oh yeah, and what if that line hadn't worked? What pickup line would you use then?" I laughed.

He stopped laughing and gazed into my eyes, "I would have just told you that you are one of the most amazing women I have seen in a long time."

After we finished our dinner and Jaxon had paid the tab, we

left the restaurant and walked through the casino toward the exit.

"Thank you for paying for dinner Jaxon. That wasn't necessary you know." I smiled demurely, as I walked by his side.

"My pleasure, Pam. I'm going to walk you back to your truck," he said as he gallantly held the casino door open for me. The rush of cool January evening air felt good as I stepped through the door and into the lot, on which hundreds of trucks sat idling.

"Thank you…that would be nice" I smiled.

"Would it be ok if I held your hand?" he asked politely.

"Of course," I smiled while offering my hand to him. His large hand felt comforting to me as he took my hand in his.

As we walked across the lot toward my truck, it felt good to be with him, my hand in his. Although my first impression of him was bland, he had slowly begun to take on a different persona. I was beginning to find him very attractive, and I did not know why.

"Well, this is my truck, BJ" I said when we arrived at my parking spot.

"BJ? You named your truck BJ? As in blow job?" Jaxon laughed.

I slapped his chest playfully, "No silly, her name has nothing to do with blow jobs. It has to do with her number."

Jaxon stood back and looked at my truck number for a moment. He had a contemplative expression on his face, and his brow furrowed as he seemingly tried to decipher and translate the number.

"Ok I give up. How do you get "BJ" out of thirty seven-thirty eight?"

"Give it some thought, Jaxon. When you think of the answer, give me a call."

"But I don't have your phone number."

"I'm going to give it to you. But you have to promise to use it, ok?"

"Ok, I promise to use it, on one condition. Will you let me kiss you?" he asked hopefully.

"Yes" I gasped.

Jaxon leaned forward and gently placed his lips on mine. I had no idea what kissing a man would be like, but I soon discovered that it felt quite good. As he kissed me, his strong arms wrapped around me and pulled me close to his muscular body. I felt as if I was floating.

My heart pounded inside my chest as I watched him walk away. Once he had disappeared into the sea of trucks, I climbed into BJ and shed my clothes. After brushing my teeth, I climbed into the sleeper berth and rapidly drifted away to a very satisfying and tranquil night of sleep.

As promised, Jaxon called me the next morning. We talked for an hour while I drove eastward on Interstate 80 toward Baltimore, and he was heading north on US 95 with his load destined for Ontario, Oregon. We talked on the phone daily, some days more than once. With each phone conversation, we learned more about each other, and I found myself becoming more and more attracted to him.

During the next few months, as we each traversed the country carrying freight to and from various cities, we often found ourselves on the same highway, and took those opportunities to rendezvous at a truck stop or casino. One of our favorite meeting spots was the Eureka Casino in Mesquite, Nevada; just north of the California state line. Truck drivers were a big part of the casino business, and outlying venues such as Mesquite, featured casinos surrounded by enormous truck parking lots. The Eureka was no exception, catering to truck drivers by offering discounted rooms and food to anyone with a CDL.

Jaxon did not like playing card games, but instead favored the slot machines or the roulette wheel. Conversely, I did not care to gamble on games over which I had no control, so I spent my time at the blackjack or poker tables. Jaxon seldom won much, if anything, in the casinos, while I normally left the tables victorious. On my worst night, I lost $40 before wisely calling it quits.

"So, what are you doing with all this money you've been

winning? I see you raking in the chips all the time, but I don't see you spending money on clothing or jewelry," Jaxon asked one evening after we had enjoyed an 'after casino' dinner in the restaurant. As he spoke, he held my hands across the table, gently caressing them with his large fingers.

"I'm saving it," I answered coyly. I had been very secretive whenever Jaxon asked me a personal question. However, I knew that eventually I would have to disclose my past to him if this relationship flourished, but was holding off as long as possible.

"What are you saving for? Buying that dream house in Minnesota?" he winked.

I laughed, "No not that. Actually, I'm saving for some rather expensive surgery that is not covered by insurance." I continued with my ambiguous responses to his questions, although it was getting harder and harder to keep from blurting out something that would reveal my secret. In time, I would have no choice. I had no idea that the time was now.

"Your sex change surgery?" he asked calmly, while gently squeezing my hands.

I gulped, "You know? How long have you known? How?..."

Jaxon laughed, "Actually, it was just an educated guess. Certain things that you have said and done gave it away. Your evasive answers to my questions, and your nervousness tipped me off too. One of the women in the office is a transsexual, and I told her about you. She's convinced that you are, and told me to just ask you."

"Oh wow, I don't know what to say. Are you ok with it?" I felt slightly reassured by the fact that he was still gently kneading my hands with his.

He paused for a few moments before replying, clearly in deep thought over how he would respond. He looked into my eyes and smiled. "Pam, I'm pretty sure I'm ok with it. I like you as a person and this is just something that I will have to adapt to."

I sighed with relief, "Thank you Jaxon. That means a lot to me."

"I'm not sure how my family will take it though," he laughed. "But I guess we'll just have to cross that bridge when we get to it."

We continued our ritual of daily telephone chats, and rendezvoused whenever possible. My dispatcher, Charlotte, was very cooperative in getting me loads that took me toward what I now referred to as my boyfriend. Although we slept together whenever we were together, we limited our sexual activity to petting. We seemed to have an unspoken understanding that sex would wait until after my surgery. At this point, living in Minnesota was becoming more and more appealing.

Conversations with Jaxon had become more comfortable for me now that he knew about my past, and I was much more forthcoming with the answers to his questions. He now knew all about my three children and my two ex-wives. I had discussed at length my reason for leaving the magazine publishing business and becoming a truck driver, as well as my plans to quit driving in another year.

"So, what are you going to do when you quit driving?" he asked during one of our telephone conversations.

"I'm planning on going back to what I know best, journalism, media, or magazine publishing. I have a lot of contacts from my twenty years in the business and I'm sure I can get back in."

"Even with them knowing about your sex change? They all knew you as a male, right?"

"Yeah, I know that is going to be a challenge. Hopefully someone will overlook that minor detail and give me a job with a magazine. I probably won't get a job as a Publisher right away, but that's ok. I'll take whatever I can get."

"Well dear, good luck with that. I hope it works out for you. Maybe you can get a job in Minnesota," he laughed.

"Maybe so" I chuckled. "Only time will tell.

Jaxon called me early in the morning on August 25th. "Ok miss Dallas Cowboys, you ready to make a wager?"

"Um, ok what in the world are you talking about?" I

laughed.

August 31st on ESPN. Minnesota Vikings against the Cowboys. I reserved a room for us at the Eureka. We can watch the game, have dinner, do a little gambling in the casino, and then spend the night together."

Oh, okay. That sounds delightful," I laughed. "I get to watch the Cowboys beat up on the Vikings."

"We'll see who beats up on who," he snickered. "Can you get your dispatcher to get you to Mesquite on the thirty-first?"

"I sure can!" I exclaimed. "You said something about a wager. What's the bet?"

"If the Cowboys win, I will give you a full body massage. When the Vikings win, YOU will give ME a full body massage" he chuckled.

I laughed, "OK Mr. Confidence. It's a bet!"

Charlotte got me a load to Los Angeles that was not due until September 2nd, which allowed me to stop in Mesquite to enjoy some time with Jaxon and to watch the game.

I arrived at the Eureka at 4:30 and parked my truck in the parking lot. Jaxon had already checked into our room and had given me the room number, so I simply went up the elevator to the room. After a few minutes of kissing and hugging, we went down the elevator to the casino to watch the game on the enormous television in the casino bar.

The fourth quarter ended in a 10-10 tie, and the game went into sudden death overtime. Jaxon and I had chided one another throughout the game as we each routed for our favorite team. It looked like I was about to win the bet when the Cowboy's kicker lined up for the game winning field goal at the 32-yard line. It should have been a chip shot, but he missed it. I held my head in my hands in disgust, while Jaxon whooped in delight.

My hopes of winning the bet were renewed, when once again the Cowboys lined up for an easy field goal, this time from the 33-yard line. Once again, he missed, and the game ended in a 10-10 tie.

"So I guess neither of us wins the massage, huh?" I laughed as we headed into the casino.

"I guess we could give each other a massage as a consolation prize, couldn't we?" he smiled.

"Sounds good, but first I have some gambling to do," I said as I dashed off to the blackjack tables.

I held my own at the blackjack tables for the next hour, drifting from table to table trying to find a hot streak. Jaxon had vanished somewhere amid the sea of slot machines doing what he loves best. After a while, he magically appeared behind me just as the dealer began dealing a hand.

"I'm ready to go up the room whenever you are," he spoke softly into my ear.

"Yeah, I'm ready. Right after this hand, ok?"

My first two cards were a three and a seven, not the best cards, but not the worst cards if you know how to play them. The dealer was showing a king. In my strategy, had the dealer been showing a card less than a seven, I would have 'doubled down', which basically means I would double my bet, but would only be given one more card. The odds would have been in my favor. However, with the dealer showing a face card, I opted to just take a hit.

My next card was another three… a horrible card to get in this situation. I now had 13, and with the dealer showing a face card, I had no choice but to take another hit. I turned and rolled my eyes at Jaxon, who was standing behind me with a perplexed look on his face.

I signaled the dealer to give me another card, which she deftly peeled from the shoe and tossed in front of me. It was the perfect card… an eight, which gave me twenty-one. The dealer then flipped over her hole card and revealed an eight, giving her eighteen.

"Hey look, Pam. Those cards are your truck number… 3-7-3-8" Jaxon laughed as the dealer placed my winnings in front of me and scooped up the cards.

"They sure are" I beamed as I tossed a chip at the dealer and began to gather up my winnings from the table.

Suddenly, the dealer, the players, and the pit boss looked behind me in astonishment as Jaxon yelled out, at what seemed to be the top of his lungs,

"Son of a bitch!"

I turned around to find Jaxon standing a few feet behind our table, looking up at the ceiling, and holding his head in both hands. He was laughing hysterically.

"Son of a bitch!" he repeated.

I left the table and walked over to Jaxon, who now seemed to be the center of attention in the casino. A nearby security guard was muttering something into his lapel microphone.

"Son of a bitch!" he laughed. That's why you named your truck BJ. Blackjack! 3738 add up to 21!"

"See honey, I told you you'd figure it out" I smiled while giving him a hug.

"Let's get up to the room Pam. I think I owe YOU a massage. Geez girl, you are really something." Jaxon swept me off my feet and into his muscular arms, and carried me to the elevators.

In November, Jaxon invited me to his home to join him and his family for Thanksgiving dinner. I was thrilled by the fact that he thought so much of me to include me as part of his family for the holiday, but at the same time, I was apprehensive about meeting them.

"I'm going to tell them about you ahead of time, Pam. They will have to find out eventually, and I don't want anyone to think we were deceiving them," Jaxon told me.

"How do you think they will take it?" I asked nervously.

"I really don't know for sure. Some of my family members are very conservative. I'm not worried, though. Whatever they think, I'm sure you can win them over with your charm," he laughed.

During the weeks and days leading up to Thanksgiving Day, I inquired on a daily basis. "Have you talked to them yet?"

"Not yet, but soon" he would respond.

I felt a wave of apprehension as I pulled into the TA in St.

Cloud and parked the truck. I had stopped at an outlet mall along the way and purchased a new dress and shoes so that I would make my best impression tomorrow. I had also purchased a Christmas gift for Jaxon, a pair of Superman boxer shorts.

It was now the day before Thanksgiving, and the plan was that Jaxon would come by the truck stop on Thanksgiving morning with his car, and drive me to his family's home. I was excited and thrilled to be meeting his family, but also very anxious. He hadn't shared with me if he had told them, nor how they had reacted. I hadn't talked to him since Monday, but I wasn't concerned, as I assumed he was busy with his family preparing for the holiday and my arrival.

I called his number, and immediately reached his voice mail greeting. After leaving him a message that I was in St. Cloud, I went into the sleeper berth to take a nap. I woke up two hours later and called him again, and once again left a voice mail message.

I woke up early on Thanksgiving morning, and excitedly dashed into the truck stop to take a shower and get dressed in my new holiday dress. I had not received a return call from Jaxon, but I knew he would be coming to pick me up soon. When I returned to the truck, I called his number again. This time I did not get his voice mail greeting. Instead, I heard a message informing me that the number was disconnected. I must have misdialed, I thought. I dialed the number again… and again… and again. The realization that Jaxon's cell phone was disconnected began to crystallize in my mind.

I sat in my truck for hours as I stared hopefully through the windshield for Jaxon to appear and take me to his home for Thanksgiving dinner. Darkness slowly descended, as I waited for my dream to come true. It never came.

I spent Thanksgiving 2006 alone in the St. Cloud Pilot, where I dined in McDonald's, while wearing my new dress and shoes. 2006 had begun with an unexpected treat. A man had entered my life and given me hope for a future of happiness. I had envisioned being with him forever. Once again, I had been delusional; and once again, reality had reared its ugly head and bit me.

"Be strong, Pam" I told myself. "You WILL get through this."

Yes, I would have to be strong. I would need to be strong in order to get through this… I will not let it affect me.

As hard as I tried to stop it, a tear managed to escape from my eyes, then dribbled down my cheek and landed on my Thanksgiving hamburger.

Chapter Twenty-Three
San Mateo

On Christmas morning, I awoke at the Loves truck stop in Rolla, Missouri. I had left the truck idling during the night with the heater running, as the temperature was well below freezing. I glanced at the thermometer on my console, which indicated an outside temperature of twenty-three degrees. The dashboard clock showed that it was 3:47 am.

After packing my shower bag with fresh clothing, and covering myself with a heavy winter jacket, I slid the curtain back just enough to be able to open the door and climb down onto the pavement. A thin layer of crunchy snow covered the ground. My exhaled breath floated in front of my face in a cloud, as I walked gingerly across the slippery parking lot toward the building. Most drivers were home celebrating Christmas with their families, leaving the truck stop parking lot unnervingly quiet. Even the familiar lot lizards, who were normally busy soliciting sex, were absent. The only sound I could hear was the crystallized snow that crunched beneath my footsteps.

Christmas 2006 marked my second consecutive holiday spent in a faraway place. 'Faraway from what?' I asked myself. I had travelled so far from home that I had forgotten where home was. It had been a long and lonely journey, with many miles behind me, and many yet to travel. I had become feral, with no home, no ties, no past, and seemingly no future.

"Merry Christmas," the young woman behind the counter greeted me cheerily as I paid for my coffee and presented my plastic card to redeem points for a free shower.

"Merry Christmas to you too," I replied dolefully, as I accepted the shower key from her, trying my best to smile. Later in the day, she would most likely be celebrating the holiday with her family, while I stared silently through my windshield, at yet another road, to another truck stop. There would be no opening of presents for me… no 'Chestnuts Roasting by the Open Fire'. There would only be the steady drone of the diesel engine as I hauled freight to another city.

As always, the combination of morning coffee and the hot water pulsating on my body lifted my spirits, and revived my mental capacity.

Why am I feeling so blue? Isn't this what I signed up for when I made the decision to become a truck driver? The price that a person is willing to pay for something should be commensurate with how badly they want or need it. I needed to do this… needed to transition into my true self. Driving a truck, and the loneliness and isolation that came with it, was my ticket to freedom. I knew from the start, that this was only a temporary job, and that I would eventually leave it behind. Soon, I would begin the planning for my future, and eventually this all would be in my past.

After a pre-trip inspection, including the added step of checking the brakes on each wheel to ensure they were not frozen, I started my log for the day, and pulled out of the truck stop parking lot, onto Interstate 44. I had picked up a load of cereal yesterday in Battle Creek, Michigan, which was due in Oakland, California in four days. From there I was to pick up another load in nearby Walnut Creek and take it to south to Los Angeles. I had an electrolysis appointment scheduled with Layla, and Charlotte was kind enough to make sure I had a load home.

The morning sun was barely peeking above the horizon behind me, as I headed westbound on the Interstate. The road was virtually void of traffic as I made my way, but I knew that in a few hours it would be replete with cars, occupied by joyful families, on their way to celebrate the holiday with relatives and friends. Later in the day, I would call Candy, Cheryl, Greg, and Steven to wish them each a Merry Christmas, and ask if they liked the presents that I had sent them. Those calls would consume no more than five minutes each. I would push hard today, covering 750 miles before I shut down for the night in Tucumcari, New Mexico, where I would grab a bite to eat and go to sleep. This would be the extent of my 2006 Christmas celebration.

At dawn the day after Christmas, I left Tucumcari, and made it as far as Kingman, Arizona. At 5:00 the following morning, I left Kingman and was back on the road on my way toward Oakland. It was now two days past Christmas, and 2006 was winding down. As I drove west along Interstate 40 through the Mojave Desert, I began to formulate my plans for 2007. During the first week of January, I would begin the process of calling my contacts in the magazine business to let them know that I was back on the market. I realized that it would be awkward explaining my gender situation to them, yet hoped this would not be an issue. During my twenty plus years in the field, I had established a good reputation; and I was confident that my talents and experience would overshadow any discomfort regarding my new gender.

Afternoon rush hour was just beginning by the time I reached the outskirts of San Francisco and drove along Interstate 880 through Freemont, California. I was in the right lane, easing along at 50 miles per hour, in pace with the dozens of vehicles around me. From here, I had only another 26 miles to my destination in Oakland. After dropping the trailer, I would head over to Walnut Creek to pick up my load, and drive down to Los Angeles. After my session with Layla and her daughter, I would then enjoy a couple of days off in Fontana, where I would update my resume, and begin to plan my job hunting strategy.

The violent explosion in the front of my truck suddenly interrupted my thoughts, as pieces of BJ's red hood, left fender, and front end suddenly flew toward me. Pieces of the truck hit my windshield, which instantly became a spider web of cracked glass. The truck suddenly pulled violently toward the left, and it took every bit of my strength and composure to pull BJ back to the right. I gradually slowed down and ushered her onto the right shoulder.

After I had come to a stop on the shoulder and set the brakes, I killed the engine, switched on my emergency flashers, and looked in the left hand mirror. Behind me was a trail of rubber, red fragments of my truck, and cars that had collided with each other, while attempting to avoid the flying debris. Traffic had come to a virtual standstill.

I opened the door and leaped down to the ground, then ran to the three cars that had been involved in a collision with one another. Fortunately, there were no injuries, which quickly became apparent as each of the drivers emerged from their vehicles with nothing more than stunned expressions on their faces. In an instant, while casually driving home from their jobs, a big truck had exploded beside them and showered them with debris.

Without saying a word, I walked back to my truck to assess the situation. All that remained of the left front tire were a few threads of rubber wrapped around the bent rim. The rest of the tire was in strips on the highway, or wrapped around the tie rod of my truck. The left front end of my truck was gone, with nothing left but the now punctured radiator, and a dangling set of wires where there had once been a headlight.

"What happened?" asked one of the drivers that had been involved in the collision.

"It looks like I had a blowout on my left steer tire. Apparently, the tire unraveled when it blew, and demolished the front of my truck," I replied pensively.

"Thank God nobody was hurt," another driver interjected.

After exchanging insurance information with the other three

drivers, the California Highway Patrol arrived, followed by a fleet of tow trucks to clear the carnage from the road. Within an hour, traffic was back to normal; the only evidence that an incident had even occurred being my demolished truck on the shoulder. I had called Charlotte to report the incident, and she in turn had called the closest International dealer, who then dispatched a tow truck.

It was nearly 7:00 pm by the time the goliath tow truck arrived and maneuvered in front of me and onto the shoulder; backing up within a few feet of BJ's bloodied nose. I hopped down from my truck and stood at the side of the road to meet the driver, as he climbed down from his rig.

"Diaaaaam" the operator exclaimed after he had walked from his rig and accessed the damage to my truck. "It looks like someone planted a bomb under your hood!"

"Yeah, well, apparently the left steer tire blew and caused all this damage. It also caused quite a bit of chaos on the freeway," I replied ruefully.

Within ten minutes, the tow truck operator had skillfully hooked his equipment to BJ, and lifted her damaged front end off the ground.

"The nearest International dealer is over in San Mateo, but they're closed now. We'll drop your rig off in their yard and you can call them in the morning. There's a hotel right across the road from them where you can stay. Want me to drop you off there?" the driver asked as he connected the necessary cables and chains from his tow truck to my truck.

"Yeah, that would be good," I replied halfheartedly. The last thing I needed right now was to be down for several days, plus bear the expense of a hotel room.

"By the way, my name is Tony," he said while removing his gloves and tossing them behind the driver's seat of his rig. "Sorry this happened to you."

"Under any other circumstances, I'd like to say it's nice to meet you, Tony," I replied sardonically as I climbed into the passenger seat of his truck.

It took us forty-five minutes to get to the International dealer in San Mateo, despite the fact that it was just slightly more than 20 miles across the San Francisco Bay. Along the way, Tony prattled about one thing or another, but I did not hear a word he said, I simply stared though the window at the passing scenery, while reflecting on the events of the past few months. The year had begun with what I had thought to be a robust relationship, which had then come to a crashing halt because of negative peer pressures stemming from the fact that I am transsexual woman. Following the demise of that relationship, I had endured yet another Thanksgiving and Christmas on the road with no celebration. Now, the year would end with my truck disabled for an undetermined period, and an uncertain future.

Bayshore International is located on the frontage road, on the southbound side of US 101, in San Mateo. Tony parked his rig and my truck in front of the dealership, and we each climbed down.

While Tony was busy lowering BJ to the ground and disconnecting the cables and chains, I climbed inside my truck and stuffed enough clothing into my shower bag to last a few days, along with a few other personal items that I would need to have with me. I grabbed my bag and my laptop, and climbed back down to the ground. If I discovered that I needed anything else, I could get it in the morning when I came to discuss the repair work that they would need to perform in order to get me back on the road. The Super 8 Motel was on the opposite side of the highway, with a walking bridge located conveniently close by.

Before climbing back into the tow truck, I stood for a moment and gazed at BJ's damaged front end. It was sad to look at her like this, but I knew that things could have been a lot worse. In just a few days, she would be back to normal and we would be back on the road.

Tony drove for what seemed to be a mile as he maneuvered his enormous rig up one street, then down another, to get over to the northbound side of the highway. We finally pulled into the parking lot of the motel and came to a stop in front of the lobby entrance.

"Why don't you go in and make sure they have a room available?" Tony said while writing onto a clipboard. "I'll have your invoice ready for you when you come back."

"Good idea," I replied, as I opened the passenger door and climbed down.

"Can I help you?" the woman behind the counter greeted me with a smile as I entered the lobby.

"I need a room for a few days, do you have a non-smoking room available?"

"I have a queen size, non-smoking room on either the first or second floor. Do you have a preference?"

"I'll take the first floor. How much is it?"

"It will run $72 per night, including tax" she smiled.

"Ugh!" I replied, extracting my CDL and credit card from my wallet, and handing them to the clerk. "I'll be right back; I just need to get my bags."

I went back to the tow truck to get my bags, and thanked Tony for waiting for me. He handed me the invoice and after I had climbed back down to the ground and closed the door, he pulled his rig out of the parking lot and departed.

My room was as austere as you would come to expect at a cheap motel. However, this was San Mateo, on the southern fringes of San Francisco, where 'cheap' meant $72 per night. I felt somewhat grateful that there was a Super 8 Motel across the road from the International dealer, rather than an expensive hotel. There is no telling what that would cost.

After checking in and entered my room, I unpacked my bags, and readied myself for bed. After sliding under the covers, I lay on my back staring blankly at the ceiling. Tomorrow morning would begin with my visit to the repair shop to assess the damage, then a busy day of phone calls and resume writing.

"Merry Christmas and Happy New Year," I murmured to myself before falling asleep.

The next morning, after a shower, I enjoyed complimentary coffee and stale pastries in the lobby. I then walked across the highway on the footbridge, and headed to the International dealer to discuss the repair work on my truck.

"We're looking at a minimum of three days of work to get you on the road, ma'am," the Service Manager said as he finished writing up the worksheet. "There is a lot of damage here, and we have to order most of the parts."

"So this means I won't get my truck back until Sunday?" The thought of sitting idle for that long horrified me.

"Well, actually we are closed on Sunday's, and Monday is a holiday. Depending on how long it takes to get the parts in, it will be Tuesday or Wednesday," he replied unapologetically. "Most likely it will not be ready until Wednesday."

"Wednesday? That's six days!" I exclaimed. "I can't just sit here for six days!"

"I'm sorry miss, but there's nothing we can do about it. I can try to get it finished by Tuesday, but I wouldn't count on having it before Wednesday."

I went back to the truck to gather up a few more days' worth of clothing, which I stuffed into a plastic trash bag. I then headed back across the freeway to my motel room. As I walked across the footbridge, visions of money evaporating from my savings pranced through my mind.

As soon as I returned to my motel room, I called Charlotte to let her know how long I would be down. She arranged for another truck to pick up my trailer and take it to Oakland. She then transferred me to Cindy in payroll, who, after I had briefed her on my situation, agreed to defer the next two lease payments so I could catch up.

"Pam, If you need an advance, let me know," Cindy said with a tone of compassion.

"Thank you, I will." I was very appreciative of her offer, which I would only accept if I absolutely had to.

My next call was to Layla to cancel my appointment. "Layla,

my truck is broke down and I am stuck for several days. I am not going to make it to my appointment." I felt no need to go into the details.

"Oh dear, I'm sorry. Where are you?"

"I'm up in San Mateo. They say my truck won't be ready until Wednesday. I'm sitting in a motel room twiddling my thumbs until I get back on the road."

"Do you want to get some electrolysis done while you are there? I know someone who is not far from San Mateo."

"Sure, I may as well get some work done as long I'm stuck here."

"Her name is Sorcha. She works out of her home in Redwood City, which I think is only about five or six miles from San Mateo."

"Sorcha? That's a unique name." I laughed.

"Well, she is a unique woman. She is very good at what she does, and I think you will like her."

After Layla had given me the phone number and address for Sorcha, we said our goodbyes and disconnected. I called Sorcha, and made an appointment for a two-hour session at 5:00 pm on Monday. I was pleasantly surprised to hear that she would be working on New Year's Day.

My next call would require all the courage I could muster, and I simply sat and stared at the phone for what felt like hours.

Art Fields and I worked together in the mid-1980s and early 1990s, during the glory days of the personal computer industry; first at Rupert Murdoch's Magazine Group, and then Ziff-Davis Publishing. Art had moved up in the ranks to become publisher of a new computer magazine that Z-D was launching, and had taken me with him to help with the launch. He was my mentor, and we had become close friends; a friendship that had survived well after each of us had departed Ziff-Davis for other publishing opportunities.

I hadn't spoken to Art for several years, but I was certain that he would still be living in San Francisco, the city that he swore he would never leave. 'They will bury me in San Francisco,' he would often say. As I punched his number into my cell phone, I inwardly hoped that hadn't happened.

"This is Art, who art thou?" He answered cheerfully after two rings. I had always loved the poetic manner in which he answered the phone.

"Art, my name is Pamela. I'm calling about a mutual friend by the name of Philip Anders," I said nervously. A knot had developed in my stomach.

"Philip? I haven't heard from him in years. Is something wrong?" he asked.

'Oh no, he is fine… well actually he doesn't exist anymore but he is doing fine."

"He's dead?"

"No he's not dead. He is actually… well, he is me…or I am him. I had a sex change…" I stumbled with the words, not sure how to convey this news to my old friend.

"You don't sound like Philip," Art replied suspiciously.

"Art, I'm a female now. I am still the same person inside, but on the outside, I am now a woman. It's hard to explain, and I know this is a shock to you," I explained.

"This is a crank call isn't it?" he laughed. "Who is this?"

"Art, think back to 1991… Comdex in Vegas… Bally's… Frank Sinatra. We had a table at the front, within ten feet of the stage. We had invited the marketing department from Microsoft to the Sinatra show. Remember?"

"Yeah, I remember that night," he replied skeptically.

"Okay, remember the one Product Manager from Microsoft… we had eaten a bunch of appetizers, and he had a glob of cheese hanging from his chin when Sinatra came on stage and started singing?"

Art chuckled, "Yeah, and Sinatra looked at our table and started laughing right in the middle of 'Luck be a Lady Tonight'. None of us had the nerve to tell this guy that he had a glob of cheese hanging from his chin, which was why Sinatra was laughing."

"Yes! And then the cheese finally dropped into his martini. Remember that?" I laughed.

"Oh my god… yes," Art roared. "And then he drank the martini without even noticing there was cheese in it!"

"Art, you and I laughed about that night for years afterward" I chuckled.

"Yes, we did…" Art quickly changed the subject. "So, you are Phil? You actually had a sex change? This is for real? You're a woman now?" He asked a barrage of questions, now with a more journalistic tone.

"Yes Art this is for real. It is me, and I am a female now. I need to talk to you. I'm in San Mateo for a few days. Can we get together?"

"You're in San Mateo? That's great, why don't you come up to the city tonight, and we'll have dinner. This I've got to see!" he chortled.

After hanging up with Art, I dialed the number for Alamo Car Rental. I would need transportation to get to my dinner with Art in San Francisco, and for my appointment with Sorcha in Redwood City. The brochure on the nightstand in the motel room indicated that I would be entitled to a discounted rate as a reward for being a guest at the Super 8 Motel. After providing the needed information to the reservation agent, she promised that a driver would deliver a car to the motel by 3:00 pm.

Scoma's Restaurant is a casual dining establishment located on the west end of Fisherman's Wharf. From the Super 8 Motel, it took me 40 minutes to drive the 20 miles up the 101 to pier 47 where I pulled up, and my rental car was valet parked by the attendant. I had enjoyed the drive, taking in the sites of San Francisco along the way.

When I entered the restaurant, I immediately spotted Art sipping on a bottle of Anchor Steam beer at a table in the far corner of the dining room. I informed the hostess that I was joining him, and headed towards the table. As I approached, he peered curiously at me above the rim of his glasses.

"Hello Art. You look great" I smiled while standing next to his table.

Art lowered his beer bottle to the table and gawked at me for a moment before speaking.

"Jesus, you look completely different. What… are you in the witness protection program or something?" he laughed.

I chuckled, "I've been asked that before, but the answer is no. My reasons for doing this are a lot more complicated than that."

"Well, don't just stand there. If you're waiting for me to come around and hold the chair out for you, you've got a long wait!" he chortled.

I smiled as I took the chair across the table from Art. A waiter appeared at our table the moment I sat down, and asked if I would like something to drink.

"I'll have one of those," I said while pointing to Art's bottle.

"Bring me another one as well," Art added with a smile.

After the waiter had departed, my former boss and I gazed wordlessly at one another for several minutes before he broke the silence.

"So, what do I call you? Did you say Pamela on the phone?"

"Yes, my legal name is Pamela now, but you can call me Pam," I smiled.

"Do you realize how confusing this is? I hope you won't be offended if I accidently call you Phil," he laughed. The waiter had dropped off our beers and we both took a swig.

"Yes, Art… I can only imagine. I will explain it all to you, and hopefully you will understand," I said, while examining the menu.

"So, what the hell have you done to yourself? You look different and you sound different. Did you get your balls cut off? Is that why your voice sounds so different?"

I laughed, "No, Art. It doesn't work that way in real life, only in the movies. I have had to go through extensive voice training to get my voice this way. I still have a long way to go. though"

Art ordered the filet mignon with rock lobster, and I selected the Dungeness crab. Art also instructed the waiter to bring a bottle of 2001 Beringer Private Reserve with our entrees. I hadn't looked at the wine list, but I knew that this dinner was going to be quite expensive.

While Art and I enjoyed our food and wine, I explained everything to him. I began my dissertation with the strange feelings I had experienced as a child, the challenges of living life in the wrong gender, my desire to conclude my unhappy life in the jungles of Vietnam, failed relationships and marriages, and finally my decision to become a truck driver while transitioning from male to female. Art listened attentively as he ate his dinner, often interjecting questions along the way. It was clear to me that my former boss was truly interested in what I had to say. I concluded my soliloquy with the incident in Fremont, and my reason for being in San Mateo.

Art poured the last of the bottle of wine into each of our glasses and placed the empty bottle upside down in the wine bucket. We each took a sip of wine and gazed into each other's eyes for a moment, while Art digested all that I had just told him. A busboy deftly cleared the dinner plates and utensils from our table, then quietly scampered away with the oval tray full of dinnerware on his shoulder. Art set his wine glass on the table and smiled.

"Phi...... er, I mean Pam, I have always detected a rather secretive aspect in you. Even your wife... what was her name? Linda?"

"Laura.... it's 'ex-wife' now," I smiled.

"Yeah Laura.... even Laura confided in me once when we were all out to dinner that you were very secretive with her about a lot of things."

"Yeah well unfortunately, I had a pretty big secret" I mused.

"Well, what you just told me certainly does explain a lot of things," he laughed.

""Yeah, I get that a lot," I smiled.

"The main thing is that you are happy. Are you happy

now?"

"Art, for the first time in my life, I am comfortable in my own skin. Am I happy? Yes, in most ways…" I said as my thoughts trailed off.

Art signaled for the waiter, who promptly appeared at our table. Art ordered a snifter of cognac, and I ordered a glass of port. The waiter returned almost instantly with our after dinner drinks.

"In 'most ways'…? In what ways are you not happy?" he asked, sipping on his cognac.

I took a sip of my port and savored its tawny flavor for a moment, trying to conjure up an answer to Art's question. After nearly a minute, I conceded that I had no answer.

"Art, I honestly don't know. I just have this feeling that something is still missing in my life, but I don't know what it is." I sighed.

The waiter appeared at our table with a dessert cart. Art smiled and pointed to the cheesecake, then held up two fingers. The waiter and the cart vanished, and a few minutes later two small plates with slivers of cheesecake had appeared in front of each of us.

"So, is this what you wanted to talk to me about?" Art asked as he took a bite of the dessert, followed by a sip of cognac.

"Actually no, it's something else." I inserted a forkful of the cheesecake into my mouth. "I want to get back into the publishing business, and I'm hoping you can help me out."

"Okay, so you are thinking you can just re-enter the business after all this time, and pick up where you left off, only this time as a woman?" Art replied sarcastically.

"Well yeah, that's pretty much what I was thinking" I said sheepishly.

"First of all, I've been retired for a few years now. I don't have the clout that I used to have, so I don't know how much help I could be. Secondly, why the hell would you even want to get back into that rat race?"

"It's what I know Art. It's what I have done for all these

years."

"Ph...... geez I mean Pam, have you seen what has happened to the magazine business over the past several years? You had to have seen it when you were running your business magazine over there in Colorado. Magazine pages have been on a steady decline since the internet search engines began to gain popularity. We used to be the kings of information… people would be lining up at the magazine racks to buy the latest issue, so they could find out what was the latest and greatest, and where to buy it, or how to fix it. Now all they have to do is type in a few keywords and click their mouse button. They don't need us anymore."

"Yes Art, I am well aware of that, but there are still magazines, and I think there always will be. There must be a place for me somewhere, even as an entry level journalist."

"Journalist?" he laughed while sipping his cognac. "There are no decent journalists anymore. Now, it's all bloggers pretending to be writers. The only requirement to be a blogger is a keyboard and an internet connection. The only real magazines left are the crapper magazines."

"Crapper magazines…?" I laughed.

"Magazines like People, where you can read an entire article about what movie star is cheating on what other movie star while sitting on the crapper" he chortled.

"That's funny… but true," I smiled. "Maybe I should just start up another magazine of my own."

"Are you crazy? Have the hormones eaten away your brain?" Art now sounded like the mentor that I knew so many years ago. "Getting back into this business would be like throwing a rope around a bull while it's running downhill. Don't do it, Phi…. Pam."

I laughed at his metaphor, "Okay, Art. You've convinced me. Honestly though, I don't know what else I can do. I don't want to drive a truck for the rest of my life, and magazine publishing is all I have to fall back on."

"What about your degree? Don't you have an engineering

degree? Get a job as an engineer."

"I went to college for engineering in the 70's, Art. They were still teaching us how to use a slide rule and tee square back then. Nowadays they are using all kinds of technology that I don't know. I would have to start all over. Besides, I never really cared to be an engineer in the first place."

"Why don't you go to law school and become a lawyer. As I recall you have a fascination for law. You and that woman judge… I forget her name, from Dallas. You and she babbled on about law for over an hour when we were all seated together at that fund raiser a few years ago."

"That was Judge Catherine Crier, and it was more than a few years ago. I think it was around 1988." I laughed. "At the end of the night she told me that I should have been a lawyer. Now she is on CNN, or Court TV, or one of those shows."

"So that settles it…. You should go to law school and become a lawyer."

"Art, it would take me at least three years to get a law degree. I don't have that kind of time… not to mention the money. Besides, I don't think I want to be a lawyer."

"Then why not be a paralegal? I have a niece who does that, and she loves it. You would be working in the legal field assisting the lawyers, and not have all the pressures or responsibilities of the attorneys. I think you can get a paralegal degree in two years."

I pondered that idea for a few moments. "Yeah, I hadn't thought of that. That sounds like a good idea, Art. I will definitely look into that."

The waiter dropped a leather folder onto the table, which Art quickly snatched, as I began to reach for it.

"This one is on me. You can treat me to dinner when you get your first job as a paralegal," he laughed, sliding his credit card into the folder and holding it in the air for the waiter.

"Thank you Art, I really appreciate your help, and your treating for dinner," I replied graciously.

"It was my pleasure. It was great to see you again…whoever

you are," he laughed.

After signing the check, Art escorted me to the exit where we each handed our tickets to the valets. As two drivers brought each of our cars to the entrance at the same time, I extended my right hand to say goodbye to my old friend Art.

"Screw the handshake," he said as he put his arms around me with a hug. I hugged him back and thanked him one more time before getting into my rental car and heading back to the hotel.

It had been nice to see Art, yet a bit disappointing. I had hoped to be ending the evening with hope for my return to the magazine business, but instead left with the revelation that my career in magazine publishing was over. Art had offset my disappointment however, by providing new hope with the idea of a career in the legal field, not as a lawyer, as Judge Crier had once suggested, but as a paralegal. I was invigorated by this prospect as I made my way south on US 101 toward San Mateo.

Chapter Twenty-Four
Gypsy Moon

My first day of 2007 began at 10:00 am, when my brain slowly began its return to existence. As my eyelids reluctantly peeled themselves away from my eyeballs, my first vision of the New Year was the slivers of sunshine that rudely invaded my room through crevasses in the closed draperies, casting an eerie light on the ceiling. My head throbbed violently, as my brain began its slow metamorphosis from sub-consciousness to consciousness. I turned my head away from the light that danced on the ceiling, and through foggy vision, I spotted the two empty wine bottles on the dresser, a blatant reminder of why I felt as though a train had run over me during the night.

I rolled out of bed, and gingerly wobbled to the bathroom on my rubber legs, where I filled a plastic cup with water and immediately poured it down the desert trail that had once been my throat. I was certain that cacti had begun to grow in the recesses of my throat as I poured down cup after cup of water.

My hands trembled as I filled the carafe with water and poured it into the coffee maker. After pushing the button to start the brewing process, I fumbled through my shower kit until I found the bottle of Advil. With feeble hands and a great deal of effort, I finally managed to open the childproof container and shake two of the magical capsules into the palm of my quivering hand, quickly popping them into my mouth. Two more cups of water followed the capsules down my parched throat, as I glared hopefully at the coffee maker, which was slowly but mercifully brewing my morning elixir.

I had spent New Year's Eve in my motel room, in the company of a pizza from the nearby Papa Johns, and two bottles of wine purchased at the Draeger's Market in downtown San Mateo. Dick Clark had smiled at me from my television screen, as he rang in 2007, while I watched the ball drop on Times Square from the comfort of my motel room bed; a slice of pizza in one hand and a plastic cup of Chenin Blanc in the other. After the televised festivities ended, I finished the wine, while watching a late night movie. I could not recollect what movie I watched, nor did I care.

The diamond point needles of hot water immediately began to sooth my aching head and body as I stepped into the shower, with a Styrofoam cup of steaming coffee in hand. The ibuprofen delivered through the Advil capsules was now coursing through my bloodstream, and its soothing affects were slowly manifesting. My brain began its slow process of functioning normally, and the muscles in my legs began to awaken to perform their daily task of supporting my body. I shampooed my hair three times, and scrubbed my body repeatedly, as if I was attempting to remove the skin. In time, the hot water began to wane, and cool water sprayed on my body in its place. The huge motel water heater, exhausted by my lengthy shower, was commanding me to stop, in its own subtle way.

I had nothing to do between now and my 5:00 pm appointment with Sorcha, but I wanted to do something other than waste time languishing in my motel room. After dressing in a pair of jeans and a polo shirt, I opened the drapes to let the bright sunlight fill the room. The sudden burst of light briefly blinded me, but my vision rapidly returned, and I was able to focus. The thrashing headache had subsided, and I felt alive again. I had a car with a tankful of gas, and I was intent on enjoying this lovely Northern California day.

I drove north on US 101 into the city. Due to the holiday, there was very little traffic, and I enjoyed taking my time, without the normal pressure. I drove slowly, enjoying the scenery of San Francisco. I passed the San Francisco airport, to which I had flown many times during my publishing career. I drove through South San Francisco, with its familiar 'ticky tacky' houses. I passed Candlestick Park, where on so many occasions I had shivered in the cold, while attending Giants baseball games with clients.

After passing through the city, I crossed over the Golden Gate Bridge into Sausalito, where I enjoyed lunch at The Lighthouse Café. After lunch, I visited some of the quaint shops in Sausalito, and then drove back across the bridge through the city and back to my motel in San Mateo. I would enjoy a brief nap, before heading down to Redwood City for my appointment with Sorcha.

I awoke from my nap at 4:00 pm, and after brushing my teeth and dressing in fresh clothing, I climbed back into my rental car and headed south on the 101. I exited at Woodside road, following Sorcha's instructions to get to her house in the Oak Knoll neighborhood of Redwood City. It was 4:55 when I pulled up on the tree lined street and parked in front of her house. Her house was modest, surrounded by a white picket fence and nestled amidst trees. I walked up the sidewalk to her front door, and pushed the doorbell button. I heard the chime of the bell through the door.

"You must be Pamela" the woman smiled as she opened the door. "Please come in."

I followed her into the foyer, and she closed the door behind me. I looked around at the interior of the house. The exterior, neatly manicured and meticulously kept, was in sharp contrast to the disheveled mess of the interior. There were sofas and chairs of all different colors and styles crammed into the living room. The dining room was crowded with a table that was much too large for the room, surrounded by eight unmatched chairs. There were stacks of books everywhere the eye could see, on the floors, on the tables, even on the kitchen counter. A piano reposed in the corner of the parlor… it too covered with books. This house looked as though a library had exploded here, leaving thousands of books in its wake.

"I'm Sorcha. It's nice to meet you Pamela. Or should I call you Pam?" she smiled, as she extended her right hand.

I shook hands with her and smiled, "Pam will be just fine"

Sorcha was the same height as me, with long, wavy gray hair that fell down past her waist. She was wearing a long black dress and black sandals. Her black rimmed glasses appeared to be much too large for her face, giving the appearance that she was wearing two large magnifying glasses over her eyes.

"Pam, my treatment room is upstairs. Please come with me." She headed up the stairway, and I followed.

The upstairs portion of Sorcha's house was, in contrast to the disaster downstairs, meticulous. I stood in a huge den, surrounded by contemporary furnishings, a small kitchen with an island counter, and an adjacent room filled with electrolysis equipment and a table. To the rear of the room, French doors led to a balcony. I found it difficult to believe that the woman who kept the upper level of this house so neat and orderly, could manage to maintain such chaos on the lower level.

Sorcha laid a white sheet on the treatment table, and patted it gently as a way of inviting me to lie down. Once I was on my back, she began to sterilize the skin on my face with a soft pad, soaked with solution. Once she had completely sterilized my face, she inserted the probe into the first follicle, and pressed the pedal. I braced myself as the first of hundreds of bee stings that I would endure during the next two hours began. I listened to the hiss of the electrolysis machine each time she stepped on the pedal, and imagined that I was listening to the screams of the dying follicles.

"Where do you live, Pam?" she asked.

There was that question again…the question that so many people have asked me, to which I could not find the answer. I gave

Sorcha the same response that I had given so many times before.

"I really don't know Sorcha. My roots are in Chicago, I lived in Texas for much of my adult life, now I get my mail in California. My family is scattered all over the country. I just live in my truck and wake up each day in another city. I'm a feral cat."

"Ah, you are a lone wayfarer. You are walking the lonely road of the traveler," she replied warmly, while continuing with the bee stings on my face.

"Yeah, I guess you could say that," I laughed.

After a brief pause, Sorcha continued.

"Are you happy with your decision?"

What decision?"

"Are you happy with your decision to transition from male to female?"

"Yes, of course I am," I replied tentatively. "Why do you ask?"

"I feel a great deal of discord inside of you," Sorcha said while moving her probe from hair to hair and applying the deadly heat.

I laughed as best I could. The fact that my face was under attack by angry bees made laughter difficult. "I tend to be a bit tense when someone is zapping me with an electric needle, Sorcha."

"No Pam. What I am sensing in you goes way beyond the pain and discomfort of the moment. There is something deeper. I sense a great deal of turmoil in your being. You are a very unhappy person," she replied while continuing her deathly attack on my facial hairs.

"Could it have something to do with the fact that my truck is disabled and I have been stuck in San Mateo for several days, with no source of income?" I asked sarcastically.

"No." she answered in a clinical tone, as she continued with her work. "You are filled with turmoil. There are things in your past that are causing a great disturbance within your soul. I felt the negative energy the moment I touched your skin."

"How can you tell just by touching my skin?" I asked.

"I just can. We'll talk later" she replied flatly. She continued with her work without speaking another word.

I closed my eyes, and absorbed what Sorcha had just said. The repeated stings of the electrolysis needle became nonexistent as my mind drifted back in time.

I thought of my mother laying in her deathbed at the hospital. She had asked me simply to give her one last hug before she died, and I refused. I let her die alone and unloved, simply because of my bitterness.

I thought of my daughter Cheryl, who I have always loved; a love that I was unable to express. Would she spend her life carrying the same umbrage toward me?

I thought of my future. I had no home. My publishing career had vanished into a puff of smoke. Where would I live? What would I do? Would I be able to endure two years of paralegal college? Was I destined to be a lonely and homeless truck driver for all my days?

The ding of Sorcha's timer snapped me out of my meditation. The two-hour session had gone by quickly, and Sorcha was now busy applying a medicating ointment to my face.

"Have you had dinner?" she asked while cleaning up the work area.

"No, I was going to grab a burger or something on the way back to the motel," I answered, while sitting up on the table.

"Nonsense, you will eat here…but first, a glass of wine."

Sorcha walked to the kitchen and pulled a bottle of wine from the refrigerator. In another instant, she had removed the cork and poured two glasses. She handed one of the glasses to me, and ushered me to the French door that led to the balcony.

"Please, have a seat on the balcony and enjoy the wine. I will prepare food for us to enjoy." She opened the door and motioned me through the doorway.

A variety of deck furniture, including chairs, tables, and chaise lounges appointed the balcony. I settled into one of the chairs, and set my glass of wine on the adjacent table. Sorcha's house was nestled on the backside of a hill, and her balcony overlooked the houses behind hers. I had a perfect view of the sky.

The moon was full on this night, and was so large that it seemed to be hanging in Sorcha's backyard like an ornament. I took a sip of my wine and stared at the moon, tempted to simply reach out and touch it… it appeared to be that close. I have had a fascination with the moon since childhood, and have often imagined that it spoke to me. I took another sip of my wine, and then set the glass back on the table. I continued to stare… mesmerized by the huge, brilliant moon before my eyes.

"It's a gypsy moon."

My fixation was interrupted by Sorcha's voice, as she laid a large tray, covered with assorted cheeses, cold cuts, pate', fruit, and crackers on the table to my left. She then settled herself into the chair to the left of the table and grabbed a handful of grapes from the tray.

"Gypsy moon?" I asked, as I took a piece of cheese and a cracker from the tray.

Sorcha stared silently at the moon for several minutes while eating grapes. She held her head cocked to one side, as she appeared to be communicating with the huge orb, awaiting instructions on how to answer my question.

"Pam, my ancestors were Romany Gypsies. Do you know anything about that culture?"

"I'm not sure Sorcha… I mean, I think I know what a gypsy is, but…"

Sorcha smiled, "That's ok Pam. The gypsies are probably the most misunderstood people in the world. It's actually a wonderful culture."

"I'm sure it is. But what is the gypsy moon?"

"Gypsies have honored the moon since ancient times. Throughout history, gypsies have recognized the moon as the Goddess, the protector and savior of the homeless wayfarer. The gypsy belief is that the Goddess watches over them and takes their souls to the moon when they die."

"You said I am a wayfarer. Does that mean…?

"Yes, Pam. The gypsy moon is watching over you, even as we speak."

Sorcha took a sip of her wine, grabbed a piece of pate from the tray, and placed it into her mouth, while continuing.

"When there is a bright full moon like this one..." Sorcha waved toward the moon as she spoke. "...it is believed to be the Goddess, protecting the gypsy people and lighting the path for them, so that they may find food and shelter. For that reason, it has come to be called the gypsy moon."

"That's very interesting, Sorcha," I said, staring at the moon. I took a sip of my wine, and then set the glass back onto the table. "I don't think I have ever met a gypsy before"

"You haven't?" Sorcha leaned forward and studied me over the black rims of her huge glasses. "Go look in the mirror."

"Me? No Sorcha, I am not a gypsy," I laughed.

"No, you are not Romany, but you are a gypsy nonetheless. Where is your home? You live in your truck, right?"

"Yes, I live in my truck for now. However, this was only a temporary job to get me through my transition. Once I am finished, I will have a home somewhere."

"So you find a home somewhere and settle down. Does that make you any less a gypsy? You are wandering alone through this life, trying to connect your past to your future, and you have no idea how to do it. This conflict is causing you to be a very unhappy person."

"Sorcha, how could you possibly know all these things about me? What makes you think I am not a happy person? I am very happy." I protested weakly.

"Are you?" Sorcha asked skeptically, as she lifted the bottle and refilled my wine glass.

"Okay, I admit it... there are certain things in my past that I would like to change. But how can I go back and change what has already been done?"

"You cannot change the past, Pam. However, you can touch it, and try to change the way you feel about it. By changing the negative thoughts about your past into more positive thoughts, you will have in a sense, changed the past. By doing so, you will then be able to shape a more positive future for yourself."

I gazed at the moon while digesting the sage words of this unique woman. As I had experienced previously throughout my life, the moon seemed to be talking to me. I felt the presence of her enormous power. My thoughts wandered back, for just a moment, to the many notes I had received on my truck, and their always present cryptic message.

Sorcha went on. "Don't worry Pam, the gypsy moon will watch over you… but first, you must make amends with your past. Your present and future will then take care of themselves. Your life is broken and you need to mend it. You will not find happiness until you stitch your wounded past back together, just the same as your wounded truck is now being stitched back together."

"But how do I do that Sorcha?"

"I cannot give you an answer to that question. You must go back to your beginnings. The answers will find you," she said.

"Sorcha?" I asked. "Would you mind looking at something for me?"

"Of course not, my dear, something that has been troubling to you, yes?"

"Yes," I replied, rummaging in my purse for the stack of notes I had so carefully saved. I handed the notes to Sorcha. "I have received these notes over the last two years. Each message was different, but always had the same cryptic message at the end. Would you, by chance, have any idea what the language is? What it might mean?"

Sorcha glanced at a few of the notes, her brow rising and a smile crossing her lips. "Ahhh, it seems as though you have had a bit more than the gypsy moon watching over you." She read aloud from one of the notes, "călătorie în siguranță, dar ai grija de pericol." This, my friend is Romanian, it translates to, "travel safely, but beware of danger. "

Rising from her chair, Sorcha said, "Now my wayfaring

friend, I must bid you farewell. This old woman is tired."

As I departed, I could not help but feel the warmth of my guardian, who for so long had been watching over me, warning me, trying to keep me safe.

As I drove northbound on the 101 toward San Mateo, my head spun wildly, as thoughts of what Sorcha had implored me to do swirled around in my brain. The drink had lightened my head, but Sorcha's words were twice as intoxicating as her wine.

I parked the rental car in front of my room, and stood next to it for a moment, gazing upward at the sky. The gypsy moon seemed to have followed me back to the motel…it was right there above my head, watching over me.

"Yes" I spoke aloud to the moon above. "I believe I know what I have to do."

Chapter Twenty-Five
Why-Oh-Ming

Four months after my chance encounter with the mystical and mysterious Sorcha, I took the leap of faith, and submitted my two-week notice to my dispatcher Charlotte. The company and I had agreed that my lease would terminate upon my return to the facilities in mid-May, where I would submit final paperwork and settle up on my final pay. On that day, my career as an over the road truck driver would conclude.

From the day I picked up my repaired truck on January 3rd until April 30th, I had logged over 50,000 miles. During that 116-day stretch, I had taken only 12 days off. I was pushing myself hard, making as much money as I could; partly to make up for the lost income while BJ was disabled in San Mateo, but mainly to salt away enough money so that I could comfortably make my exit from truck driving.

After my conversation with Art, I had begun researching colleges that offered paralegal programs. I had found a suitable paralegal college, which offered a two-year degree program at which I could attend online classes. The ability to attend live online classes was appealing to me for two reasons: The primary reason for my interest in online classes was the fact that I would be working as a waitress and bartender while working toward my degree, which meant an unpredictable work schedule. The second, and perhaps most critical reason, was that I would be in Bangkok in January 2008 for my GRS. The hospital had assured me that a wireless internet connection would be available to me, and I would be able to attend classes from my hospital bed.

After I had submitted the transcripts from my previous college program, and the credits were transferred to the paralegal program, it was determined that I would be able to obtain my degree in only sixteen months. My first classes would begin in the fall.

I had enjoyed working with Charlotte, and she seemed to have enjoyed working with me. She often referred to me as her 'Go To Girl', because she knew that she could rely upon me to get critical loads delivered on time, even if it meant my having to bend the hours of service rules in the process. In return, Charlotte had been very accommodating of my needs, frequently getting me loads to Dallas or Florida so that I could visit my kids.

I had spent April 29th in Dallas, where I celebrated Greg's fifteenth birthday by taking him and Steven bowling, and then out for pizza. From Dallas, I had taken a load up to Vancouver, Washington, and then picked up a load from Portland destined for Orlando. My plan was to deliver that load on Wednesday, and then head over to Daytona to have dinner with Cheryl. This would be the first time that Cheryl and I would spend time together without her boys. It would also be the first time she would see me as Pam. It was time for me to stop pretending, and tell her the truth. It was also time for me to make amends with my daughter.

I left Portland yesterday morning, and after shutting down in Ogden, Utah last night, I was now driving across Wyoming on Interstate 80. The air was damp and cold; and the sky was grey and overcast. As usual, swirling snow blew across the Interstate. I had grown to despise the state of Wyoming, with its seemingly endless winters and unreliable cell phone service. Blizzards had stranded me for countless days in Wyoming, with no internet or cell phone service. My telephone call from Mike Leary, banning me from the ladies room, came while I was driving through Wyoming. I had vowed never to set foot in this state again, once my truck driving days were over. This would be my last time in Wyoming, and it would be quite memorable.

The first of the snow began to fall as I passed though Rock Springs. It began as a light snowfall at first, but then gradually became heavier as I progressed eastward, with huge snowflakes quickly piling up on my windshield. I turned the wipers on low speed to clear the snow, but I soon had to switch them to high. The snow rapidly covered the front of my truck, with the only clear spot being the wedge shaped portions of my windshield that the wipers cleared as they flopped back and forth. Ahead of me, visibility was diminishing.

The snow had completely covered the road, with only one lane of traffic crawling along at 5 miles per hour. Visibility rapidly became worse, and soon, all I was able to see were the flashing lights of the truck in front of me. I turned on my flashers as well, so the truck behind me could follow me in the same way. It was a complete whiteout, and the only thing that guided each driver along were the flashing lights of the preceding truck.

My wipers were at full speed, yet were barely able to keep up with the relentless snowfall. I had never seen such a rapid accumulation of snow, not even in my years living in Chicago and Colorado. As each wiper blade swung from one side to the other, the falling snow quickly re-covered its cleared path before it could traverse and clear it again. Even with the wipers working at full speed, it was very difficult to see through the windshield.

Suddenly, as if things could not get any worse, the driver's side wiper blade detached from the arm and sailed away into the blizzard. Now, all that remained on the driver's side of the windshield was the small metal arm, which was now scraping impotently back and forth. Within seconds, snow had completely covered the left side of the windshield, and I was driving blindly.

While holding the steering wheel with my left hand, I leaned as far to the right as I could and peered through the passenger side of the windshield. Had this happened at any other time, I would have simply exited the freeway, but huge snowdrifts and snowbound vehicles blocked the exit ramps. There was no shoulder to pull onto, and stopping in my tracks was out of the question, as doing so would most certainly cause a chain reaction collision behind me. I had no choice but to keep going until I made it through this horrible nightmare.

For the next thirty miles, and what seemed to be an eternity, I gripped the steering wheel with my left hand, while holding my left foot on the accelerator pedal. My body leaned far to the right so that I could peer through the only side of the windshield that was clear. Traffic moved at a snail's pace, so I kept BJ in third gear and simply guided her along the grooves in the snow that the traffic in front of me had created.

The snowstorm gradually began to wane, and by the time I reached Wamsutter, it had stopped completely. The road was now drivable, and the defroster managed to melt away the snow that remained on the windshield. As I pulled into the Love's Truck stop in Wamsutter, the only indication that there had been a snowstorm were the snow covered eastbound trucks. An unexpected spring blizzard had hit a small section of Wyoming, just as I was driving through!

After I had backed into a parking spot and set the brake, I let out a huge sigh of relief. I felt as though I had just landed a crippled jet onto the deck of an aircraft carrier. I sat for a moment, gazing mindlessly through the now completely clear windshield, and then burst into laughter.

"Another fond memory of Why – frigging – Oh-Ming" I chuckled aloud as I climbed down from the truck and headed into the building to buy a wiper blade.

Three days after the windshield wiper incident in Wyoming, I made my delivery in Orlando. While the dockworkers were busy unloading my trailer, I called Charlotte.

"Charlotte, can you get me a load to Chicago before you put me on my final load back to LA?"

"Chicago? You are actually requesting a load to Chicago?" she laughed. "Pam, nobody ever asks for loads to Chicago."

"I know Charlotte. But I need to get to Chicago."

"That's right; you are from Chicago aren't you? Is something wrong with a family member?"

"No it's nothing like that. I just need to go to Chicago one last time before I quit driving. I have some unfinished business to take care of."

"Okay, hold on. Let me see what we've got." I could hear Charlotte's fingers clattering on her keyboard as she spoke. After a minute, the clattering stopped.

"When do you need to be in Chicago, Pam?" she asked.

"There is no particular day that I need to be there Charlotte. I just need to get there on my way back to LA" I replied.

"OK… well there is absolutely no Chicago bound freight out of Florida right now. I do have a load out of Titusville that needs to get to Allentown on Friday though. I could put you on that load and then find something from Pennsylvania to Chicago. I'm sure I can find something."

"That would be great, Charlotte. Go ahead and put me on that load."

"You got it 'Go to Girl'. I'm going to miss you when you leave."

"I'm going to miss you too Charlotte. You have been awesome!"

It was an hour drive from Orlando to the distribution center in Titusville, where I dropped my empty and picked up the loaded trailer. From, there, I headed north along the east coast of Florida, on Interstate 95 toward Daytona.

Cheryl and I had arranged to meet at 6:00 in the Wal-Mart parking lot in Port Orange, just outside of Daytona. I arrived at 5:30, and after a quick visit to the restroom, where I freshened up my makeup and brushed my hair, I sat in my truck and waited for her bright yellow pickup truck to arrive. I was nervous, as this was the first time that Cheryl would see me as Pamela. Although I was presenting as a female, I had dressed down for the occasion, wearing jeans, a casual top, and tennis shoes. The only hints that I was female were the light makeup, pink fingernails, and earrings.

I had no idea what the conversation with Cheryl would consist of, but I knew there were words that I needed to say, and things that needed explanation. Rather than prepare a speech, I had sent her an email outlining the change that I had gone through, and why I had done it. Tonight she would ask questions. I hoped to have the answers.

At 5:55, Cheryl's yellow pickup arrived and parked next to my truck. I climbed down and met her in the parking lot where we exchanged hugs.

"My, you look… um… different," she laughed while opening the passenger door of her truck.

"Yeah, well it's the new me. At least I'm not wearing a skirt," I laughed as I climbed into her pickup truck.

The Applebee's restaurant was less than a mile from the Wal-Mart. Cheryl parked the truck, and we walked across the parking lot and into the entrance, where we were greeted by a cheery hostess holding a stack of menus.

"Table for two, ladies?" she asked cordially.

Cheryl glanced at me with a wane smile.

"Yes, just the two of us," I answered. "Could we please have a booth somewhere where we can have a private conversation?"

"Sure thing. Follow me, ladies," she said as she headed toward the back corner of the dining room. After Cheryl and I were seated, she laid two menus on the table in front of us.

"Your server will be Jessica. She will be right with you," she bubbled, and then scurried back to the hostess stand.

"So you are really doing the girl thing, huh? When I got your email, I figured this was just another one of your crazy pranks," Cheryl laughed.

"Not this time Cheryl. This is for real. As I told you in the email, this has been an issue for me my entire life. I finally decided to do something about it."

"So have you um…" she struggled for the words. I knew what she was asking.

"Had the surgery?" I smiled.

"Yeah that…" she replied.

Our server interrupted our conversation as she arrived at our table. "Hello ladies, my name is Jessica, can I take your drink orders?"

I ordered a bottle of Heineken. Cheryl concurred. Jessica headed to the bar to get our drink orders.

After Jessica had disappeared, I continued with my answer to Cheryl's question.

"No, I have not had that surgery yet… it's called GRS by the way… Gender Reassignment Surgery. I am going to Bangkok in January to have that done."

"Are you scared?" she asked with a concerned tone.

Jessica appeared at our table with two bottles of Heineken and two frozen mugs.

"Are you ladies ready to order?"

I glanced at the menu, then smiled at the server, "I'll have a burger with Swiss cheese and grilled onions."

"I'll have the same thing," Cheryl smiled while handing her menu to Jessica.

I pushed my frozen mug aside and took a sip from the bottle of Heineken, and then answered my daughter's question.

"Cheryl, I am not scared… that's not really the word I would use. It's more like, 'apprehensive'. This whole transition from male to female has been very stressful. I've endured over a hundred hours of electrolysis, plus a few facial surgeries. I have been displaced from, my home, family, and job, and have had to suffer unspeakable insults. Going to Bangkok and getting the surgery will just be the happy ending to a Greek tragedy.

"You sound like you are not happy. Why did you do it?" she took a sip of her beer.

Jessica suddenly appeared at our table and placed two platters in front of Cheryl and me. I nodded silently to her, and she vanished.

I took a bite of my burger, followed by a swig of beer. I then answered Cheryl's question pensively.

"Cheryl, I am at peace with myself. For the first time in my life I am who I had meant to be at birth…a female. But, am I completely happy? Probably not."

Cheryl took a bite of her hamburger, then a sip of her beer. She gazed at me for a moment while she chewed, and then asked.

"If you are so comfortable in your decision to change genders, and you are at such peace with yourself, why are you still unhappy?" I sensed a tone of facetiousness in her question.

"Cheryl, it's because of a lot of things. I need to resolve many issues. One of them is you," I replied as I took a swig of my beer.

"Me? What about me?" she asked as the popped a French fry into her mouth.

"Cheryl, I have let you down in so many ways. I have been a terrible parent. In spite of all that, I want you to know that I have always loved you. From the moment you were born, you have always been my baby girl. There are so many things that I wish I would have done differently, but that is all in the past… I cannot change that. All I can say to you is that I am sorry for all the hurt that I have caused you."

Cheryl set her hamburger onto the platter and gazed at me. She then picked up her bottle of beer and took a long swig before responding.

"So now you are a female and everything is different? In your email you said that you are the same person inside. Now you are telling me that you want to make amends for everything in the past. If you are the same person, how do you expect me to believe that anything will be any different than it was before?"

"Look, I know my absence from your life during your younger years caused you a lot of pain. You have done well, in spite of your unhappy upbringing, but blaming me or anyone else in your family for the outcome of your life can only lead to unhappiness. Can we just get past that now, and move on to a more positive future relationship?"

"I'm willing to try. But don't expect it to happen overnight."

"I don't."

Cheryl and I finished our dinner, with the remainder of the conversation centered on topics other than our strained relationship. We discussed her two boys and how they were doing in school, her business that she had started in Daytona, my split up with Laura, and finally my future after truck driving.

"Are you going to go back into the magazine publishing business as a female?" she asked.

"No, I am afraid that career is pretty much over. The magazine business is in a decline, which means fewer opportunities. I have had to face the reality that it would be just about impossible to reenter that field," I said while extracting my credit card from, my wallet and waving it at Jessica.

"Yeah, that makes sense. I hardly read any magazines or newspapers anymore, I get everything I need from the internet," she replied. "So what are you going to do?"

"I'm going to become a paralegal. I have already enrolled in an online degree program and will have my paralegal degree in December 2008," I proclaimed proudly.

"Wow, that's cool. So where are you going to live… LA?"

"No, I'm going to Portland, Oregon. I have a friend there who has offered me a place to stay until I get on my feet financially. I have lined up a job as a cocktail waitress at the Portland Trailblazers games," I smiled.

Cheryl laughed, "It sounds so funny to hear you refer to yourself as a 'waitress'."

"I know…. but it is what I am now." I smiled while signing the bill and returning the plastic card to my wallet.

"So what should I call you now?" Cheryl asked as we walked back to her pickup truck. "It seems a bit strange to call you 'dad'."

"Cheryl, I will always be your dad, no matter what. But you

are right, it would seem a bit strange. I guess since 'mom' is already taken, you can call me Pam if you want," I answered after we had seated ourselves inside her truck.

"Okay… Pam it is" she smiled. "So where are you going from here?"

"I'm heading up to Allentown, Pennsylvania. From there I will be heading to Chicago, and then my last load will be back to LA."

"Say hello to Chicago for me. I miss it sometimes," she said as she parked her yellow pickup in front of BJ.

"I will… I will also be taking care of some unfinished business while I am there," I replied pensively, as I got out of her truck. Cheryl also got out and came around to the passenger side.

"Good luck dad… I mean Pam. Thanks for talking to me, I feel a little better now. It's going to take a lot of time though."

"I know it will. All I ask is that you and I work together to patch things up. Is that a deal?"

"It's a deal!" she said, as she wrapped her arms around me.

"I love you Cheryl, I always have, and always will. You are still my baby girl," I said as we embraced.

"I love you too," she said as she hopped into the driver's seat of her truck, closed the door, and started the engine.

After watching Cheryl's yellow pickup leave the Wal-Mart parking lot, I climbed into the truck and headed five miles north on Interstate 95 to the Love's truck stop, where I spent the night.

On the morning of Friday, May 11th, I made my delivery in Allentown. After the trailer was unloaded, I checked the Qualcomm. Charlotte had once again come through for me. I was to take the empty trailer to Bethlehem, where I would get a live load of bicycle parts and take them to Chicago. The load was due in Chicago on Sunday.

The live load took several hours, which did not please me, since I do not earn any money while sitting at a dock. By the time the dockworkers finished unloading, and I had received my bills of lading, It was 3:30. I decided to spend the night in nearby Allentown, then head to Chicago early in the morning.

My alarm woke me up at 2:30 the next morning. I quickly packed my shower bag and headed into the truck stop for my morning coffee and a quick shower. A thin dusting of spring snow had fallen during the night, and the parking lot, shrubberies, and trees glistened with the white snow.

After my shower, I started the truck, and then hopped down to perform my pre-trip inspection. I dusted the snow off the headlights, and returned to the cab. A quick flick of the wipers, and the windshield was clear of snow. After starting my log for the day, I put the truck in gear and headed out of the truck stop. The dashboard clock told me it was 4:00 am.

I was in good spirits as I made my way north on Interstate 476 toward Interstate 80, on which I would head West. In just a few days, I would be in Chicago, where I would take care of what needed doing, in order to touch my past, as Sorcha had so eloquently put it. I would then head to Los Angeles where my truck driving days would end. In a few months, I would be in paralegal college, and on my way to a new career. It was time to start my new life.

As I merged onto Interstate 80 in Stroudsburg, I checked the clock and quickly performed the math in my head. I would reach Gary, Indiana by 3:00 pm, where I would shut down for the night at the TA, and then make my delivery in Chicago early in the morning. From there, Charlotte would have found a load for me to Los Angeles.

I had just passed the Mifflinville weigh station, when I heard a faint popping sound behind me. A glance in my rear view mirror revealed a large black object flopping along on the highway. The object appeared to be an 'alligator', which is the trucker term for the long strips of rubber left behind on the highways by blown truck tires. The crackling of the CB confirmed my suspicions.

"Westbound big truck, you just blew a trailer tire," the voice from another truck informed me.

I grabbed the microphone and pressed the key, "Ten-four driver. There is a TA up ahead in Bloomsburg. I'll jump off there and get it replaced."

Chapter Twenty-Six
The Itsy Bitsy Spider

As I crossed the state line from Indiana into Illinois, I glanced at the 'Mom' license plate that reposed on the dashboard of my truck. After my blowout in Pennsylvania, I had managed to make it from the Bloomsburg TA to Angola, and then on to Chicago, without any more blown tires, blizzards, or lost windshield wiper blades. However, the spring storm that Hoppy had warned me about was brewing, and snow flurries were in the air. Snow seemed to have been following me during the past week.

After delivering my load of bicycle parts in Chicago, I headed east to Gary, Indiana to pick up a preloaded trailer of 'Puffs' tissue at the Proctor & Gamble distribution center, which I was to deliver to Los Angeles. How ironic that the last load of my driving career would be identical to my first load, two and a half years ago.

It did not take long to find my assigned trailer at the DC, which I skillfully backed under, with the familiar clank of the fifth wheel engaging with the kingpin of the trailer. After the obligatory tug test to ensure the safe coupling of the tractor and trailer, I hopped out of the truck to hook up the cables and hoses, and to perform the last pre-trip inspection of my brief career as a truck driver. As I walked back to the truck, I spotted a pointed wooden stake lying on the ground next to the trailer, which I picked up and tossed behind the driver's seat while climbing back into the cab.

From Gary, I took Interstate 90 into Chicago, and then the Stevenson Expressway to Cicero Avenue. Driving south on Cicero toward 63rd Street, I reminisced, as I passed the parking lots on which Eddie had once tutored the small boy. Once again, his voice reverberated in my head.

'You'll be the king of the road someday'

I turned onto 63rd Street and headed east, until I found a parking spot large enough in which to park my 70-foot tractor and trailer. After maneuvering my enormous vehicle into the parking spot, setting the brake, and killing the engine, I stared blankly through the windshield and took a deep breath. Sorcha's voice echoed in my brain:

'Go back to your beginnings. The answers will find you'

I climbed down and stood for a moment next to my truck, as traffic on the two lanes of 63rd street zipped by. After a few minutes, I found an opening, and dashed across the street. I began to walk east toward Homan Avenue.

63rd street had changed considerably over the years. Many of the once familiar shops had new names, and most of the doors and windows now sported steel burglar bars. 'Just a sign of the times,' I told myself as I reached Homan, and then turned south toward 65th Street.

I had somehow imagined that I would find Gertie in The Yellow Store grumbling at her young customers from behind the candy counter. Instead, I discovered that the building was vacant, the windows now covered with plywood. Tall weeds adorned the faded yellow bricks. There was no telling how many different businesses had occupied this building since my childhood, but apparently, the building had outlived its usefulness.

I walked around to the west side of the building and leaned against the brick wall, watching the light Sunday traffic along the intersection of 65^(th) Street and Homan Avenue. Cars passed, with women seated in the passenger seat wearing their Mother's Day corsages. I imagined the patrol boys with their white baldrics, halting traffic so that the hordes of children could safely cross, as they scampered to their homes.

Beneath my feet, at the base of the wall, years of dirt and debris had accumulated. I transferred my weight onto one foot and began to swing the other foot back and forth like an eraser. As I kicked at the ground, my heavy driving boot pushed years of dirt, dead leaves, candy wrappers, and cigarette butts aside into two separate piles. I looked down and watched, as my efforts slowly exposed the concrete footing of the building. Soon, the concrete scroll began slowly to materialize at my feet.

I squatted at the footing, and used my fingers to finish clearing the last remnants of dirt and debris. Light snow swirled around my hands as I worked. Soon, the message, inscribed so many years ago by the hopeful young boy, became clearer. There it was, like a time capsule… a message in a bottle. The concrete was cracked and discolored, but the message was nearly as vibrant as if it had been written only days ago.

I brushed my hands together, to remove the dirt from my fingers, as I stood and gazed pensively at the artwork from the upside down year. The boy who wanted nothing more than simply to be the person he was really meant to be, had left his message for all time.

I continued south on Homan, then turned the corner on 66th toward the main entrance to Eberhart Elementary School. The brick building somehow looked smaller than it had in the past, as if it had shrunk over the years. I passed the first wrought iron fence that surrounded the boy's playground, stopping briefly at the entrance. I then continued past the walkway to the faculty entrance with its grass buffer that separated the two playgrounds.

I entered the once forbidden girl's playground and stood silently as I gazed across the asphalt. This was the hallowed ground permitting only girls, and I now belonged here.

My eyes fixed for a moment on the iron fence beyond the grass buffer. The light powder of snow continued to swirl about me, as the cool wind blew my hair across my face. I turned my face upward, in the faint hope that I might see the gypsy moon, but instead saw only grey sky. I closed my eyes, as the flurries fell upon my face, and felt myself slowly fading into a trance.

Suddenly, I heard the sounds of shrieking, frolicking children. I opened my eyes and looked around me to find a sea of pastel colors, as little girls flocked to the entrance of the school. I then turned my head, and looked across the grass buffer toward the boy's playground. There, standing at the wrought iron fence, was a slight, dark haired boy.

As he stared at me through the iron bars, I smiled and raised my arm waving for him to come over. He hesitated. I waved to him again, and then a third time. Finally, as though the iron bars that imprisoned him had dissolved, he ran through the barrier that held him in place, and joined the throng of girls as they entered the building. I turned and watched, as the frolicking children slowly dissolved before my eyes.

The playground was now empty and quiet. Swirls of light snow danced across the ground as I exited the playground, beginning the walk back to 63rd Street. I enjoyed a feeling of exhilaration as I trudged north on Homan, with a sense that I had just accomplished something important. However, one more vital task remained.

The light snow flurries continued as I drove west on 63rd Street toward Archer Avenue, where I turned southwest into the suburb of Willow Springs. The windshield defroster quickly melted the snow as it landed on the glass, and I had to engage the wipers only intermittently.

I had not been to Archer Woods cemetery since the cold February day in 1970, when I watched emotionlessly, as my mother's body was interred. Her death certificate states the cause of her death as cirrhosis of the liver, but she was also close to death by the cancer that had invaded her throat and tongue. She had been a heavy drinker and smoker; and I had spent my life irrationally blaming her for her own demise.

Weeks earlier, I had utilized the internet to obtain information and directions to Archer Woods. In doing so, I had discovered several websites claiming that the cemetery is haunted… haunted in particular by a mysterious woman.

One website trumpets:

'She seems to be content staying inside the cemetery, although it is passing motorists who usually notice her. People who are sometimes driving along the road in front of the cemetery at night claim to have heard the sound of a sobbing woman from the other side of the gates. They report the apparition of a woman in a white dress, walking among the tombstones and crying loudly, her face covered by her hands'

"Of all the places for my mother to be buried, it had to be a haunted cemetery," I ruminated as I parked the truck on Archer, near the Kean Road entrance.

"Or perhaps she is the one doing the haunting?"

I climbed down from cab, opened the small door next to the driver's side door, and extracted a small mallet from my toolbox. I then reached behind the seat, and grabbed the pointed wooden stake that I had picked up at the distribution center in Gary. After closing the door, I walked the remaining quarter of a mile to the entrance of the cemetery. In one hand was the mallet; in the other hand was the wooden stake. The miniature 'MOM' license plate was in my coat pocket.

The falling snow flurries intensified as I walked aimlessly through the cemetery in search of my mother's grave. I had no idea where she was, and was certain that her grave did not have a large headstone. Finally, after examining dozens of small markers on the ground, I found the one that bore her name:

Jacqueline Smith Mair

I let the mallet and stake fall out of my hands, as I stood over my mother's tomb. The area on and around her grave was unkempt, as surely in all these years not a single person had come to visit her, or tend to her final resting place. The weeds and brown grass that covered her like a blanket were shrouded with white crystals, as the snow continued to fall. Above me, the grey sky had become darker, as nighttime began to creep up on me.

I stood silently for several minutes, unable to think of the words to say to my deceased mother. I felt that she could somehow feel my presence, and would hear my words. It did not matter to me whether or not she heard them, however. I simply needed to get them out of my system.

"Happy Mother's Day, Mom. It's me… I'm your daughter now. How do I look?" I asked as if to anticipate an answer.

I dropped to my knees and began to pull weeds from the ground as I continued.

"Mom, I'm sorry that I haven't been back in all these years to visit you, but I was really hurt and angry. I know now… I should have given you a hug when I had the chance. If I could, I would do it now."

After I had finished pulling weeds, I stood and piled them next to a nearby tree. The knees of my jeans were cold and wet, but I barely noticed. I then picked up the mallet and stake from the ground, and stood over the small plaque, which bore my mother's name. Three swift blows, securely anchored the stake to the ground next to the plaque.

"Mom, I want you to know that I am no longer angry with you. I think I understand you now, and somehow I know why you reacted to me the way you did. Will you try to understand me, and why I did the things I did?"

I watched contemplatively over my mother's grave for one last moment. I felt at peace now, and hoped that my mother was at peace as well. With mallet in hand, I turned and headed back toward the entranceway. With one last glance over my shoulder as I walked, I smiled at my mother as she rested peacefully, with the 'MOM' license plate attached to the wooden stake above her head.

My final run as a professional truck driver took me across Illinois, Iowa, Nebraska, Colorado, Utah, Nevada, and then into California. I was in no hurry. I stopped frequently along the way and reminisced at many of the landmarks that had become part of my journey during the past two and a half years.

I spent Monday night at the Pilot in Big Springs, Nebraska, where two years earlier a voice had crackled over the CB announcing that she had seen a transvestite in the ladies room. This time, I stood at the mirror for several minutes as one woman after another briefly glanced at me without as much as a blink of the eye.

I stopped for fuel at the Pilot in Kearney, where I had met my dear friend Marla. In a chance encounter, on a day filled with emotional defeat and disappointment, I had forged a friendship that would be everlasting.

On Tuesday, I shut down at the Eureka Casino in Mesquite, Nevada. I played blackjack for an hour and lost $100, but I did not care. Afterward, I dined on prime rib and a Heineken in the casino restaurant, where a capricious romance had begun a year earlier. After dinner, and on my way to the exit, I passed the bank of elevators to which a tall man had once carried me in his strong arms; proclaiming in a fleeting moment his adoration for me.

In a thirty-month period, I had driven nearly 400,000 miles, and hauled enough freight to fill a cargo vessel. During that time, I had endured moments of fear, loneliness, and despair. I had encountered hate and bigotry. However, the laughter, the joy, and the enduring friendships that I had developed along the way, mitigated all those things. All in all, it has been an incredible journey.

Winston Churchill once said, "When you are going through hell, keep going." I had come close to the brink on several occasions, and the thought of conceding to defeat had crossed my mind. Perseverance won over, however, snatching victory from the jaws of defeat.

Sorcha had implored me to touch my past.

"The answers will find you."

She was right. Answers to questions I did not even know to ask had been bestowed upon me. I now felt complete. I had made my amends. I had connected my past to the present and future, and I no longer felt disjointed. Finally, I was happy and at peace.

I made my delivery in Los Angeles at 5:00 am on Wednesday. From there, I drove to the Stugel terminal, where I dropped my empty trailer in one of the available slots. It would be two more hours before the office was open and I would be able to complete my final paperwork, so I spent this time emptying the truck.

I drove over to the driver's parking area, and began the process of moving my personal belongings into my car. I emptied the cubbyholes where I stored my clothing. I gathered up my CD collection and my laptop. I packed my shower bag; which I had toted across truck stop parking lots hundreds of times. I transported all of it from the truck to the car.

By 7:00, I was finished, and the truck was empty. I drove her over to the service area and parked. Before opening the door and climbing out of BJ for the final time, I stood and looked around. I gazed pensively at the sleeper berth, where I had spent so many lonely nights, often crying myself to sleep. I looked at the desk, where I had checked my email, written letters, and talked to friends on the phone. I looked at the driver's seat where I had spent thousands of hours hauling freight across the country.

I climbed down to the ground and closed the door, then stood for a moment and stared. BJ had been my cocoon, while I morphed from a caterpillar to a butterfly. She had been my best friend. She had sheltered and protected me. In a sense, she had been my mother. Leaving her was bittersweet.

It would be another hour before the office was open, so I walked over to the Schneider driver's lounge to say my goodbyes.

The driver's lounge was as it was every morning. CNN and the Weather Channel blared from the two televisions. Drivers were scattered about the tables eating breakfast, drinking coffee, and engaged in conversation. The cadre of trainers sat at their usual corner table.

I filled a Styrofoam cup with coffee, and after paying the cashier, I walked over to the service desk to say my goodbyes to Sly, Glenda, and Stella.

"So, what are you going to do now?" Glenda asked.

"I'm going to be a paralegal" I responded proudly.

"I think you will do well, Pam. Best of luck," Stella added.

"Whatever you do, be safe out there," Sly said with his usual smile.

I sat at one of the tables and sipped my coffee. At a nearby table, solemn faced students sat with looks of anticipation and wonderment of what was to come. I scanned their faces and wondered what was behind the façades. What secrets did each of them have that brought them here? Who among them was in the midst of a life changing transformation? Who among them would meet the gypsy moon?

"Hey lady, aren't you going to say goodbye to an old friend?"

Gennipher, who was now standing next to me, interrupted my contemplation. I stood up and gave her a hug.

"Gennipher, you are one of my favorite people on the planet. I would never dream of leaving without saying goodbye to you."

"Geez, Pam. It seems like it was just yesterday when I was teaching you how to drive a truck," Gennipher said ruefully.

"Yeah, the last few years have just flown by. I'm a completely different person now too," I smiled.

Gennipher laughed, "Yes, you certainly are a different person from when I first met you. Quite different!"

"I'm going to miss you Gennipher. You have been a great friend though all of this."

"I'm going to miss you too, Pam. Let's stay in touch."

I walked back to the Stugel terminal and went to the office to sign off on all of the paperwork. When I finished, I stopped by Charlotte's desk.

"Charlotte, you have been an awesome dispatcher, and I am going to miss you."

Charlotte stood from her chair and wrapped her arms around me. "I'm going to miss you too, 'Go To Girl'."

I left the building, and walked slowly to my car. A chapter in the book of my life was coming to a close. Although it was a happy ending, and the beginning of a new and positive chapter in my life, it was nonetheless a bittersweet moment. I almost didn't want it to end.

As I opened my car door, I glanced one last time across the yard to where BJ stood. Soon, the men in the shop would strip my name from her doors, clean her up, and put her on the market. I hoped that she would fall into the hands of someone who would love her as much as I did.

I climbed into my car, stared the engine, and shuffled through my CD collection until I found the one I was searching for… Carly Simon's 'Coming Around Again'. I slid the disc into the player, advancing to the track I wanted.

I sat and listened to what had become my anthem during the past few years. 'I'll be coming around again'. As the song ended, Carly and her chorus of children sang the song that has been my inspiration throughout my life, and particularly through the challenges of these past years. I turned up the volume and sang along.

The itsy-bitsy spider climbed up the water spout.
Down came the rain and washed the spider out.
Out came the sun and dried up all the rain.
And the itsy-bitsy spider climbed up the spout again.

While singing along with Carly and her chorus of children, I eased my car to the exit gate. As the arm rose, I looked in my rear view mirror. There was BJ staring at me. I froze, fixated on her… I did not want to leave her.

But she seemed to be waving to me, urging me on… like a mother butterfly encouraging her young to fly away from the cocoon.

"Fly away butterly, you are ready. You will be fine," I heard her say.

"Okay BJ," I laughed.

I put my car in gear and headed home.

Chicago native Pamela Rose Anders has penned two satirical humor books entitled, "How to Lose Friends and Influence Enemies" and "Rules of the Rude". Gypsy Moon is her first Narrative Non-Fiction work.

Pamela resides in Phoenix, Arizona, where she operates an independent paralegal business.

In keeping with her vow, she has never returned to the state of Wyoming.

Visit her website at www.pampurrs.com

CPSIA information can be obtained at www.ICGtesting.com
Printed in the USA
LVOW041148100911

245706LV00002B/3/P